The Coinage of the Bosporan Kingdom

The Coinage of the Bosporan Kingdom

From the First Century BC to the Middle of the First Century AD

Nina Frolova

Stanley Ireland

BAR International Series 1102
2002

British Archaeological Reports are published by John and Erica Hedges Ltd and by Archaeopress

This volume has been published by:
John and Erica Hedges Ltd
British Archaeological Reports
7 Longworth Road
Oxford OX2 6RA
England
Tel/Fax +44(0)1865 511560
E-mail: publishing@barhedges.com
www.barhedges.com

Enquiries regarding the submission of manuscripts for future publication may be sent to the above address

BAR S1102

The Coinage of the Bosporan Kingdom: From the First Century BC to the Middle of the First Century AD

Volume Editor: Erica Hedges

Printed in England by Digital Books Logistics Ltd

ISBN 1 84171 322 8

All BAR titles available from:

Hadrian Books
122 Banbury Road
Oxford OX2 7BP
England

The current BAR catalogue with details of all titles in print, prices and means of payment, is available free from Hadrian Books

All volumes are distributed by Hadrian Book Ltd

Preface

In two earlier publications (*Coinage of the Kingdom of Bosporus, AD 242-341/2*, Oxford BAR 1983, and *Coinage of the Kingdom of Bosporus, AD 69-238*, Oxford BAR 1979) Nina Frolova analysed the products that characterised the region in the three hundred years between the reforms introduced under Nero in the 60s AD and the final demise of autonomous Bosporan coinage in the mid-fourth century. The present volume takes that historical process one stage back in time by detailing the issues produced between the incorporation of the Bosporus into the kingdom of Mithradates VI of Pontus and the Neronian reforms. Unlike the earlier volumes, on the other hand, the present one seeks not so much to analyse the material as to present it for further study to a wider audience than has hitherto had access to it. By providing a detailed catalogue of the material held in the State Historical Museum in Moscow and the Hermitage Museum in St. Petersburg, together with subsidiary collections elsewhere within Russia and a selection of specimens from western museums, it is hoped that this will enable scholars throughout the numismatic world to renew their interest in a region which for so long has suffered from the isolation imposed by politics. The rupture in contacts over a number of decades not only substantially robbed the west of direct access to primary information, leading at times to a conflation of distinct coin-issues, or conclusions as to rarity and authenticity that in the light of present evidence may seem misplaced, but also isolated many within Russia from those developments in numismatic scholarship that were taking place elsewhere. This latter factor has often shown itself through a reliance upon sources of information and analysis dating from the 19th and early 20th centuries largely unobtainable in the west because of age, impenetrable to many in terms of language, and now of questionable value in the conclusions they reached. Notwithstanding this it was my firm belief that the information presented in the present volume would be of significant benefit to scholars that led me to undertake the task of putting it into a form acceptable for publication. I have attempted on occasion to point out where problems may continue to arise or where further expansion of evidence is available, and to add references to some of the more important recent publications relevant to the area. The volume's main purpose, however, continues to be the presentation of a corpus of material designed to allow a more detailed study of developments within Bosporan coinage. A part of this inevitably involves the very rulers in whose name bullion coins were issued, but whose period of control and relationship to one another have long been a matter of contention. In addition, there is the question of the status and meaning of the monograms found on so many coins of all metals, the significance of the typology adopted, and the opportunity for gaining some idea of the volume of material produced. By expanding available information concerning existing specimens we hope that the study of Bosporan coinage will, in consequence, be able to occupy the position within numismatics that it clearly deserves.

Stanley Ireland
University of Warwick

Contents

COINAGE OF THE BOSPORAN KINGDOM,
1st century B.C. - middle of the 1st century AD

INTRODUCTION

One of the most persistent problems concerning the coinage of the Bosporus in the first century BC is the chronology of its issues. A brief survey of the coinage of Bosporus in the late 2nd - 1st century B.C. was given by A. N. Zograph,[1] but despite the appearance of new scholarly publications[2] within the last twenty years, the conclusions reached have often either been formulated upon insufficient numismatic information or have reached conclusions which are questionable. The present work aims to provide scholars with a broader baseline of evidence upon which future work might be more profitably constructed. The purpose of this Introduction on the other hand is to provide a brief overview of developments and the problems that these engender within the existing literature.

Coins of the end of the 2nd century to the first half of the 1st century B.C.

Like many others Zograph drew attention to the watershed event in the history of the Bosporan kingdom when in 110-109 BC the last local ruler, Pairisades V, ceded control of the territory to Mithradates VI of Pontus. This event not only drew the Bosporus into close association with one of the most powerful states in Asia Minor, engaged as it was in a period of rapid aggrandisement, but also, through the conflict with Rome that this expansionist policy inevitably brought about in the subsequent fifty years, eventually brought the Bosporus into the orbit of the eternal city as a vassal state (see further Nawotka 1989).

The close connection between Bosporus and Pontus which evolved during the reign of Mithradates VI is reflected in many of the motifs that were adopted on the coinage, especially that referring to Dionysus, with whom Mithradates associated himself. Significantly, however, it is clear that there remained major differences in the monetary circulation of the two areas. Whereas, for instance, bullion coinage specifically in the name of Mithradates existed in Asia Minor, this was absent from the Bosporus. There is evidence instead for the circulation of staters of Lysimachus minted in Byzantium, while silver is represented by local products issued in the name of cities such as Panticapaeum, Phanagoria and Gorgippia rather than any individual. A complicating factor exists in the form of a gold stater bearing the name of Mithradates Eupator (von Aulock 5, Anohin 213) which has been regarded by many as the sole survivor of a royal Bosporan issue, but the degree of difference it bears compared to all other known Mithradatic gold coins in terms of motif and the absence of those letters and monograms normally present on such Mithradatic bullion issues, creates severe problems in the way of accepting it as genuine. It is also worth noting that no other gold coins of Mithradates have been found either within the territory of Bosporus or anywhere nearby.[3]

Bronze coinage of the period seems to have taken two basic forms: those bearing the names of issuing cities and anonymous issues bearing only monograms as marks of difference. Bronze coins also exist in a number of denominations. To take the earliest issues of this period as an example, we find obols bearing obv. the head of Poseidon, rev. a prow (Zograph pl.XLIII,1; Anohin 191; here pl.II, 1)[4]. Below these come tetrachalkoi with obv. the head of Artemis, rev. reclining stag, minted in both Panticapaeum and Phanagoria (Zograph pl.XLIII,2-3; Anohin 192, 194; here pl.II, 2-III,20),[5] and still

---

[1] A. N. Zograph, *Ancient Coinage*, BAR 33(ii) 1977 p.297ff.; cf. S.A.Zhebelev, 'The Last Pairisades and the Scythian Uprising in the Bosporus', *The Northern Black Sea Littoral*, p. 82-113; V.F.Gajdukevich, *Das Bosporanische Reich*, 1971, p. 313 ff.; E.A.Molev, 'The Power of Mithradates in the Bosporus', *The Ancient World and Archaeology*, II, 1974, p. 60 ff.; id., *Mithradates Eupator*, 1976, p. 39 ff.; id., *Bosporus in the Hellenistic Period*, 1994; id, *The Ruler of Pontos*, 1995, p. 41; D.B.Shelov, 'The Cities of the Black Sea Coast and Mithradates Eupator', *VDI*, 1983, p.45 ff.

[2] B.C. McGing (1986, p. 50-55, 166), K. Nawotka (1989, p. 326-338; 1992, p. 21-48), A. Burnett, M. Amandry, P.P. Ripollès (1992), W. Leschhorn (1993, p. 44-64), H. Heinen (1994, p. 63-79), F. de Callataÿ (1997).

[3] The unique nature of the coin cannot be used as an argument against its authenticity in view of the fact that the later gold coinage of Queen Dynamis is even now represented by only two specimens. Comparison of Mithradates' coin (star and crescent within wreath; above, ΒΑΣΙΛΕΩΣ; below, ΕΥΠΑΤΟΡΟΣ) with the rev. typology of Dynamis' stater (star within crescent; above ΒΑΣΙΛΙΣΣΗΣ; below, ΔΥΝΑΜΕΩΣ) suggests a deliberate echo by a ruler who was, after all, Mithradates' grand-daughter. S.I.

[4] See further, D.B.Shelov, 'Materials toward the History of Monetary Circulation in the Cities of the Bosporus in the VIth – Ist cent. B.C., *NE*, 5, 1965, p. 42-43; K.V.Golenko, 'Bronze Coins of the Cities of Pontos and Paphlagonia in the Time of Mithradates Eupator among Bosporan Finds'. Palestina's Symposium, 11 (74), 1964, p. 68; id., 'On the History of the Currency in the Bosporus in the 1st Century B.C., *NE*, 2, 1960, p. 28 ff.; id., 'On the Coinage of the Anonymous Bosporan Obols', *NSph*, 2, 1965, p. 47.

[5] K.V.Golenko, 'The Bronze Coins of Pontus in the Bosporus', *Klio*, 46, 1965; D.B.Shelov, 'Materials toward the History…', pl. 6 which is a study of the finds of coins of the II – I cent. B.C.; K.V.Golenko, 'Imitations of the Bronze Coins of Pontos and Paphlagonia in the Time of Mithradates Eupator', *VDI*, 1966.

smaller denominations bearing obv. head of Athena, rev. trident (Zograph pl.XLIII,4; Anohin 184[6]). Perceived similarities with Pontic issues over the ensuing decades has also led to hypothesised orders of production. Zograph (1977, p.297ff.), for instance, listed seventeen types of coin issued over the period of Mithradates VI's reign. Points of chronology and typology were subsequently treated in a series of articles by Golenko,[7] and some aspects of their chronology were reconsidered by Anohin,[8] but the lack of an overall study invites further special attention to be paid to the coinage of the Bosporus in the late 2nd - early 1st centuries BC.

As a starting point we might note the difficulties which the length of Mithradates VI's reign (109-63BC) itself creates for any system of ordering the coins. So, for instance, in his catalogue Anohin assigned the five periods of issue, into which he divided Mithradatic coins, to specific decades (109-100, 100-90, 90-80, 80-70, 70-63),[9] and while it is clear that this system was chosen to indicate order of production rather than exact dates, the regularity of the chronology he provides can give a misleading impression of certainty to a situation where there is no exactitude.

To the first group dated between 109-100 B.C. Anohin attributes the following types of silver: Apollo / bow in case (A., no.189), Dionysus / thyrsus (A., no.190; here pl.VII,17) as well as several bronze issues: Poseidon / prow (A., no.191, here pl.II,1) and Artemis / stag (A., no.192; here pl.II,2). He presumes that these series are reliably dated to the first years of Mithradates' reign over Bosporus, as there are drachms overstruck on coins of Amisos. However, there is no agreement among scholars on the date of the above-mentioned silver.[10] In the article by Golenko, cited by Anohin, the Apollo / bow in case (no. 189) type is attributed to the time of the Spartocids (200-140 B.C.). Golenko had only suggested that these coins could belong to the final issues of the Spartocids.[11] None of the scholars dated them later than the 2nd century B.C. At the same time the fact that some coins of Panticapaeum were struck over silver coins of Amisos cannot help us with the dating of the Bosporan silver of the Apollo / bow in case type since the female head / owl coins of Amisos were minted from the 4th century B.C. to the late 2nd - early 1st century B.C.[12] It was assumed that the silver coins of Amisos had ceased to be minted not long before the enthronement of Mithradates Eupator (121/120 B.C.).[13] Golenko attributed that event to the very beginning of Mithradates' reign.[14] Anohin still has to prove that the Apollo / bow in case type drachms (A.189) could have been issued between 109-100 B.C. However, there is no evidence for this at present. Golenko has also mentioned that the influx into Bosporus of coins minted in the cities of Pontus had nothing to do with the subjugation of the kingdom to Mithradates Eupator - the process had started before that, under the Spartocid dynasty.[15] Consequently, Golenko dated the issue of these drachms in the period before 109 B.C. To the same chronological group Anohin attributed the Artemis / pomegranate flower type of Phanagorian silver coins (A.193) as well as silver coins of Gorgippia of the type Helios / cornucopia between stars (A. 195 - numbered 196 on pl.7). This Gorgippian coin was considered doubtful by Golenko.[16] Anohin states that the coinage of the above mentioned Phanagorian and Gorgippian silver coin types is reliably testified under Mithradates,[17] at the same time providing no actual evidence confirming his statement. Joint finds of these Gorgippian and Phanagorian coins with those of the cities of Pontus issued under Mithradates could have proved that they had been minted within the same period, but

---

[6] V.A.Anohin, *The Coinage of Bosporus*, Kiev 1986 places this denomination in the period 125-115 BC. On pl.6 he wrongly numbers the coin 187.

[7] K.V.Golenko, 'The Kerch Hoard of Bosporan Coins of the 1st cent. B.C.', *NE*, 9, 1971, p. 38 ff.; id., 'The Phantalovski Hoard of Bosporan Didrachms of the 1st C. B.C.', *VDI*, 1965, p.158; id., 'The Staters of Asander in the 20 Years of his Reign', *NE*, 10, 1972, p. 103 ff.; Golenko, Karyszkowski, 'The Royal Gold Coinage of King Pharnaces of Bosporus', *NC*, 12, 1972, p. 25-38, pl. 2-3.

[8] Anohin p. 72 ff.

[9] One should note that there is some variation in the dating of periods 4 and 5 given in the text (p.74-6) and catalogue (p.144-6) of Anohin's work.

[10] Bertier de la Garde A. L., 'Materials for the Metrological Study of the Monetary Standards of the Ancient Greek Cities and Kings of Sarmatia and Tauris', *NS*, II, 1913, p. 87, dated the coins to the 3rd-2nd cent. B.C.; Zograph, p. 290 gave the date as the 2nd cent.B.C.; D.B.Shelov , *Coinage of the Bosporus VI-II Centuries B.C.* Oxford 1978, p.139, and K.V.Golenko, 'Two Coins of Pantikapaeum of the 2nd C. B.C.', *NE*, V, 1965, p. 60, supposed the second half of the 2nd C. B.C.

[11] K.V.Golenko, 'Some Silver Coins of Panticapaeum during the 2nd Century B.C. with Traces of Overstriking', *NE*, 7, 1968, p. 38-40, pl. I. 3-4.

[12] *SNG BM*, London 1993, pl.XL-XLI.

[13] Waddington, Babelon., Reinach,. *Recueil général des monnaies grecques d'Asie Mineure*, Paris, 1925, p. 53.

[14] K.V.Golenko, 'On the History of the Currency in the Bosporus in the Ist C. B.C.', *NE*, 2, 1960, p. 32-44.

[15] Golenko, 'Some Silver Coins of Panticapaeum...', *NE*, 7, 1968, p. 39.

[16] Golenko, 'On the History of the Currency...', p. 35, n. 32; id., 'The Phantalovski Hoard...', p. 152, n. 60.

[17] Anohin, p. 73.

Anohin cites no such cases. Gorgippian coins (A.195) and those of Phanagoria, of the Artemis / flower type (A. 193), were dated by Zograph to the 2nd century B.C.[18]

Within the second chronological group (100-90 B.C.) Anohin included the silver coins of Panticapaeum and Gorgippia of the Dionysus / running stag type (A.196-197). He states that both types were often overstruck on drachms of Amisos[19] referring to the authority of Golenko. But the article by Golenko cited by him contains nothing which could be taken as evidence of Gorgippian coins ever being minted from the drachms of Amisos.[20] It is true that in the list summing up the coins known to Golenko, ten of the fourteen Dionysus / running stag type coins of Panticapaeum were restruck from the drachms of Amisos. But only five coins of Gorgippia are known; four of them bear no traces of restriking; one is too badly preserved to tell anything. At the same time the dates suggested for them by Golenko are different: he thought, on the basis of these restrikes, that the spread of Amisos silver could be dated to the end of the 2nd century B.C.[21]

The third chronological group is dated by Anohin to 90-80 B.C. It comprises the Dionysus / wreath coin types bearing the names of Panticapaeum, Phanagoria and Gorgippia, but all were produced by the mint of Panticapaeum (A.198, 204, 209; here pl.V). Anohin argues that a study of die-sequence for these coins does not prove that they were all minted in Panticapaeum.[22] However, Golenko not only verified the date of these coins but he also published coins of Panticapaeum and Gorgippia struck from one obverse die, as well as coins of Panticapaeum and Phanagoria struck from one obverse die.[23] This fact made him assume that there had been no mint at all in Gorgippia and that the mint of Phanagoria had been functioning only in the 2nd century B.C. and may have also functioned under Asander.[24] It appears that there was one and the same official supervising the minting of all these coins, though bearing different city-names, ΠΑΝΤΙΚΑΠΑΙΤΩΝ, ΦΑΝΑΓΟΡΙΤΩΝ, ΓΟΡΓΙΠΠΕΩΝ; they are all marked with the same monogram (1).[25]

The fourth group consists of anonymous bronze obols of the Dionysus / bow in case type (A. 212, here pl.XIII-XIV), which Anohin dated to 80-70 BC in his catalogue (83-70 in his text, p.73). However, whether this dating is to be accepted is open to question. The Patraeus hoard of 1950[26] contained forty such anonymous obols and thirty four coins of Sinope of the Zeus / eagle on thunderbolt type, on some of which was the date 223 of the Pontic era (75/4 BC).[27] The question arises as to whether this was the first year of their issue. We have a clearer understanding of the final date for their issue - 70 BC - since in that year Sinope fell to the Romans, but the question of whether they found their way to Bosporus before this date or after must remain open. Another question is the status of such Dionysus / bow in case coins. The absence of city names for the Bosporan coins suggests that they are different from issues specifically giving their place of origin, but does this imply that they were the product of Mithradates's son Machares, who ruled Bosporus at this time?[28]

Anohin's fifth issue, which he dates to 70-63 in the catalogue and 65-3 in the text, consists of two types: (i) Apollo / eagle (A. 214; here pl.XV) (ii) Apollo / tripod (A. 215; here pl.XVI). Others, like Golenko, preferred to date the coins to the reign of Pharnaces who had usurped Mithradates' power in Bosporus in 63, but the question of their dating remains contentious.[29] Golenko produced no evidence over and above what was already known to Oreshnikov.[30] His arguments are confined only to the fact that these coins are struck over anonymous obols of the Dionysus / bow in case type and coins

---

[18] Zograph, *Ancient Coinage*, p. 291f., pl. XLII, 12, 14

[19] Anohin, p. 73.

[20] Golenko, 'On the History of the Currency...' p. 30, pl. I.

[21] *Ibid.*, p. 31-34.

[22] Anohin, p. 75.

[23] Golenko, 'On the History of the Currency... § 2, p. 34, pl. III,1 (Panticapaeum), 2 (Gorgippia). This problem was discussed by B.V.Köhne and Chr. Giel: Köhne, *Description of the Museum of Prince V.V.Kochubei, and Investigation into the History and Numismatics of the Greek Colonies in Russia and Likewise of the Kingdom of Pontos and of the Cimmerian Bosporus*, St Petersburg, vol. I, 1857, p. 418; Chr. Giel, *The Bosporan Coins with Monograms BAE, BAM and* . Odessa, 1888, p. 1-8, pl. I. They regarded these coins as minted in Panticapaeum.

[24] Golenko, 'On the History of the Currency...', *NE*, 2, p. 34, pl. III, 3 (Panticapeum), pl. III, 4 (Phanagoria); id., 'The Phantalovski Hoard ..., p. 149.

[25] The figure in brackets associated with a monogram refers to the list which follows the catalogue.

[26] Yu.S.Krushkol, 'Coins with Monograms from the Patraeus Hoard of 1950 (Taman)', *VDI*, 1952, p.145; id., 'The Patraeus Hoard of 1950'. *KSIIMK*,1956, 66, p.116-117.

[27] Imhoof-Blumer F., 'Die Kupferprägung des mithradatischen Reiches und andere Münzen des Pontos and Paphlagoniens', *NZ*, 1912, p.182 no.77; pl.II,27.

[28] D.B.Shelov, 'Machares as King of Bosporus', *VDI*, 1973, p.63-65; id., 'The Cities of Black Sea Coast and Mithradates Eupator',*VDI*, 1983, p.52-54.

[29] Golenko K. V., 'On the History of the Currency..., p.32-44.

[30] A.V.Oreshnikov, *Catalogue of the Collection of Antiquities of Count A.S.Uvarov*, VII, Moscow,1887, p.60-61.

of Sinope of the Zeus / eagle type. We should mention here that Oreshnikov did not consider these coins to have been issued by Pharnaces: he suggested only that they had been struck under him, in the name of Panticapaeum.[31] Golenko, in contrast, went further, suggesting that they had indeed been minted by Pharnaces, to which Anohin rightly objects.[32] As for the dating of the Apollo / eagle and Apollo / tripod types, the fact that most of these coins were overstrikes brings them closer to the overstruck coins of Asander. Golenko is obviously right in suggesting 60-53 B.C. for their date, but we should note that all these coins bear the inscription ΠΑΝΤΙΚΑΠΑΙΤΩΝ, which obliges us take them for a city coinage, not one of the king's. To the king's coinage belong only staters bearing the actual name of Pharnaces.[33]

Further problems introduced by Anohin concern his interpretation of minting authority, including his suggestion (p.74) that some silver coins were sponsored not by the cities involved but by temples, religious communities or by private individuals. But we should remember that all the coins involved have the name of the city, ΠΑΝΤΙΚΑΠΑΙΤΩΝ, inscribed on them. From this we cannot but infer that it was the city which produced the coins, not temples or individuals. The problem arises in attempting to use the monograms present on the coins as indicative of temples or individuals as issuing authority, but the evidence of such monograms on Pontic coinage has never led to the suggestion that these were anything but either royal issues, in the case of bullion coinage, or city issues in the case of bronze. The same must hold true also of Bosporus, which has a number of features in common with Pontic issues. Further, between 90 and 80 BC silver coins for three cities were struck at the mint of Panticapaeum from one obverse die, and one and the same monogram was placed above the city-names.[34] The same monogram appears on bronze coins issued by Panticapaeum,[35] Phanagoria[36] and Gorgippia,[37] often along with one or more other monograms. The monogram common to all the three series was taken by Anohin for an abbreviation of the name of Mithradates Eupator. In this connection we ought to draw attention to arguments militating against his suggestion. First of all there is no evidence that Mithradates VI used monograms to indicate his name. His Pontic gold and silver currency employed his full name and title: ΒΑΣΙΛΕΩΣ ΜΙΘΡΑΔΑΤΟΥ ΕΥΠΑΤΟΡΟΣ, and it follows from this that the monograms also found on such coins can have no connection with the royal name; indeed their variety tells against any such suggestion. On the analogy of this it follows that Pontic material which does not bear the Royal name (i.e. the bronze city issues) was not minted under the direct authority of Mithradates and that the wide variety of monogram found on Pontic bronze is unconnected with his name. Transferring this to a Bosporan context suggests that we have just as little reason for seeing Mithradates' name behind monograms found either on silver issues bearing the name of the cities producing such coins or on any of the bronze. Any attempt indeed to interpret the monograms must immediately become a quagmire of hypothesis and uncertainty,[38] and can even lead to the dubious dating of material; hence Anohin's locating of coins of the Apollo / eagle or Apollo / tripod type to the final years of Mithradates' reign, while others attribute them to the time of his successor, Pharnaces. Similarly, in the case of bronze coins of the tripod / star type (A.203), which Anohin dates to 90-80 BC, others have not been so prescriptive. So, for instance, Zograph (p.299) dated them to the first quarter of the 1st century BC, while Golenko, who published a specimen of the tripod / star type struck over the Athena / prow type[39] gave them a wider date - within the reign of Mithradates Eupator.[40] Later, however, Shelov published coins of the tripod / star type overstruck on earlier coins of the Apollo / bow in case, Athena / prow, and bull's head / plough and corn-ear types,[41] Golenko found these facts persuasive and agreed with

---

[31] *Ibid.*

[32] Anohin, p.73.

[33] Golenko, Karyszkowski, 'The Gold Coinage of King Pharnaces', p.25-38. The question of the distinction between whether these coins were minted by or under Pharnaces is hardly worth pursuing. The fact that in the depiction of Apollo's head they manifest a shift away from the use of Dionysus (surely signifying Mithradates VI) is enough to indicate a deliberate distancing from the past which one might have expected from Pharnaces - S.I.

[34] Anohin, 198, 204, 209, pl.40, no.15.

[35] Anohin, 202; here pl.X.

[36] *Ibid.*, 208a; here pl.XII.

[37] *Ibid.*, 211д; here pl.XII. We might note that some Gorgippian coins have variants of this: pl.XII no.16.

[38] So, for instance, Anohin p.75 takes the monograms on the coins of Bosporus of 90/80 B.C. for abbreviated names of temples, religious communities, private citizens, tax-farmers, 'newcomers from the retinue of Mithradates Eupator', representatives of local nobility and even of the king of Pontus himself. There is, of course, no evidence for this, and the varied form for Gorgippian coins given above suggests a variety of interpretation.

[39] Burachkov, pl.XXII,176. For the type see Anohin no.183.

[40] Golenko, 'The Date of the Bronze Coins of Panticapaeum. The end of the III - II B.C'. *KSIIMK*, 58, 1955, p.137, fig.55, n. 7.

[41] Burachkov, pl. XXI.114 - Apollo/bow in case; id., pl.XXII,176 – Athena/prow; id., pl.XXIII,188 - bull's head/plough, corn ear, cf. Anohin 165, 169, 183; Shelov, 'Materials toward the History…', p.44; id., 'On the History of the Currency …, 1982, p.45-50.

the dating proposed by Shelov that such coins belong instead to the end of the 2nd century BC.[42] Anohin, however, does not accept the overstrikes discovered by Shelov as a fact convincing enough to date the tripod / star type coins to the end of the 2nd century B.C.[43] There is, however, every reason to accept the dating suggested by Shelov because these are overstrikes which are beyond doubt, and there is nothing wrong in the fact that coins minted by the end of the second century B.C. were still circulating at the beginning of the first century and even later.

The coinage of Pharnaces (63-47 BC)

The assumption of power over Bosporus by Pharnaces, son of Mithradates VI, brought with it the promise of more amicable relations with Rome, something acknowledged by Pompey in granting him the title 'friend and ally of the Romans' (Appian *Mith.* 113).[44] However, there is no evidence of Pharnaces ever referring to this in any known inscription, suggesting that in terms of local politics he pursued a continuing line of independence, and his subsequent attempt to expand his power and, by exploiting hostilities between Pompey and Caesar, to recover the Pontic elements of his father's kingdom only resulted in his defeat by Caesar at Zela in 47 and the end of his reign. In numismatic terms the major point of contention lies in the date given to Pharnaces' last issue of gold coinage. Anohin confuses the issue by giving two different dates for the staters involved: 247 of the Pontic era = 51/50 BC and 248 = 50/49.[45] However, the year 50 / 49 BC could only be taken for the last year of the staters issue if staters of Pharnaces dated to year 248 of the Pontic era existed and were known to Anohin. But no such coins are listed in the Anohin's catalogue; the register of Pharnaces' staters ends at year 247.[46] Consequently, for want of evidence to the contrary, 51/50 BC remains the final date for the mintage of Pharnaces' coins.

The coinage of Asander (49/8-21/20 BC)

One of the main problems in the history of Bosporus in the second half of the 1st century BC is the Chronology of Asander's reign.[47] As part of his attempt to recover Pontic territory Pharnaces appointed Asander Archon of Bosporus while he himself was engaged in military operations in Asia Minor. Dio Cassius 42.9.2 and 42.45.2 says that Pharnaces took the field at the time of the civil war between Pompey and Caesar, i.e. no earlier than 49. On the evidence of Appian, *Bellum Civile* 2.87-8, and Dio 42.6.2 the actual campaign itself probably began in 48,[48] and it was while Pharnaces was engaged in this that Asander revolted against him, after which Pharnaces was defeated at Zela in 47. But when exactly did Asander's rule begin and when did it end? The question is complicated by the fact that Asander did not make any reference on his coins to the Bosporan era, but preferred instead simply to indicate the regnal year in which individual coins were produced. However, the discovery by Novichenkova at Yalta in 1983[49] of a new stater of Queen Dynamis dating from the year 277 B.e. – 21-20 BC, together with the testimony of ancient authors,[50] makes it possible to consider this question afresh in the context of the transfer of power.[51] The gold coins of Asander testify that he first held office as Archon and in the fourth year assumed the title of king.[52] The stater issued by Dynamis in 21-20 BC, taken in the context of Dio (54.24) that Dynamis received power from her husband

---

[42] K.V.Golenko, 'Some Silver Coins of Panticapaeum During the 2nd century B.C. with Traces of Overstriking', *NE*; 7, 1968, p.41.
[43] Anohin, p.75.
[44] There may be a hint of similar close ties with Machares, son and viceroy of Mithradates VI in Bosporus, on the basis of Plutarch *Lucullus* 24, cf. Appian *Mith.* 83; Nawotka , 1989, p.327. The whole period is usefully surveyed by W.Leschhorn, *Antike Ären*, Stuttgart 1993, p.44ff.
[45] Ahohin, p.76, 77.
[46] *Ibid.*, no.220.
[47] P.O.Karyszkovski, N.A.Frolova, 'The Reign of Asander in the Bosporus Based on Numismatic Data', in *The Ancient Black Sea Littoral*, Odessa, 1990, p.89-112, pl.VII-IX; Leschhorn p.46ff.
[48] N.A.Frolova, P.O.Karyskovskij, M.Delfs, 'Zur Chronologie der Herrschaft Asanders im Bosporos', *Chiron* 23, 1993, p.65f.
[49] N.G.Novichenkova 'A New Find of the Yalta Archaeology Expedition in 1983', *Symposium of the Institute of Archaeology of Russia (March 1984)*.
[50] Appian, *Mith.* 120; *De Bell. Civ.* II.91-2; Plutarch, *Caesar* 50; Dio Cassius 42.47.
[51] P.O.Karyszkovski, N.A.Frolova, 'On the History of the Reign of Asander in Bosporus 49/48 - 21/20 B.C.', *The Ancient Black Sea Littoral*, Odessa, 1989, p. 32-34; Karyszkovski, Frolova 'On the History of the Reign of Asander in Bosporus', *Numismatic Investigations of the History of South-East Europe*, p. 39-100; Karyszkovski, Frolova 'The Reign of Asander in the Bosporus…', p.89-112. See also N.A.Frolova, 'Dating the Reign of Dynamis', *SA*, 1978, p.49-60, Leschhorn p.50f.; Frolova, Karyskovskij, Delfs 'Zur Chronologie…'; K.Nawotka, 'Asander of the Bosporus: His Coinage and Chronology', *AJN* 3-4, 1991-2, p.29ff.
[52] This is shown by the existence of Δ = 4 as the last numeral to appear on the Archon coins and the first that has been found on staters with the title King.

Asander, makes it likely that this was also the last year of Asander's reign.[53] Since Asander's coinage is marked with his regnal years, the final figure known, 29, thus suggests that the first year of his archonship fell in the period October 49-September 48.[54] On the evidence of Dio Asander revolted against Pharnaces most probably in 48, though 47 remains a possibility.[55] Following the battle of Zela Pharnaces attempted to return to Bosporus but was killed by Asander (Dio 42,47,5; Appian *Mith.* 120). Thereafter Asander had to contend with Mithradates III of Pergamum (Dio 42.48.4, Appian *Mith.* 121, Caesar *Bellum Alexandrinum* 78), to whom Caesar awarded Bosporus for the help he had given in Egypt. Asander's victory in the ensuing struggle (Strabo 13,4,3) may have been the signal for his assumption of the title King, but the absence of a firm date for the final clash prevents certainty.[56] What must be certain, however, is that the defeat of Mithradates, backed as he was by Rome, indicates an initial coolness of relations between Bosporus and Rome, additional evidence for which comes in the presence or absence of the term φιλορώμαιος from inscriptions.[57]

In turn, the coinage of Dynamis and the issue of staters with monograms presents a whole series of further problems, not least the dates of her sole reign and whether one or two periods of power are involved. Following the death of Asander, which we have presumed took place in 21/20, the recognition of Dynamis as queen by Rome opens a new period in the history of Bosporus. Rostovtzeff[58] went so far as to claim that the area was actually incorporated into the Roman empire, though its nominal independence and the authority of its ruler were preserved. He suggested that Dynamis had twice obtained confirmation of her position from Augustus: first after the death of Asander when staters dated to 21/20 and 17/16 BC were issued in her name and then after the death of Polemo, whose wife she had become on the command of Augustus (Dio 54,24). It is known that c. 12 BC Polemo married again, taking as his wife Pythodoris, Queen of Pontus, (Strabo 12.3.29),[59] but there is a supposition that following Polemon's death in 9/8 BC Dynamis held power again. The evidence for this, however, lies solely in interpretation of the monogram  (2) found on a series of staters bearing the dates 289-304 B.e. = 9/8BC - AD 7/8.[60] The presence of a male head on each side, usually interpreted as Augustus and Agrippa, also led to the idea that having been granted the right to strike gold by Augustus in 8BC Dynamis honoured her overlords by renaming Panticapaeum as Caesarea and Phanagoria as Agrippia.[61] This idea, first tentatively suggested by Oreshnikov, was soon accepted by Rostovtzeff and others as an established fact.[62] However, Oreshnikov considered the coins bearing the new city names as contemporary also with staters marked with the monogram KNE issued in 305-6 B.e. = AD 8-9, a monogram which can in no way be associated with an abbreviation of the name Dynamis. Furthermore, Bertier de la Garde regarded gold staters with the monogram  (2) and bronze coins with the monograms BÂE and BAM as contemporary, again suggesting a more fluid situation than simply a second reign by Dynamis.[63] Indeed, once identification of the monogram

---

[53] We might note, while not accepting, Dio's dating of Asander's death to 14 BC (54.24.4).

[54] cf. *RPC* I, 1842. Leschhorn p.50-1. Nawotka (1991-2, p.29-31) gives a useful summary of the evidence, but questions the assumption that Dynamis began coining only after her husband's death, cf. Leschhorn's mention of this possibility p.51. Nawotka himself (p.38) gives Asander a reign of 31 or 32 years between 46 and 16/15 BC. One possible explanation he gives for the discrepancy is that coins minted in Asander's final years are not known. Other possibilities he considers are that Asander may not have counted his regnal years from the time he took power and that some of the busts shown on his staters belong to Mark Antony and Octavian, which would require shifting the whole series to a later time-span, to between 44/3 and 16/15. However, this leaves the question of Dynamis' coinage unresolved.

[55] Leschhorn p.47.

[56] Frolova, Karyskovskij, Delfs, p.67. Leschhorn p.51 suggests c.47/46 as the date.

[57] Thus *CRIB* 913 contains no reference to the term, while *CRIB* 30 does. This suggests that with time Asander's relations with Rome improved to the extent of recognition of him as king of Bosporus. There is also the evidence of Dio 42,46,4, who says that in revolting against Pharnaces Asander hoped to gain Rome's favour and be recognised as ruler of Bosporus.

[58] *Iranians and Greeks in Southern Russia*, Oxford 1922, p.152; contrast Nawotka (1989) p.328-9, who points out the emphasis Dynamis herself placed upon her descent from Mithradates VI in inscriptions, Leschhorn p.51-2.

[59] Oreschnikov A.V., 'Pythodoris and her Origin in the Pontic Kingdom', *IAK*, 34, 1902, p.12; Baldus H.R. 'Die Daten von Münzprägung und Tod der Königin Pythodoris von Pontos', *Chiron*, 13, 1983, p.541 ff.; *RPC* I p.331.

[60] Rostovtzeff, 'A Bronze Bust of the Bosporan Queen Dynamis at the Time of Augustus. *Drevnosti*, XXV, 1916, p. 18; id., 'The Bronze Coins of Dynamis and Aspourgos', *ITUAK*, 54, 1918, p. 49; id., 'Queen Dynamis of Bosporus', *JHS*, 39, 1919, p.100-101; Gajdukevitch V.F., *The Kingdom of Bosporus*, 1949, p. 222, 316-317; Zograph, *Ancient Coinage*, p.307; Blavatsky, *Panticapaeum*, 1964, p. 32; Shelov, *Tanais and the Lower Don in the IIIrd - Ist cent., B.C.*, p. 231; Boltunova, 'On the inscription *IOSPE*, II, 400', *VDI*, 1954, p.174; Golenko, 'The Kerch Hoard of Bosporan Coins of the Ist cent. B.C.', *NE*, 9, 1971, p. 41.

[61] Nawotka (1989) p.328, in contrast, suggests that the presence of the heads was a propaganda ploy by Dynamis to assure Rome of her loyalty while engaged in a power struggle with Polemon.

[62] Oreshnikov, 'Excursus on the Ancient Numismatics of the Black Sea Coast', 1914, p.40; Rostovtzeff, 'A Bronze Bust of the Bosporan Queen Dynamis at the Time of Augustus' p.14-18.

[63] Bertier de la Garde, 'The Coins of the Kings of the Cimmerian Bosporus determined by Monograms', *ZOOID* 29, 1910, p.190. Burnett, Amandry, Ripollès (*RPC*, I p. 331) in fact, rightly attribute the staters with the monograms (289-304 B.e. = 9/8 B.C. - A.D. 7 KNE (305-306 B.e. = A.D. 8-9) and (307-310 B.e. = A.D. 10-13) to a period of 'Uncertain Kings'.

(2) with Dynamis is rejected, the alternative scenario of the queen's death shortly after the accession of Polemo in 15/14 BC, followed by Polemo's marriage to Pythodoris in 12 BC becomes a far more satisfactory interpretation of events. However, the question of the date when Panticapaeum and Phanagoria were renamed remains to be resolved. It is reasonable to suggest that the most likely period for the inception of coinage recording the event would be between 18 BC and the death of Agrippa in 12 BC, the period of his greatest influence in the empire. The appearance at Rome of coins commemorating Augustus and Agrippa in 13-12 BC might well provide the spark for the renaming, though Agrippa's intervention in the area in 15-14 BC, as suggested by *RPC* I p.334, is also a distinct possibility.[64]

In addition to staters bearing the monogram  (2) and KNE mentioned above the period also saw issues of gold with the monogram  dated to 307 and 310 B.e. = AD 10/11 and 13/14, as well as bronze issues bearing the monograms BAE, BAM, and BAP. The last of these certainly refers to Aspurgus, whose staters, bearing the same monogram, span the period 311-334 B.e. = AD 14-37.[65] The similarity of bronze coins bearing BAP (pl.XLVI, 8-14) to others bearing the monogram BAM (pl.XXXIX, 23-26) suggests that they are associated in time, the BAM coins preceding the other. Interpretation of the BAE monogram, however, is more problematical. Frolova, for instance, points out that one of the BAM types (pl.XXXIX, 18-21) is close to a series marked with the BAE monogram (pl.XXXIV, 18), suggesting connection in time, a factor strengthened by a similarity of denominations. She concludes from this that the series belongs to the period between the death of Polemo and the accession of Aspurgus.[66] In contrast, *RPC* I p.331 points to the presence of BAE together with the date A on a unique stater (*RPC* I 1865) which has been attributed to the reign of Polemo.[67]

Thus the coinage between the death of Asander and the accession of Aspurgus may be divided into three major periods:

1. 21/20 - 14 BC, the reign of Dynamis, when relations with Rome continued along the lines set by Asander.
2. 15/14 - 9/8 BC, the reign of Polemo. The existence of the stater marked with the monogram BAE, whether it belongs to the reign of Polemo or later, ushers in a period when the head of the Roman emperor regularly occupied the obverse of gold coins, which in turn suggests Bosporus' recognition of Roman overlordship.
3. 9/8 BC - AD 13, the period of 'uncertain rulers', the coinage of which is characterised by monograms and the imperial head.

The coinage of Aspurgus[68] (AD 14-37)

Epigraphic and numismatic evidence brings us to the conclusion that the reign of Aspurgus starts from the time when staters of 311 B.e. = AD 14 with the monogram BAP were minted in Bosporus since it cannot be doubted that his name is concealed in the monogram. However, until recently the problem of the beginning of his reign remained open. Various dates were suggested: 8 BC,[69] AD 8[70], AD 10[71] and AD 14.[72] This variety of dates was caused by the attempt to relate the staters of Aspurgus with the above-mentioned monogram to gold coins marked with monograms  (2) (9/8 BC - AD 7), KNE (AD 8-9) and (AD 10-13). So, for instance, although the representations

[64] *RPC* I p.334 also points out that the presence of coins of Caesarea and Agrippia together with others bearing the monogram BAE in the Kerch hoard of 1961 strengthens the idea of their appearance towards the end of the 1st century BC.

[65] In addition to the numismatic evidence there is also inscriptional evidence; see further Blavatskaya, 'Inscriptions of King Aspurgus' *SA* 2, 1965, p.197; id., 'Aspurgus and Bosporus in AD 15', *SA* 3, 1965, p.26; *CRIB* 39, 985.

[66] Frolova, 'Dating the Beginning of Aspurgus's Reign in Bosporus', *VDI*, 1979, p.139-147, pl. I-III; id., 'Bronze Coins of the Bosporus from the End of the First Century BC - Beginning of the First Century AD', *NE* 15, 1989, p.3-18. Frolova also argues that the dating is confirmed by typologically similar Roman denarii, citing Cohen, *Description historique des monnaies, médailles imperiales*, I, Paris 1880, p.141, no.529.

[67] Cf. Leschhorn p.60. Interpretation of the monogram as ΒΑΣΙΛΕΩΣ ΕΥΠΑΤΟΡΟΣ invites comparison with Mithradates VI, but as Leschhorn p.58-60 points out, the evidence of the gold stater militates against a reference to Rome's former enemy, and the monogram may instead represent ΕΥΣΕΒΗΣ, which Polemo I assumed.

[68] The dynastic origins of Aspurgus cannot be established. Nawotka (1989) p.329 makes him son of Dynamis, though the intervening period of dynasts and the lack of any evidence prevents such an assumption.

[69] Latyshev, *ΠΟΝΤΙΚΑ*, St Petersburg, 1909, p.106.

[70] Gajdukevich, *The Kingdom of Bosporus*, p.322; Shelov, *The Ancient World in the Northern Black Sea Littoral*, p.153; Blavatski, *Panticapaeum*, p.132.

[71] Rostovtzeff, 'A Bronze Bust of Bosporan Queen Dynamis', p.17; id., 'The Bronze Coins of Dynamis and Aspurgus…', p.51; id., 'Queen Dynamis...', p.103; Golubzova, *The Northern Black Sea Littoral Between the Centuries BC. and AD*, p.87-88.

[72] Bertier de la Garde 'The Coins of the Kings of the Cimmerian Bosporus Determined by Monograms', *ZOOID*, 29, 1910, p.120.

on staters with BAP are different from the others, attempts were made to ascribe coins with [monogram] to Aspurgus. Rostovtzeff, ascribing the [monogram] stater to Aspurgus, also took bronze coins with a different monogram - BAE - for the earliest bronze issue of that king.[73] It followed from this that Aspurgus was apparently issuing coins with three different monograms: [monogram] , BAE and BAP, though it is clear that these must conceal different names. Certainly, however, the decipherment of BAP as of the name of Aspurgus is confirmed by Bosporan inscriptions of A.D. 15/16, 16/17 and 23 mentioning the name and the title of the king and by the minting of contemporary gold coins marked with that same monogram. It is also worth mentioning that three types of bronze coins with the monogram were issued, while there were no bronze coins with the monogram [monogram] . We can also point out that the monograms of the later Bosporan kings Cotys I and Rhescuporis II are the same on both gold and on bronze coins suggesting a similar system should have operated in the case of Aspurgus also, and that the only universal monogram for him is BAP. Consequently, the first year of Aspurgus' reign in Bosporus must correspond to the time when staters with the monogram BAP first make their appearance: 311 B.e. = AD 14. From the inscription of 312 B.e. set up for Aspurgus by the Gorgippians it follows that Augustus was the emperor who had confirmed the rights of Aspurgus on the throne of Bosporus.[74] The typology of Aspurgus' bronze coins also supports the idea. The death of Augustus evidently made Aspurgus seek a new confirmation of his rights from Rome. We may be sure that those rights were ratified in turn by Tiberius and Caligula, something testified by the inscriptions on Aspurgus' coins issued in the reigns of the two emperors. In this way we get the initial date of his reign – AD 14, while the end of Aspurgus' reign should be seen as coinciding with the latest dated issue of staters, 334 B.e. = AD 37 - not to 38/39 as suggested by some.[75] It has been suggested indeed that Aspurgus' relations with three emperors indicates he signed a treaty of friendship (*amicitia*) with Rome on three occasions, and that he was the first of the kings of Bosporus who, along with the titles φιλόκαισαρ and φιλορώμαιος, was granted Roman citizenship - evidence for a new stage in the relationship between Bosporus and Rome.[76] One suggestion, however, that the numismatic evidence does not support is that of Aspurgus taking a second, Thracian name - that of Rhescuporis.[77]

The Coinage of Gepaipyris (AD 37-8)

With the exception of a single silver plate inscribed with her name and titles (found in Scythian Neapolis),[78] Gepaipyris is mentioned neither by any of the ancient authors nor by other epigraphic texts from Bosporus. Only coins issued in her name provide confirmation of her existence, and make us consider the question of her autonomous rule in Bosporus and her relationship to Aspurgus, Mithradates[79] and Cotys I.[80] These questions have never, in fact, been considered properly. Gepaipyris has been taken either for the wife of Mithradates or his mother.[81] Following the suggestion made by Bertier de la Garde, that the bronze coins of Cotys (pl.LIII, 1-3) bore the portraits of the king's parents, along with monograms constructed from their names: BAP and [monogram] , Rostovtzeff came to the conclusion that the portrait of Cotys' mother was close to Gepaipyris' representation on bronze coins of Mithradates, and he suggested reading the monogram as containing the name and title of Gepaipyris. The identity of monograms on the copper coins of Cotys I, and on gold coins of 334 B.e = A.D. 37 (3 specimens) and 335 B.e. = A.D. 38 (2 specimens) makes it possible, in fact, to consider that Gepaipyris was the wife of Aspurgus and the mother of Mithradates and Cotys. Further

[73] Rostovtzeff, 'A Bronze Bust of Queen Dynamis…', p.51.

[74] Vinogradov, 'Epigraphy in the USSR', *Archeologysk Vestnik. Acta Archaeologica*, 31, 1980, p.309, n.100.

[75] Gajdukevich, *Das Bosporanische Reich.*, p.340, n.16

[76] Nawotka (1989) p.329 with refs. While *amicitia* treaties are well attested, the idea that Aspurgus was enrolled in the Senate is highly speculative.

[77] The basis for the assertion that king Aspurgus bore the additional name Rhescuporis is the monogram BAP on the coins of this king. The idea was advanced in 1884 by Burachkov (*General Catalogue*, p.237-239), by Bertier de la Garde ('The Coins of the Kings of the Cimmerian Bosporus…', p.157, 164, 179 ff.), and by Zograph (*Ancient Coinage*, p. 315). Further work by Blavatski, 'On Rhescuporis I', *SA*, 4, 1976, p.56-61 and Frolova, 'The Copper Coins of Cotys I as a Historical Source', *SA*, 3, 1976, however, supported the idea that Aspurgus did not take a second Thracian name, Rhescuporis I.

[78] Yazenko , 'The Queen Gepaipyris Dish from Scythian Neapolis', *Istoriko-Archeologicheski Sbornik*, Moscow, 1962, p.101-103.

[79] The numbering of this Mithradates within the royal succession of Bosporan kings varies greatly in the literature. To Zograph (p.315-17) he is Mithradates III; Nawotka (1989) p. 329f. makes him Mithradates VIII, while *RPC* I p.329 has him as Mithradates I. In view of this we prefer in this introduction simply to record his name without the complication of a number.

[80] That Mithradates and Cotys were brothers is established by Dio Cassius 60,28,7 and Tacitus *Ann.* XII,18), cf. *CIRB*, 41

[81] Köhne, *Description of the V.V. Kochubei Museum*, St Petersburg, 1857, p.202-215ff; Bertier de la Garde, 'The Coins of the Kings of the Cimmerian Bosporus...', p.195. Köhne, and after him, Bertier de la Garde supported the idea that Gepaipyris was a wife of Mithradates, but Rostovtzeff regarded Gepaipyris as Mithradates' mother: Rostovtzeff, 'A Bronze Bust of the Bosporan Queen Dynamis...', p.21.

confirmation of this can be extracted from a study of the bronze coins which bear the name of Gepaipyris.

Two types of coin exist with the name of Gepaipyris: one has the queen's bust and a legend bearing her name and titles on the obverse, and on the reverse the bust of Aphrodite and the mark IB (12 units),[82] which testifies to her autocratic rule over Bosporus, since there is no reference to Mithradates. This bronze series can be compared only to the staters of Dynamis. The second bronze issue with the name of Gepaipyris (represented by ten known specimens)[83] has the bust of Gepaipyris on the obverse, that of Mithradates on the reverse. It reflects another stage in her legal status, the beginning of her son Mithradates' reign over Bosporus. However, if we assume that this latter issue showed not the mother but the wife of Mithradates, then, taking into account the bronze issue showing Aphrodite, we would have to conclude that the wife, being accorded an issue in her name alone, had been given more authority and power than her husband. We have every reason to think, therefore, that Gepaipyris was the mother of Mithradates, not his wife. Her gold staters, dated to 334 and 335 B.e. = AD 37/8 and 38/9, also demonstrate that her sole reign was not long.

Thus, taking into account the typology of the issues, we are able to establish an autonomous reign of Gepaipyris separate from those of Aspurgus and Mithradates, and to consider her coins, earlier attributed to the coinage of Mithradates, as a distinct group. We also see now that the two series of Gepaipyris' coins reflect two stages in her legal status. The first type testifies to her autonomous rule; the second reflects the enthronement of her son.

The Coinage of Mithradates (AD 39-45?)

Mithradates, inheriting the throne of Bosporus from his mother Gepaipyris, who had obviously received confirmation of her titles and the right to issue gold coins from Caius Caligula,[84] was denied both of these privileges. Caligula granted the Kingdom of Bosporus instead to Polemo II, (Dio, 59, 12, 2), though whether the latter ever exercised any power in the region is doubtful. For his part Mithradates, whose legitimate right to the throne of Bosporus had been brought into question, evidently wished to display his royal dignity by issuing gold coins somewhat different from those of his predecessors.[85] Staters of the three years of his reign are known: 336 B.e. = AD 39/40 (3 specimens), 337 B.e. = AD 40/41 (2 specimens) and 338 B.e. = AD 41/2 (2 specimens). But, while on the obverse the coins in question have a portrait of the emperor Gaius Caligula (a sop to Rome?), the reverse motif shows Nike holding a wreath and a palm branch, together with the name and title of Mithradates inscribed around: ΒΑΣΙΛΕΩΣ ΜΙΘΡΙΔΑΤΟΥ. There are, in addition, two bronze issues: one has on the obverse the king's portrait and an inscription containing his name and title, ΒΑΣΙΛΕΩΣ ΜΙΘΡΑΔΑΤΟΥ. On the reverse there is the portrait of his mother along with her name and titles, ΒΑΣΙΛΕΩΣ ΓΗΠΑΙΠΥΡΕΩΣ and the mark IB (12 units). The issuing of this type can be dated to AD 38 because of their similarity with the type of bronze coins bearing no value-marks issued in the lifetime of Gepaipyris. The second type has on the obverse the portrait of Mithradates, and on the reverse the club of Heracles with a lion's pelt over it. This second type can perhaps be dated to AD 39, the year when staters with the name and title of Mithradates were first issued. The appearance of gold and bronze issues of Mithradates glorifying his royal dignity suggests the king's wish to carry on his own independent policy. It resulted in Polemo II never becoming king of Bosporus; on the contrary, in AD 41 the emperor Claudius recognised Mithradates, descendant of the great Mithradates Eupator, as king of Bosporus, while Polemo II was given instead the province of Cilicia (Dio, 60,8,2). The only known inscription of Mithradates, dating to A.D. 41, gives a new formulation of his title: he is called 'the friend of the allies and the friend of the fatherland' instead of the usual 'the friend of Rome and the friend of Caesar'. This suggests that his second *cognomen,* 'the friend of the fatherland' indicates his desire to make the kingdom more independent of Roman overlordship, while at the same time retaining relations with the Empire. Mithradates' separatist attitude was denounced by his brother Cotys before the emperor Claudius. It caused military intervention from Rome, with Roman troops invading Bosporus, and Cotys being proclaimed king.[86]

[82] Pl.XLVII,1-18, XLVIII,1-3; N.A.Frolova, 'On the Period of the Reigns of Gepaipyris and of Mithradates III', *VDI*, 1977, p.169, pl. I, 8.
[83] Pl.XLVIII,5-8.
[84] This much is indicated by the presence of the emperor on the obverse of staters: pl. XLVI,15-19. Identification of the 'Roman' bust on the reverse and its significance is open to question.
[85] CIRB, 1123. N.A.Frolova, 'The Gold Coins of Mithradates III (338 B.e. = A.D. 41), from the Collection of GIM', *VDI*, 1986, p.54-59.
[86] Tacitus *Annals* XII, 15-21.

The analysis of the bronze issues of Mithradates, now carried out for the first time, demonstrates that coins with the monogram BAM, formerly attributed by Zograph to Mithradates,[87] could not have been issued by him. For the time of his reign in Bosporus the first date is marked by the issue of the staters of 336 B.e. = AD 39, the last by the first emission of gold in the name of Cotys in 342 B.e. = AD 45.

The Coinage of Cotys I (A.D. 45- 68)

In contrast to those of his predecessor the coins of Cotys I display unquestionable marks of his submission to Rome, prompted partly perhaps by his reliance upon Rome for his throne and partly by the presence of Roman troops in his territory. One of the features of his coins, for instance, is the presence of imperial effigies on both the obverse and the reverse, Cotys' own name and titles being confined to the monogram BAK. Staters of Cotys I with the monogram are known from 342 to 357 B.e. = AD 45-60. In 359 B.e. = AD 62 his monogram on gold coins was replaced by that of Nero himself NEP (74). The issue of gold coins of Cotys was thus limited to AD 45-62; no staters minted after AD 62 have yet been found. The types of his coins demonstrate the dependence of this king of Bosporus upon Rome: events taking place in Rome found a quick response in Bosporus. This is true also for the bronze coins of Cotys. Investigation of the chronology of his bronze issues is based on the study of the portraits of Romans and the titles which appear on them.[88] For the earliest series of Cotys' bronze (AD 45-50) three types of his coins are included bearing the value marks Δ, ϛ and H – 4, 6 and 8 units. The second series, all marked IB (12 units / asses) and including four types with the portrait of Claudius on the obverse and that of Agrippina on the reverse, is dated to AD 49-50 because it could be issued only after Claudius had married Agrippina in that year.[89] However, coins belonging to the series could well have continued to be minted to the end of Claudius' reign (AD 54). To the third series (AD 54-59) belongs only one type, again of 12 units, representing Nero and Agrippina. Its dating is determined by the year when Nero was proclaimed emperor (AD 54) and by the time of Agrippina's death, the end of AD 59. To the fourth series (AD 63), likewise a single series of 12 units, belong coins representing Nero and Poppea. To the fifth series of bronze (AD 63-68) two new large denominations were added: sestertii (MH = 48 units) and dupondii (KA = 24 units). Dupondii were of three types: 1. Nero / Nike; 2. temple – KA- ΠΕ / monogram BAK within wreath; 3. temple – KA- ΠΕ / monogram BAKY or BAKY (75-76) within a wreath.

The reform of coinage carried out by Nero in the kingdom of Bosporus, discontinuing the issue of gold coins after AD 62 and changing the minting of bronze to bring it more readily into line with the Roman system, has been regarded by some as a first step towards the unification of the money system within the Roman Empire as a whole. It was mentioned earlier that Nero substituted his own monogram on gold coins for that of Cotys in AD 62; one might also hypothesise that the apparent discontinuance of stater-production thereafter was paralleled by a prohibition on native bronze coins.[90] However, this finds no parallel in Roman history. Antioch, Alexandria, the cities of Asia Minor, Crete, Cappadocia and Caesarea all minted autonomous local bronze and silver coins under Nero. There is, therefore, the possibility of the new denominations of the 5th series coins being minted not in the reign of Cotys, but at the beginning of the reign of Rhescuporis II in A.D. 68/69 when the production of staters was resumed.

An additional problem concerning the coinage of the period centres upon coins showing a curule chair, crown and sceptre together with the inscription ΤΕΙΜΑΙ ΒΑΣΙΛΕΩΣ ΚΟΤΥΟΣ (*RPC* I 1934). Ostensibly these are products of Cotys I, but there is no easy location for them within the various series produced by him and they omit the monogram BAK which is characteristic of his coins. It is tempting, therefore to assign them instead to a later reign (coins of a similar obverse type were produced, for instance, by Cotys II, AD 123-32, but as sestertii[91]), or to the successor of Cotys I, Rhescuporis, who is known to have produced TEIMAI coins in his own name.[92]

---

[87] Zograph p.316; cf. Nawotka (1989) p.330.
[88] Bertier de la Garde, 'The Coins of the Kings of the Cimmerian Bosporus...', p.161-165, 204; Zograph, p.317; Karyszkovski, 'Bosporus and Rome in the 1st Century AD...', *VDI*, 1953, p.179-183.
[89] Karyszkovski p.182-189; Frolova, 'The Coinage of Cotys I, the Son of Aspurgus (A.D. 45-68)', *NS* GIM, V,1977.
[90] Bertier de la Garde 'The Coins of the Kings of the Cimmerian Bosporus...', p. 214; Zograph, p. 318ff. The question of weight standards for the Bosporan and Roman issues, which may have a bearing on their denominational relationship, is discussed by Zograph, p.319f.
[91] Frolova, *The Coinage of the Kingdom of Bosporus AD 69-238*, p.149; pl. XVIII, 12-30.
[92] cf. *RPC* I p.334; *RPC* II, p.84; Frolova, *The Coinage of the Kingdom of Bosporus AD 69-238*, p.16; pl. IV, 1, 6, 7.

CATALOGUE OF THE BOSPORAN COINS

After the Bosporan Kingdom had been incorporated into Mithradates VI's state its coinage and currency followed that of Pontus and Paphlagonia (Zograph, 1977, p.298): as in the case of Pontus, the largest bronze denominations were obols (= 8 chalkoi, wt. = 17-18 g.). Below this was a middle denomination – tetrachalkos (= 4 chalkoi or ½ of obol, wt. = 8-9 g.), followed by the smallest – chalkos (wt. = 2 g.) (Zograph, 1977, p.299).

§ 1. The end of the 2nd century B.C. - the beginning of the 1st century B.C.

Panticapaeum

Chalkoi

Obv. Tripod.
Rev. Star; between the rays, ΠΑΝΤΙΚΑΠΑ or ΠΑΝΤΙΚΑ.
Anohin 203; *SNG BM* 941-4; Stancomb 587-8.

A.N. Zograph dated this type of coin to 100 - 75 B.C. (A.N. Zograph, *Ancient Coinage* p.299 pl.XLIII, 18). D.B. Shelov ('Materials Toward the History of Monetary Circulation in the Cities of the Bosporus in the VIth - Ist Centuries B.C.', *NE*, V, 1965, p.44) dated them to end of the 2nd century B.C.. K.V. Golenko supposed that this type was minted in 90-80 BC - 'The Bronze Coins of the Cities of Pontos and Paphlagonia in the time of Mithradates VI Among Bosporan Finds', *Palestina Sbornik*, II (74), 1964, p.63.

Dies		Wt.	Dia.	Mus.	Mus. No.	Plate	Notes
A-a	1)	3,62	15 mm	GE	865	pl.I,1	
B-b	1).	2,67	16 mm	GE	866	pl.I,2	
C-c	1)	2,33	15 mm	GE	867	pl.I,3	
D-d	1)	1,95	15 mm	GE	868	pl.I,4	
E-e	1)	3,06	17 mm	GE	869	pl.I,5	
F-f	1)	3,22	16 mm	GE	870	pl.I,6	
J-j	1)	2,90	15 mm	GE	871	pl.I,7	
I-I	1)	2,93	14 mm	GE	872	pl.I,8	
K-k	1)	3,08	15 mm	GE	873	pl.I,9	
L-l	1)	2,96	15 mm	GE	874	pl.I,10	
N-n	1)	3,20	16 mm	GE	875	pl.I,11	Anohin 203
Ai-ii	1)	3,20	15 mm	A		pl.I,11a	
O-o	1)	2,48	15 mm	GE	876	pl.I,12a	Overstruck on type: Obv. Head of bull. Rev. Plough, ear of wheat, ΠΑΝ. The end of the 3rd B.C. - first half of the 2nd century B.C. (Shelov, 83)
	2)	1,83	15 mm	GE	877	pl.I,12b	Overstruck on type: Obv. Head of bull. Rev. Plough, ear of wheat, ΠΑΝ. The end of the 3rd – first half of the 2nd century B.C.
	3)	2,02	15 mm	GE	878	pl.I,13	Overstruck on type: Obv. Athena Rev. Prow. About 110 B.C. (Shelov, 102)
P-p	1)	1,61	13 mm	GE	879	pl.I,12	
S-s	1)	2,08	15 mm	GE	880	pl.I,14	
T-t	1)	1,82	12 mm	GIM	8863	pl.I,15	
	2)	2,05	12 mm	GIM	8859		
	3)	2,80	12 mm	GIM	8860		
	4)	2,10	12 mm	GIM	8862		
	5)	2,06	13 mm	GIM	8847	pl.I,15a	
G-g	1)	2,87	13 mm	GIM	8864	pl.I,16	
	2)	2,83	13 mm	GIM	8865		
	3)	1,94	13 mm	GIM	8848	pl.I,16a	
U-u	1)	2,60	13 mm	GIM	8866	pl.I,17	
V-v	1)	1,47	12 mm	GIM	8867	pl.I,18	
H-h	1)	1,82	13 mm	GIM	8869	pl.I,19	
	2)	2,55	13 mm	GIM	8868		Poor condition
	3)	2,69	13 mm	GIM	8870		Poor condition
Q-q	1)	3,21	14 mm	GIM	8871	pl.I,20	
	2)	2,60	15 mm	GIM	8872		

Z-z	1)	3,01	15 mm	GIM	8873	pl.I,21	
	2)	2,10	14 mm	GIM	8874		
	3)	1,26	12 mm	GIM	8854	pl.I,21a	
X-x	1)	1,98	12 mm	GIM	8875	pl.I,22	
	2)	1,42	11 mm	GIM	8876		Poor condition
	3)	1,27	12 mm	GIM	8877		Poor condition
	4)	2,07	12 mm	GIM	8878		Poor condition
	5)	1,22	12 mm	GIM	8880		Poor condition
	6)	3,46	13 mm	GIM	8881		
	7)	1,63	13 mm	GIM	8882	pl.I,24	
	8)	1,10	12 mm	GIM	8855	pl.I,23a	
	9)	1,80	13 mm	FMC	4469	pl.I,23	
Ah-ah	1)	2,60	13 mm	BM	941		
	2)	2,45	12 mm	BM	942		
	3)	3,05	13 mm	BM	943		
	4)	2,15	14 mm	BM	944		
Ab-ab	1)	2,00	13 mm	GIM	8883	pl.I,25	
	2)	1,64	13 mm	GIM	8884	pl.I,26	
	3)	2,07	13 mm	GIM	8885		
Ac-ac	1)	2,39	14,5 mm	GIM	8888		Overstruck on type: Obv. Head of Satyr. R. Star-crested caps of Dioscuri - last quarter of the 2nd century B.C. (Shelov, 101)
Ad-ad	1)	1,64	15 mm	GIM	8889		Overstruck on the same type: Obv. Satyr. Rev. Caps of Dioscuri (Shelov, 101)
Ag-ag	1)	2,45	13 mm	GIM	8887	pl.LIX,1	Enlarged
	2)	1,50	10 mm	GIM	8851		
		1,85	15mm	GIM	8845	pl.I,1a	
		2,10	15mm	GIM	8846	pl.I,2a	

AE Obols

Obv. Head of Poseidon r.; to l., trident.
Rev. Prow. r.; ΠΑΝΤΙΚΑ - ΠΑΙΤΩΝ.
B.V. Köhne, I, p.374, №127, pl.VI, 26; A.M. Podshiwalov, *The Moscow Public and Rumijantsev Museum, Numismatic Department, №1. Catalogue of Coins*. Moscow, 1884, p.22, №181; P.O. Burachkov pl.XXII, 152; Zograph pl.XLIII, 1; Anohin 191; Stancomb 586.

Dies		Wt.	Dia.	Mus.	Mus. No.	Plate	Notes
A-a	1)	18,82	30 mm	GE	27137		Anohin, 191
	2)	18,58	30 mm	GIM	8789	pl.II,1	Burachkov, XXII,152
B-b	1)	16,45	30 mm	GIM	8788	pl.LIX,2	Enlarged
	2)	17,32	30 mm	GE	27136		Overstruck on a Pontic coin

The beginning of the 1st century B.C.

To the 1st century B.C. belong bronze coins of two types: Obv. Artemis with bow - Rev. Stag, ΠΑΝΤΙΚΑΠΑΙΤΩΝ, and Obv. Artemis with bow - Rev. Stag, ΦΑΝΑΓΟΡΙΤΩΝ, which die linkage shows were coined at one mint - Panticapaeum.

AE Tetrachalkoi

Obv. Head of Artemis r.; at shoulder, bow and quiver.
Rev. Stag reclining l.; ΠΑΝΤΙΚΑΠΑΙΤΩΝ.
Burachkov, XXII, 170; Zograph XLIII,2; Anohin 192.

Dies		Wt.	Dia.	Mus.	Mus. No.	Plate	Notes
A-a	1)	7,42	21 mm	GIM	8790	pl.LIX,3	Enlarged
	2)	6,77	22 mm	GIM	8791	pl.II,2	
	3)	6,33	22 mm	GE	779	pl.II,3	Anohin 192
	4)	7,48	20 mm	GE	780	pl.II,4	Obv. countermark, wheat-ear

5)	7,68	20 mm	GIM	12709		Kozievsky Coll.
6)	6,45	20 mm	GIM	12710		Kozievsky Coll.
7)	5,63	20 mm				Found in Phanagoria
8)	5,63	17mm	GIM	8924	pl.II,3a	

Obv. Head of Artemis r.; at shoulder, bow and quiver.
Rev. Stag reclining l.; below, **ΦΑΝΑΓΟΡΙΤΩΝ.**
Köhne, I, p.400, №7; Podshiwalov, p.26, №206; Burachkov, XXIII, 21; Zograph, XLIII, 2/3; Anohin 194, *SNG BM* 1000-3, *Cop.* 5[93]

Dies		Wt.	Dia.	Mus.	Mus. No.	Plate	Notes
A-a	1)	6,72	22 mm	A		pl.II,5	
	2)	6,13	23 mm	GE	58	pl.II,6	
	3)	7,57	22 mm	GE	57	pl.II,7	
	4)	7,22	21 mm	GE	55	pl.II,8	
	5)	5,43	23 mm	GE	44	pl.II,9	
	6)	3,85	20 mm	GIM	14531	pl.II,10	Grandmaison Coll.
	7)	2,96	20 mm	GIM	14536	pl.II,11	Overstruck; Grandmaison Coll.
B-a	1)	6,85	23 mm	GE	45	pl.II,12	
	2)	6,14	23 mm	GIM	6650	pl.II,13	
	3)	6,71	21 mm	GIM	6651	pl.II,14	
	4)	6,43	23 mm	GIM	6658	pl.II,15	
	5)	7,79	22 mm	GE	52	pl.II,16	
	6)	7,53	22 mm	Cop	5		
B-b	1)	6,31	23 mm	GIM	6661	pl.II,17	
B-d	1)	5,08	22 mm	GE	50	pl.II,18	
	2)	7,06	23 mm	GIM	6664	pl.II,19	
B-g	1)	7,28	23 mm	GIM	6653	pl.III,1	
	2)	6,89	23 mm	GE	49	pl.III,2	
C-c	1)	7,07	22 mm	GE	51	pl.III,3	Rev. only
D-f	1)	7,61	24 mm	GE	47	pl.III,4	
	2)	6,04	23 mm	GIM	6656	pl.III,5	
	3)	5,35	23 mm	GIM	6657	pl.III,6	
	4)	7,68	23 mm	GIM	12709		Kozievsky Coll.
F-I	1)	7,46	24 mm	GIM	6648	pl.III,7	
G-h	1)	6,88	23 mm	GIM	6649	pl.III,8	
H-k	1)	5,84	21 mm	GIM	6652	pl.III,9	
	2)	6,94	22 mm	GIM	6662	pl.III,10	
I-l	1)	5,63	23 mm	GIM	6660	pl.III,11	Anohin 194
I-m	1)	5,33	21 mm	GIM	6654	pl.III,12	
	2)	3,22	18 mm	GE	53	pl.III,14	
	3)	4,48	20 mm	GIM	6655	pl.III,13	
K-n	1)	6,83	22 mm	GE	54	pl.III,15	Overstruck on a coin with monogram  (5)
	2)	6,45	21 mm	GIM	12710a		Monogram  (5) under **ΦΑΝΑΓΟΡΙΤΩΝ**; Kozievsky Coll.
L-o	1)	6,80	25 mm	GIM	6665	pl.III,16	Overstruck on a coin of unclear type
	2)	6,80	25 mm	GIM	6666	pl.III,17	
	3)			GIM	6667	pl.III,18	
	4)	6,68	23 mm	GIM	6668		
	5)	6,70	22 mm	OGAM	27894	pl.III,19	
	6)		22 mm	OGAM	28770	pl.III,20	
	7)	5,60	18 mm	BM	1000		
	8)	5,40	18 mm	BM	1001		
	9)	6,27	20 mm	BM	1002		
	10)	5,38	21 mm	BM	1003		

[93] Five other specimens are recorded in S. Ireland, 'The Ancient Coins in Amasra Museum', in R. Ashton (ed.), *Studies in Ancient Coinage from Turkey*, Royal Numismatic Soc., British Institute of Archaeology at Ankara, 1996, p.115-37.

100 - 75 B.C.

Silver Drachms of Panticapaeum

Obv. Head of Artemis r.; at shoulder, bow and quiver.
Rev. Stag feeding r.; monogram (1), **ΠΑΝΤΙΚΑΠΑΙΤΩΝ**.
Burachkov, XXII,168-169; Zograph, XLIII,8; Anohin 199; *SNG BM* 935.

Dies		Wt.	Dia.	Mus	Mus. No.	Plate	Notes
A-a	1)	3,83	18 mm	Berlin	490	pl.III,21	
	2)	4,06	15 mm	GIM	8795	pl.IV,1	20% Ag
B-b	1)	3,97	17 mm	GIM	8796	pl.IV,2	50% Ag
C-c	1)	2,79	17 mm	GIM	8797	pl.IV,3	50% Ag
D-d	1)	4,15	17 mm	GE	795	pl.IV,4	Enlarged
	2)	3,94	17 mm	GE	796		
D-a	1)	3,70	17 mm	GE	794	pl.IV,5	
E-e	1)	3,57	17 mm	GE	797	pl.IV,6	Anohin 199. Monogram (1) left
F-f	1)	3,56	17 mm			pl.IV,7	Giel, 'Description of coins which have entered my collection in 1892 and 1893'. *ZRAO*, VII., 1895, p.9, pl.XIX,49
H-k	1)	4,28	17 mm	GE	798	pl.IV,8	
	2)	3,74	17 mm	GE	799		
A-I	1)	1,92	15 mm	GIM	13749	pl.IV,9	Monogram above stag; 50% Ag
A-g	1)	4,07	16 mm	Naville, V, pl.L, 1661			
	2)	3,86	15 mm	BM	935	pl.IV,1a	
	3)	7,55		Coll. Prowe Catalogue, 1904, pl.III,388			

100 - 75 B.C.

Silver Didrachms of Panticapaeum

Obv. Head of Dyonysus r.
Rev. Ivy wreath; inside, grapes and **ΠΑΝΤΙΚΑΠΑΙΤΩΝ**; above monogram (1).
Podshiwalov, *Beschreibung der uned. Münz*, p.7, №22, pl.I,15; Burachkov, pl.XXII, 180; Giel, 'A new acquisition in my collection', 1891: 1) p.7, №36, wt.7,21g.; 2) pl.V, 36, wt.8,68g.; 3) 7,12g. with **ΠΑΝΤΙΚΑΠΑΙΤΩΝ** from the collection of Sibirsky. Zograph, XLIII,5; Golenko, 'The Phantalovski Hoard of Bosporan Didrachms of the 1st century B.C.', *VDI*, 1965, p.141-157. Golenko published 487 coins of this type, which were found in the Anapa region in 1963. Kept in the Anapa Museum, the hoard comprised 335 didrachms of Panticapaeum, 135 didrachms with the name Phanagoria and 15 didrachms with the name Gorgippia; D.B. Shelov,' The Cities of the Black Sea and Mithradates Eupator', *VDI*, 1983, p.45; Anohin p.73, 145, №198, - dates this type of didrachm to 90-80 B.C.; *SNG BM*, 932-4; Stancomb 589-90.

Dies		Wt.	Dia	Mus	Mus. No.	Plate	Notes
A-a	1)	7,65	20 mm	A	3405	pl.IV,10	
	2)	9,12	19 mm	A		pl.IV,11	
	3)	8,30	20 mm	GIM	8792	pl.IV,12	50% Ag
A-b	1)	8,50	21 mm	GIM	8793	pl.IV,13	50% Ag
B-c	1)	6,83	21 mm	GIM	8794	pl.IV,14	60% Ag
A-d	1)	8,52	21 mm	GIM	13750	pl.IV,15	Kozievsky Coll.
	2)	8,47	21 mm	BM	932	pl.IV,16	
	3)	8,41	20 mm	BM	933	pl.IV,17	
D-e	1)	6,98	20 mm	B	70	pl.IV,18	
	2)	8,00	20 mm	B	71	pl.IV,19	
	3)	8,47	20 mm	GIM	14156	pl.IV,20	Grandemaison Coll.
I-I	1)	8,17	21 mm	GE	787	pl.IV,22	
	2)	8,75	23 mm	GE	789	pl.IV,23	
L-l	1)	3,58	19 mm	A	3406	pl.IV,21	
K-k	1)	8,10	22 mm	GE	790	pl.IV,24	
	2)	8,18	22 mm	GE	791	pl.V,1	
	3)	8,82	22 mm	GE	792	pl.V,2	
	4)	7,87	20 mm	GE	793	pl.V,3	

Dies		Wt.	Dia.	Mus.	Mus. No.	Plate	Notes
	5)	8,45	22 mm	GIM	13751	pl.V,4	Kozievsky Coll.
	6)	8,42	20 mm	BM	934	pl.V,5	
M-m	1)	6,51	22 mm	GE	785		
	2)	8,50	22 mm	GE	785a		
	3)	8,33	22 mm	GE	786		
	4)	8,17	21 mm	GE	787		
	5)	8,30	21 mm	GE	788		
	6)	7,87	20 mm	GIM	14157	pl.V,6	Grandemaison Coll.
	7)	8,67	21 mm			Ars Classica, XV, 1930, pl.21, №588	
	8)	7,98	22 mm	P	31681		

Silver Didrachms of Phanagoria

Obv. Head of Dionysus r.

Rev. Ivy wreath; inside, grapes and ΦΑΝΑΓΟΡΙΤΩΝ; above, monogram (1).

Burachkov, XXIII, 24; Zograph, XLIII, 6; Golenko, *VDI*, 1965, p.155-157, Anohin 204; *SNG BM* 997; Stancomb 625.

Dies		Wt.	Dia.	Mus.	Mus. No.	Plate	Notes
A-a	1)	8,53		GMII	23516		Anohin 204
A-b	1)	8,56	20 mm	GIM	14533	pl.V,7	Grandemaison Coll.
	2)	8,49	20 mm	GIM	14534	pl.V,8	Grandemaison Coll.
	3)	8,13	20 mm	GIM	13754	pl.V,9	Kozievsky Coll.
A-g	1)	8,51	22 mm	GIM	13753	pl.V,10	Kozievsky Coll.
A-c	1)	8,73	22 mm	GE	59	pl.V,11	
	2)	8,37	21 mm	GE	60	pl.V,12	
	3)	8,34	21 mm	GE	62	pl.V,13	
A-d	1)	8,48	21 mm	GE	61	pl.V,14	
A-e	1)	8,25	21 mm	GE	63	pl.V,15	
	2)	8,58	20 mm	B	3	pl.V,16	
B-I	1)	8,15	21 mm	B	3a	pl.V,17	
	2)	6,24	20 mm	BM	997		
C-k	1)	9,11	23 mm	Naville, V, pl.LXIV, 2297			
D-l	1)	7,29				Coll. Prowe. Auction Egger, 1904, pl.V, 857	

Silver Didrachms of Gorgippia

Obv. Head of Dionysus r.

Rev. Ivy wreath; inside, grapes and ΓΟΡΓΙΠΠΕΩΝ; above, monogram (1).

Giel, 'A new acquisition...,' p.9, №50, pl.V,50 (7,94 g); Burachkov, XXIII,5; Zograph, XLIII,7; Anohin 209; Golenko, 'The Phantalovski hoard...', *VDI*, 1965, p.141, fig.69 & 73, in which there were 15 examples.

Dies		Wt.	Dia.	Mus.	Mus. No.	Plate	Notes
A-a	1)	7,26	24 mm	GE	2/27497	pl.V,18	
	2)	7,73		P			Anohin, 209
	3)	7,70	23 mm	GE	3/27498	pl.V,19	
B-a	1)	7,93	23 mm	GE	4/27499	pl.V,20	Obv. only
	2)	8,16	22 mm	GIM	14518	pl.V,21	Grandemaison Coll.

The weights of Gorgippia coins from the Phantalovski Peninsula published in *VDI*, 1965, p.141, are as follows:

Dies		Wt	Cat. No
L-k	1)	9,09	64
	2)	9,01	65
	3)	8,39	66
	4)	8,39	67
	5)	8,39	68
	6)	8,27	69
	7)	8,28	70
	8)	7,79	71
	9)	7,31	72
H-k	10)	8,49	73
	11)	8,29	74
	12)	8,27	75
	13)	8,24	76
	14)	7,79	77
	15)	7,81	78

100 - 75 B.C.

Silver Drachms

Panticapaeum

Obv. Head of Dionysus r.
Rev. Running doe (or stag?) r.; behind, thyrsus with band; ΠΑΝΤΙΚΑΠΑΙΤΩΝ.
Burachkov, XXII,150; Zograph, XLIII,9; Anohin 196.

Dies		Wt.	Dia.	Mus.	Mus. No.	Pl.	Notes
A-a	1)	3,67	15 mm	GIM	8798	pl.VI,1	Published by Golenko, 'History of the Currency of the Bosporus of the 1st century B.C., *NE*, 2, 1960, p.30, №11a
B-b	1)	3,20	15-17 mm	GIM	8799	pl.VI,2	Golenko (*NE*, 2, 1960, p.30, №12) supposed this coin to be overstruck on one from Amisus, but this is not so.
C-c	1)	3,72	15 mm	GIM	8800	pl.VI,3	
	2)	3,67	15 mm	GIM	3679		
	3)	3,89	20 mm	GE	800/27161	pl.VI,4	Anohin 196. Golenko (*NE*, 2, 1960, p.30, №12) supposed this coin to be overstruck on an Amisus issue, but, in fact, it was overstruck on a Bosporan coin of the: type Apollo/ bowcase
		3,90	17mm	GIM	8801		Overstruck
D-a	1)	4,07	17 mm	GE	801/27162	pl.VI,6	Golenko, *NE*,2, 1960, p.30, №2
	2)	3,98	17 mm	GE	802/27163	pl.VI,7	Golenko, *NE*, 2, 1960, p.30, №3
	3)	3,85	17 mm	GE	803/27164	pl.VI,8	Golenko, *NE*, 2, 1960, p.30, №8
	4)	3,62	17 mm	B	35a	pl.VI,9	
	5)	2,89	16 mm	Naville, V, pl.XLX, 1608			
	6)	3,69	16 mm	Naville, V, pl.XLX, 1658			
	7)	4,07	16 mm	Naville, V, pl.XLX, 1660			
	8)	3,95		Sotheby, Wilkinson, Hodge, Catalogue of rare coins, 1924, pl.I,43; Golenko, *NE*, 2, 1960, p.30, №4			
	9)	3,72	15 mm	Coll. Prowe, Egger, Auction, 1904, pl.IV,413; Golenko, *NE*, 2, 1960, p.30, №9			
	10)	3,35		Auction, Cahn, 60, pl.VI,306			

Gorgippia

Obv. Head of Dionysus r.
Rev. Running doe (or stag?) r.; behind thyrsus; ΓΟΡΓΙΠΠΕΩΝ
Burachkov, XXIII,2; Zograph, XLIII, 11; BMC, *Pontus, Paphlagonia, Bosporus*, 1889, pl.I,3; Minns, *Scythians and Greeks*, pl.IX,23; Anohin 197; *SNG BM* 985.

Dies		Wt.	Dia.	Mus.	Mus. No.	Plate	Notes
A-a	1)	2,21	15-17 mm	B		pl.VI,10; pl.LIX,6	Enlarged[94]
	2)	3,78	15 mm	GE	5/27500	pl.VI,11	
A-b	1)	4,08	16 mm	GE	6/27501	pl.VI,12	
B-c	1)	3,99	17 mm	BM	985	pl.VI,13	Anohin 197
	2)	3,06					Golenko, *NE*, II, p.30, №19; found in Chersonesus
	3)	2,69	17 mm	A		pl.VI,14	
	4)	3,07		Burachkov, XXIII, 2, p.176, №2			

[94] The obv. of this coin has the same die as GIM 8798 (pl.VI,1), GE 802 - 803 (pl.VI,7-8). Thus we can conclude that this type of coin was minted only at the Panticapaeum mint.

We must pay particular attention to the question of the dating of these types of coin. Anohin considered that they could be dated to 100 - 90 B.C. (Anohin, p.145, №196-199). K.V. Golenko thought that all of them were overstruck on coins of Amisus and dated to 100 B.C. ('Bronze Coins of the Cities of Pontos and Paphlagonia in the Time of of Mithradates VI Among Bosporan Finds', p.71). Our investigation of these coins gives the opportunity to conclude that Bosporan coins of the type Dionysus/doe (or stag) running, ΠΑΝΤΙΚΑΠΑΙΤΩΝ and ΓΟΡΓΙΠΠΕΩΝ were not overstruck on coins of Amisus and were issued in the period of 100 - 75 B.C. In addition, the dates of coins of Amisus, on which Golenko came to his conclusion, are not fixed yet.

§2 The first part of the 1st century B.C.

Phanagoria

Silver Drachms

Obv. Head of Dionysus r.

Rev. Thyrsus with band, ΦΑΝΑΓΟΡΙΤΩΝ.

Köhne, I, p.397, №1, monogram ΥΘ (7); Podshiwalov, *Beschreibung der unedirten und wenig bekannter Münzen von Sarmatia Europaea, Chersonesus Taurica und Bosphorus Cimmerius aus Sammlung A.M. Podshiwalov*. Moscow, 1882. p.24, №25, pl.III,49a,49b, monogram ΛΡΘ (8); Burachkov, XXIII,10; Zograph, pl. XLIII, 10; Anohin 205, 205a; *SNG BM* 998; Stancomb 626-7.

No monogram

Dies		Wt.	Dia.	Mus.	Mus. No.	Plate	Notes
A-a	1)	4,05	16 mm	B	572	pl.VI,14a	
	2)	4,06	16 mm		Naville, V, №2298		
	3)	3,84	16 mm	GE	68/27402	pl.VI,15	
	4)	3,24	15 mm	Cop	3	pl.VI,15a	
B-b	1)	3,27	15 mm	GE	69/27403	pl.VI,16	
	2)	3,59	15 mm	P	9		
C-c	1)	3,45	15 mm	GIM	6640	pl.VI,17	30% Ag
	2)	3,68	15 mm	GIM	6644	pl.VI,18	20% Ag
D-d	1)	3,50	16 mm	GIM	13755	pl.VI,19	Kozievsky Coll.
	2)	3,18	16 mm	GIM	6643	pl.VI,20	
E-e	1)	3,36	16 mm	A		pl.VII,6	
	2)	4,01	16 mm	A		pl.VII,7a	
	3)	3,55	16 mm	F		pl.VII,15	

Monogram ΛΡΘ (8)[95]

Dies		Wt.	Dia.	Mus.	Mus. No.	Plate	Notes
E-e	1)	4,80	17 mm	GE	70/24404	pl.VI,21	
G-g	1)	3,74	16 mm	GIM	6642	pl.VI,22	
	2)	3,50	17 mm	GE	72/27406	pl.VI,23	
E-k	1)	3,13	16 mm	GIM	13756	pl.VII,2	Kozievsky Coll.
E-i	1)	3,88	18 mm	GE	75/27409	pl.VII,1	
	2)	3,85	15 mm	A		pl.VII,10a	
	3)	3,26	15 mm	A		pl.VII,14	
	4)	3,66	15 mm	P	10		Anohin, 205a

Monogram ΛΡʘ (9)

Dies		Wt.	Dia.	Mus.	Mus. No.	Plate	Notes
F-f	1)	2,84	16 mm	GE	73/27407	pl.VII,3	Published by Podshiwalov *Beschreibung*..., pl.III,45a
F-af	1)	3,27	17 mm	GE	74/27408	pl.VII,4	Published by Podshiwalov *Beschreibung*..., pl.III,45b

[95] From the plates it is questionable whether there is any real difference between monograms 8, 9 and 10 other than their being variant dies of the same monogram; compare pl. VII,10a = mono.8, VII,5 = mono.9, VII,10 = mono.10. It is clear that in some cases Frolova has misread the monogram, e.g. on pl. VII,8 she misreads as P what is in fact a worn Θ. In the case of monograms 8 and 9 I reproduce what is evident on the photographs. In the case of monogram 10 I give the forms given by Frolova, though the photographs (pl. VII,8 and 10) clearly show instances of monogram 8. S.I.

	2)	4,11	15 mm	Podshiwalov, *Moscow Public and Rumijanzev Museums*, p.25, №202			
	3)	3,85	15 mm		Naville, V, №2299		
E-l	1)	3,66	16 mm	B	573/1899	pl.VII,5	Enlarged
	2)	3,24	16 mm	P	11		Monogram unclear

Monogram  or  (10)

Dies		Wt.	Dia.	Mus.	Mus. No.	Plate	Notes
A-m	1)	3,41	16 mm	GE	71/27405	pl.VII,7	
	2)	3,12	15 mm	OGAM		pl.VII,8	
	3)	3,50	16 mm	GIM	6641	pl.VII,9	50% Ag
	4)	3,78	15 mm	GIM	14535	pl.VII,13	Grandemaison Coll.
I-n	1)	3,65	18 mm	GE	76/27410	pl.VII,10	
G-l	1)	4,14	16 mm	GIM	6639	pl.VII,11	10% Ag
K-o	1)	3,24	15 mm	OGAM		pl.VII,12	
	2)	4,50	16,5 mm	GIM	6645		Poor condition, 20% Ag
	3)	3,60	15 mm	GIM	6646		Poor condition, 30% Ag

Silver Hemidrachms

Monogram  (11)

One hemidrachm was published by Chr. Giel, 'A new asquisition...', p.9, №49, pl.V,49. Anohin 206

Dies		Wt.	Dia.	Mus.	Mus. No.	Plate	Notes
A-a	1)	1,24	15 mm	GE	77/27411	pl.VII,16	
	2)	1,38	15 mm	P	13	pl.VII,16a	Enlarged; Anohin, 206

Panticapaeum. The end of the 2nd century – beginning of the 1st century B.C.[96]

Silver Hemidrachms

Monograms  (12),  (13),  (14),  (15)

Obv. Head of Dionysus r.
Rev. Thyrsus decorated with bands, ΠΑΝΤΙΚΑΠΑΙΤΩΝ, monograms.
Burachkov, XXI,101; Anohin 190.

Dies		Wt.	Dia.	Mus.	Mus. No.	Plate	Notes
A-a	1)	1,90	14 mm	GE	804/27165	pl.VII,17[97]	Enlarged; Monogram (12)
	2)	1,62	15 mm	GE	805	pl.VII,18	Enlarged; Monogram (12)
	3)	1,64	15 mm		Podshiwalov, p.6, №17, pl.I,12		Monogram
B-a	1)	1,76	15 mm	GIM	8803	pl.VII,19	cf. Anohin, 190; Monogram
	2)	1,90	15 mm	GIM	8802	pl.VII,20	Monogram (13)
	3)	1,86	15 mm	GIM	8804	pl.VII,21	Monogram (13)
	4)	1,45	15 mm	B		pl.VII,22	Monogram (13)
	5)	1,58	13 mm	BM	930	pl.VII,23	Monogram (13)
B-b	1)	1,64	14 mm	GE	807	pl.VII,24	Monogram (13)
	2)	1,87	15 mm	GE	806		
B-g	1)	1,72	15 mm	GE	808	pl.VII,25	Monogram (13)
C-c	1)	1,80	15 mm	GE	809	pl.VII,26	cf.Anohin, 1876; Monograms (14), (15)

[96] The traditional dating of these coins places them before those of Phanagoria above. However, the similarity of style has induced us to set them together for ease of comparison.
[97] Frolova also includes pl.VII,17a: 1,72g., 15mm, Giel, *Description of Coins…*, p.9.no.50.

Crude Style without Monogram.

Silver Hemidrachms

Obv. Head of Dionysus r.[98]
Rev. Thyrsus, ΠΑΝΤΙΚΑΠΑΙΤΩΝ.
Burachkov, XXII,178, Anohin 187a.

Dies		Wt.	Dia.	Mus.	Mus. No.	Plate	Notes
A-a	1)	1,93	15 mm	GE	810	pl.VII,27	
	2)	1,75	15 mm	Cop	28		

Panticapaeum 100 - 75 B.C.

AE Obols

Obv. Head of young man (Men?) in diademed Phrygian helmet.

Rev. Dionysus standing l. holding grapes and thyrsus; at feet l., panther; across field, ΠΑΝΤΙΚΑΠΑΙΤΩΝ and monogram (16)

Giel, *Kleine Beiträge*, 1886. p.34, №5, pl.IV,5; A.M. Podshiwalov, *Moscow Public and Rumijanzev Museums*, vol. 1., p.25, №200; A.B. Oreshnikov, *Catalogue of the Collection of Antiquities of Count A.S. Uvarov*, №VII, p.68, №429a; Burachkov, XXII, 79; Zograph, XLIII,13; Anohin 201; *SNG BM* 936.

Dies		Wt.	Dia.	Mus.	Mus. No.	Plate	Notes
A-a	1)	14,30	30 mm	GIM	8805	pl.VIII,1	
B-b	1)	11,40	27 mm	GIM	8806	pl.VIII,2	Poor condition
C-c	1)	18,30	30 mm	GIM	8807	pl.LIX,4	Enlarged; The metal composition of the coin is: Cu - base, Pl.-0,78; Zn-0,086; Bi-0,0025; Ag-0,1; Sb-0,37; As-0,016; Fe-0,28; Ni-0,013; Co-0,0013; Au-0,0004
	2)	17,45	27 mm	BM	936	pl.LIX,5	On Obv. and Rev. – countermark - star
	3)	13,90	27 mm	OGAM	22773	pl.VIII,2a	Rev. only
D-d	1)	17,27	30 mm	GE	821/27182	pl.VIII,3	Overstruck on a Panticapaean coin: Zeus/prow
E-e	1)	19,07	30 mm	GE	822/27183	pl.VIII,4	Overstruck on a Panticapaean coin Zeus/prow
F-f	1)	17,52	30 mm	GE	823/27184	pl.VIII,5	Overstruck on a Pontic coin Helmeted head of Athena/Perseus and Medusa
H-h	1)	17,25	33 mm	GE	824/27185	pl.VIII,6	Overstruck on a Pontic coin Zeus/eagle
I-i	1)	18,18	29 mm	GE	825/27186	pl.VIII,7	Overstruck on a Pontic coin Helmeted head of Athena/Perseus and Medusa
	2)	18,80	30 mm	GIM	12264		Kozievsky Coll.; overstruck on a Panticapaean coin of uncertain type

Phanagoria 100 - 75 B.C.

AE Obols

Obv. . Head of young man (Men?) r. in diademed Phrygian helmet.

Rev. Dionysus standing l. holding grapes and thyrsus; at feet l., panther, across field, ΦΑΝΑΓΟΡΙΤΩΝ and monogram (16)

Giel, *Kleine Beiträge*, p.34, №6, pl.IV,6; Anohin 207.

[98] Many identify the head as that of Apollo. S.I.

Dies		Wt.	Dia.	Mus.	Mus No.	Plate
A-a	1)	18,13	31 mm	GE	78/27412	pl.VIII,8

Gorgippia 100 - 75 B.C.

AE Obols

Obv. . Head of young man (Men?) r. in diademed Phrygian helmet.

Rev. Dionysus standing l. holding grapes and thyrsus; at feet l., panther; across field, ΓΟΡΓΙΠΠΕΩΝ, below monogram or (16)

Giel, *Kleine Beiträge*, p.34, №7, pl.IV,7; Burachkov, XXIII,6; Zograph, XLIII,14; Anohin 210

Dies		Wt.	Dia.	Mus.	Mus. No.	Plate	Notes
A-a	1)		31 mm	GE	1/27501	pl.VIII,9	
B-b	1)	19,20	33 mm	GE	7/27502	pl.VIII,10	Mono:
C-c	1)	17,02	30 mm	GE	8/27503	pl.VIII,11	
D-d	1)	18,27	30 mm	GE	9/27504	pl.VIII,12	Overstruck
	2)	18,65	32 mm	GE	10/27505	pl.IX,2	Overstruck
E-e	1)	16,98	30 mm	A		pl.IX,1	
F-f	1)	18,90	30 mm	GE	11/27506	pl.IX,3	Overstruck
H-h	1)	15,87	30 mm	GE	13/27508		
A-b	1)	17,62	30 mm	GIM	6674	pl.IX,4	
G-g	1)	15,81	30 mm	GIM	6675	pl.LX,1	The metal composition of the coin is: Cu-base; Sn-11; Pl 0,4; Zn-0,036; Ag-0,16; Sb-0,16; As-0,0091; Fe-0,024; Ni-0,0062; Co-0,0011; Au-0,0021

Panticapaeum 100-75 BC: AE Tetrachalkoi

Obv. Head of Apollo r.

Rev. Thyrsus leaning against tripod; to l. monogram (17); to r. monogram (1); ΠΑΝΤΙΚΑΠΑΙΤΩΝ.

Köhne, I, p.362, №89; Burachkov, XXI, 122; Giel, *Kleine Beiträge*, pl.IV,10; Oreshnikov, *Catalogue of the Collection...*, p.25, №201; Zograph pl. XLIII, 15; Anohin 202; *SNG BM* 937-40; Stancomb 591-6.

Dies		Wt.	Dia.	Mus.	Mus. No.	Plate	Notes
Ab-bb	1)	6,82	20 mm	A		pl.IX,5	Double struck
BB-ab	1)	7,50	20 mm	BM	937	pl.IX,6	Overstruck on an Amisos coin Head of Ares / sword in scabbard
A-a	1)	8,04	20 mm	GIM	8808	pl.IX,7	
	2)	7,64	20 mm	GIM	12686		Kozievsky Coll.
B-b	1)	6,35	20 mm	GIM	8809	pl.IX,8	
C-c	1)	6,36	20 mm	GIM	8810	pl.IX,9	
D-d	1)	6,10	20 mm	GIM	8811	pl.IX,10	
E-e	1)	5,32	23-24 mm	GIM	8812	pl.IX,11	
G-g	1)	6,73	20 mm	GIM	8813	pl.IX,12	
H-h	1)	6,08	20 mm	GIM	8814	pl.IX,13	
	2)	6,39	20 mm	GIM	8817	pl.IX,16	
F-f	1)	7,78	20 mm	GIM	8815	pl.IX,14	
	2)	8,54	20 mm	GIM	8819	pl.IX,15	
	3)	7,28	20 mm	GIM	8816	pl.IX,17	Rev. only
I-I	1)	6,66	21 mm	GIM	8822	pl.IX,18	
	2)	5,48	20 mm	Cop	57	pl.IX,19	
	3)	6,33	21 mm	GIM	8823	pl.X,1	
	4)	7,70	21 mm	GIM	12685		Kozievsky Coll.; overstruck on Panticapaean coin Artemis/ stag; monogram (1) only. On obv. countermark of ear of wheat

K-k	1)	8,57	20 mm	GIM	8825	pl.X,2	
	2)	6,67	20 mm	GIM	8830	pl.X,3	
L-l	1)	8,70	20 mm	GIM	8836	pl.X,4	Anohin 202. Monogram (1) only
M-m	1)	5,84	20 mm	GIM	8832	pl.X,5	Monogram (1) only
N-n	1)	6,98	21 mm	GIM	8839	pl.X,6	
	2)	6,74	20 mm	GIM	6670[a]		Poor condition
	3)	7,67	21 mm	GIM	12682		Kozievsky Coll.; Monogram (1) only

Coins from GIM in poor condition:

1)	3,79	20 mm	GIM	3699
2)	7,09	20 mm	GIM	3702
3)	5,98	20 mm	GIM	3707
4)	9,11	20 mm	GIM	3708
5)	5,89	20 mm	GIM	3700
6)	7,20	20 mm	GIM	3712
7)	6,13	20 mm	GIM	3714
8)	6,91	20 mm	GIM	3715
9)	4,54	20 mm	GIM	3716
10)	7,54	20 mm	GIM	3718
11)	7,54	20 mm	GIM	3719

Coins from GE with only one monogram -  (1)[99]

R-r	1)	7,28	23 mm	GE	828/27189	pl.X,7	
S-r	1)	9,27	21 mm	GE	829/27190	pl.X,8	
P-r	1)	8,49	22 mm	GE	831/27192	Pl.X,9	
	2)	8,77	23 mm	GE	832/27193	pl.X,10	
T-t	1)	7,85	21 mm	GE	833/27994	pl.X,11	
Ta-u	1)	7,24	21 mm	GE	834/27915	pl.X,12	
Aa-v	1)	7,04	20 mm	GE	835/27916	pl.X,13	
U-x	1)	1,40	22 mm	GE	837/27918	pl.X,14	
X-?	1)	8,45	23 mm	GE	838	pl.X,15	
F-f	1)	8,23	21 mm	GE	839	pl.X,16	
	2)	8,50	21 mm	GIM	12684		Kozievsky Coll.
	3)	7,06	21 mm	GIM	12683		Kozievsky Coll.
	4)	3,77	18 mm	GIM	12642		Kozievsky Coll.

Coins from GE with two monograms -  (17),  (1)

Ab-aa	1)	6,49	23 mm	GE	840	pl.X,17	
Ac-ab	1)	8,23	22 mm	GE	841	pl.X,18	
Ad-ad	1)	6,57	23 mm	GE	842	pl.X,19	
Ae-ae	1)	8,67	23 mm	GE	843	pl.X,20	
	2)	6,53	22 mm	GE	848	pl.XI,1	
Af-af	1)	6,09	23 mm	GE	844	pl.XI,21	
Aj-aj	1)	8,97	23 mm	GE	845	pl.XI,22	
Ag-ag	1)	5,40	22 mm	GE	846	pl.X,23	
Ai-ai	1)	8,32	23 mm	GE	847	pl.X,24	
Bi-bi	1)		23 mm	GE	849	pl.XI,2	Overstruck on Panticapaean coin
Ci-ci	1)	8,33	24 mm	GE	850	pl.XI,3	Overstruck on Phanagorian coin
Ad-di	1)	7,89	24 mm	GE	851	pl.XI,4	Overstruck on coin: Artemis/stag
Ad-ii	1)	7,17	25 mm	GE	852	pl.XI,5	Overstruck; original types defaced
Di-ik	1)	7,12	24 mm	GE	853	pl.XI,6	Overstruck on Phanagorian coin: Artemis/stag

[99] On some coins (e.g. pl.X,14,15) the monogram seems to be in the form  (6).

2)	5,83	25 mm	GE	854	pl.XI,7	Overstruck on a Phanagorian coin: Artemis/stag
3)	7,57	23 mm	GE	855	pl.XI,8	Overstruck on a coin: Artemis/stag
4)	7,38	25 mm	GE	856	pl.XI,9	Overstruck on a Phanagorian coin Artemis/stag, **ΦΑ[ ]**
5)	6,67	23 mm	GE	856[a]		
6)	8,29	25 mm	GE	857	pl.XI,10	Overstruck on a Phanagorian coin: Artemis/stag, **[Φ]ΑΝΑΓ[ΟΡΙΤΩΝ]**
7)	6,93	25 mm	GE	858	pl.XI,11	On obv. – countermark: ear of wheat
8)	7,60	22 mm	GE	859	pl.XI,12	Overstruck; on obv. countermark: ear of wheat
9)	9,89	24 mm	GE	860	pl.XI,13	Overstruck on Phanagorian coin: Artemis/stag, **[Φ]ΑΝΑΓΟΡΙΤΩΝ**; on obv. - countermark: ear of wheat
10)	7,70	23 mm	GE	861	pl.XI,14	Overstruck on Phanagorian coin: Artemis/stag
11)	7,02	25 mm	GE	862	pl.XI,15	Overstruck on Amisus coin: Aegis/Nike
12)	8,82	21 mm	GE	863	pl.XI,16	Overstruck; original illegible
13)	6,93	20 mm	GE	864	pl.XI,17	Overstruck on Pontic coin: Ares/sword in scabbard
14)	7,25	25 mm	GE	46	pl.XI,18	Overstruck on Phanagorian coin: Artemis/stag, **[Φ]ΑΝ[ΑΓΟ]ΡΙ[ΤΩΝ]**
15)	9,30	20 mm	BM	940	pl.XI,19	Overstruck on Phanagorian coin: Artemis/stag
16)	7,70	23 mm	BM	939	pl.LX,2	Enlarged; overstruck on Pontic coin: Aegis/Nike
17)	6,85	22 mm	GIM	8824	pl.LX,3	Enlarged; chemical analysis: Cu-base.; Sn-4,02; Pl-1,1; Zn-0,0093; Bi-0,011; Ag-0,31; Sb-0,59; As-0,0091; Fe-0,0023; Ni-0,013; Co-0,0011; Au-0,0001
18)	6,03	23 mm	GIM	12687		Kozievsky Coll.; overstruck on Pontic coin: Aegis/Nike
19)	7,08	20 mm	OGAM	27863	pl.XI,20	Overstruck on Pontic coin: Aegis/Nike
20)	6,70	20 mm	OGAM	27895	pl.XI,21	

Phanagoria 100-75 BC: AE Tetrachalkoi

Obv. Head of Apollo r.

Rev. Thyrsus leaning against tripod; to l., monogram (17), to r., monogram (1); **ΦΑΝΑΓΟ- ΡΙΤΩΝ.**

Köhne, I, p.398, №2, pl.VII,3 - Kohne was the first who wrote that coins of this type with the names of Panticapaeum, Phanagoria and Gorgippia were coined at the same time and at the Panticapaeum mint only and were probably the work of a single die-cutter (Köhne, I, p.363); Burachkov, XXIII,12; Zograph, XLIII,16; Anohin 208a; *SNG BM*,1007; Stancomb 628-9.

Dies		Wt.	Dia.	Mus.	Mus. No.	Plate	Notes
A-a	1)	6,11	24 mm	GIM	6671	pl.XII,1	
	2)	6,74	22 mm	GIM	6670a		Poor condition
	3)	6,44	22 mm	GIM	6670		
B-b	1)	6,71	22 mm	GIM	6673	pl.XII,2	
C-c	1)	9,30	21 mm	GE	79/27413	pl.XII,3	
D-d	1)	11,77	24 mm	GE	80/27414	pl.XII,4	Overstruck
E-e	1)	6,84	21 mm	GE	82/27416	pl.XII,5	
G-g	1)	7,95	23 mm	GE	83/27417	pl.XII,6	
	2)	8,55	21 mm	GE	84/27418	pl.XII,7	Anohin 208a
	3)	7,95	23 mm	GE	85/27419		Overstruck on Pontic coin

F-f	1)	6,43	24 mm	GE	86	pl.XII,8	Overstruck
H-h	1)		21 mm	GE	87	pl.XII,9	
I-I	1)	6,77	23 mm	GE	88	pl.XII,10	Overstruck on Pontic coin: Aegis/Nike
K-k	1)	6,83	23 mm	GE	89	pl.XII,11	
L-l	1)	7,20	20 mm	GE	90		
	2)	6,86	20 mm	F	1338	pl.XII,12	Overstruck
	3)	8,19	24 mm	GIM	6672	pl.LX,4	Enlarged; chemical analysis: Cu-bas., Sn-00,0043, Pl-7,9; Zn-4,8; Bi-0,052; Ag-0,1; Sb-0,054; As-0,13; Fe-0,32; Ni-0,0068; Co-0,0036; Au-0,0003
	4)	8,47	20 mm	GIM	6675	pl.LX,5	Enlarged; chemical analysis: Cu-bas., Sn-4,2; Pl-0,78; Zn-0,19; Bi-0,0052; Ag-0,16; Sb-0,037; As-0,02; Fe-0,38; Ni-0,0062; Co-0,0036; Au-0,0002
	5)	7,41	20 mm	GIM	12708		Kozievsky Coll.

Stancomb 630 also records for this period Obv. Head of Artemis r.; Rev. Horse grazing l.; **ΦΑΝΑΓΟΡΙΤΩΝ**; to l., monogram ; 5.09g., but see here pl. XXVI, 1 etc.

Gorgippia 100-75 BC: AE Tetrachalkoi

Obv. Head of Apollo r.

Rev. Thyrsus leaning against triopod; to l., monogram - (17), to r., (1), ΓΟΡΓΙΠΠΕΩΝ (at times monogram 17 omitted).

Köhne, I, p.418, №2, noted that this type of coin was minted by the same die-cutter as produced those of this type with the names of Phanagoria and Panticapaeum. He showed that that this type of coin was known to J. Eckhel, *Doct. Num. Veterum*, II, 339; cf. T.E. Mionnet, II, p.333, №1,2; Suppl. №4,5; D.Sestini, *Lettere e dissert.*, VII, p.29, pl.II,19,20; Burachkov, XXIII,5; Zograph, XLIII,17; Anohin 211; *SNG BM* 986; Stancomb 618-20.

Dies		Wt.	Dia.	Mus.	Mus. No.	Plate	Notes
A-a	1)	8,03	21 mm	GE	14/27509	pl.XII,13	Anohin 211a; mono
B-b	1)	6,93	19 mm	GE	15/25510	pl.XII,14	
	2)	4,72	21 mm	GIM	6719	pl.XII,16a	
C-c	1)	5,63	22 mm	GIM	6718	pl.XII,15	
	2)	8,90	20 mm	F	7336	pl.XII,16	Mono
	3)	9,06	21 mm	GIM	6720		Obv. die as the Phanagorian coin (pl.XII,9-11 = GE 87-89) and the Panticapaean coin (pl.X,23 = GE 846)
	4)	7,55	21 mm	A		pl.XII,17	
	5)	7,63	20 mm	A		pl.XII,18	Mono
	6)	7,36	20 mm	Cop	1	pl.XII,19	
D-d	1)	6,30	21 mm	GIM	6721		
	2)	6,78	19 mm	GIM	6722		
	3)	4,90	20 mm	GIM	6694	pl.XII,20	Poor condition
	4)	7,20	20 mm	GIM	6896	pl.XII,21	Poor condition
	5)	7,81	22 mm	GIM	6697	pl.XII,22	Poor condition
	6)	5,66	20 mm	GIM	12721		Kozievsky Coll.
	7)	8,61	20 mm	GIM	12722		Kozievsky Coll.
	8)	7,60	21 mm	A		pl.XII,23	

On the following coins the dies are not linked

	Wt.	Dia.	Mus.	Mus. No.	
1)	6,34		GE	27513	Anohin, 211
2)	9,23	20 mm	BM	986	Anohin 211б
3)	6,22		GE	27516	Anohin, 211в
4)	7,20		GE	1356	Anohin, 211г

§3 The end of the 2nd century B.C. - 63 B.C.

AE Obols

The chronology and typology of the coins of type: Dionysus / bow in case were discussed in several articles by Krushkol, Golenko, Shelov (Ju. S. Krushkol, 'Coins with Monograms from the Patraeus Hoard of 1950', *VDI*, 1952, 3, p.139-146; Ju.S. Krushkol, 'The Patraeus Hoard of 1950', *KSIIMK*, 66, 1956, p.116; K.V. Golenko, 'On the Coinage of the Anonymous Bosporan Obols, *NSph*, 2, Kiev, 1965, p.47; id., 'Bronze Coins of the Cities of Pontus and Paphlagonia in the Time of Mithradates', *Palestina Sb.*, II, p.63-66. Golenko supposed that the Bosporan towns were deprived of their right to mint autonomous coins by Mithradates VI and his son Machares. D.B. Shelov, 'Machares as King of Bosporus', *VDI*, 1978.

Oreshnikov was the first to consider that the coins of the type 'Dionysus / bow in case' were minted by Machares, the son of Mithradates VI Eupator: A.V. Oreshnikov, *The Cimmerian Bosporus in the Period of the Spartocids from Inscriptions and Royal Coins*, p.31; A.V. Oreshnikov, *Catalogue of the Collection of Count A.S. Uvarov*, p.60.

Golenko believed that after 80 B.C. Machares was sent by his father to Bosporus as ruler (cf. Appian *Mith.*, 67). At this time coins Dionysus / bow in case were minted. The characteristic of the issue is a complete absence of countermarked coins among them. There are monograms on the rev. of these coins, which are supposed to represent the name of the magistrate, but there is no other name on this type.

Obv. Head of Dionysus r.
Rev. Bowcase l., monograms.
Burachkov, XXIII, 25-30; Zograph, XLIII, 22-23; Anohin 212; *SNG BM* 946-9; Stancomb 597-604. (In addition to those coins bearing monograms others exist which show no sign of ever having had a monogram, e.g. Kerch hoard №935, 977, 1060, 1072).

I. Monogram  (18)

Dies		Wt.	Dia.	Mus.	Mus No.	Plate	Notes
A-a	1)	16,33	25 mm	GIM	8894	pl.XIII,1	Burachkov, XXIII, 30
	2)	15,83	25 mm	GIM	8894a		
	3)	15,60	25 mm	OGAM	23302	pl.XIII,2	
A-b	1)	14,50	26 mm	GIM	14419	pl.XIII,3	Grandemaison Coll.
B-c	1)	16,73	26 mm	GIM	8897	pl.XIII,4	
C-d	1)	15,30	25 mm	GIM	8898	pl.XIII,5	
Ca-da	1)	16,42	26 mm	A		pl.XIII,5a	
C-e	1)	14,47	27 mm	GIM	8899	pl.XIII,6	
D-f	1)	14,95	26 mm	GIM	8900	pl.XIII,7	
C-g	1)	17,17	27 mm	GIM	8905	pl.XIII,8	
A-h	1)	16,86	25,5 mm	GIM	8906	pl.XIII,9	
A-I	1)	15,59	27 mm	GIM	8909	pl.XIII,10	
E-j	1)	16,16	27 mm	GIM	8908	pl.XII,11	
F-a	1)	17,41	25 mm	GIM	8911	pl.XIII,12	
	2)	14,96	25 mm	A		pl.XIII,12a	Rev. only
C-g (?)	1)	14,09	27 mm	GIM	8912		
G-k	1)	15,12	25 mm	GIM	6328		
	2)	13,85	25 mm	OGAM	27898	pl.XIII,13	
	3)	15,50	25 mm	OGAM	23612	pl.XIII,14	

The dies on the following coins have not been linked:

	Wt.	Dia.	Mus.	Mus. No.	Plate	Notes
1)	16,03	27 mm	GE	27553		
2)	17,32	25 mm	GE	27543		
3)	16,72	25 mm	GE	27545		
4)	17,98	27 mm	GE	27547		
5)	17,82	25 mm	GIM	12672		Kozievsky Coll.
6)	16,89	26 mm	Cop	10		
7)	18,17	25 mm	BM	948		
8)	17,92	25 mm	BM	946	pl.LX,6	Enlarged
9)	16,10	25 mm	BM	947	pl.LXI,1	Enlarged
10)	16,77		GE	27544		Poor condition
11)	16,85		GE	27546		Poor condition
12)	15,29		GE	27548		Poor condition

13)	16,39	GE	27449	
14)	16,98	GE	27550	
15)	15,92	GE	27551	
16)	15,50	GE	27552	
17)	16,25	GE	27554	
18)	17,00	GE	27555	
19)	15,67	GE	27556	
20)	17,10	GE	27557	
21)	16,93	GE	27558	
22)	15,49	GE	27559	
23)	11,45	GE	27560	
24)	22,00	GE	27561	
25)	16,31	GIM	8913	
26)	14,96	GIM	8901	
27)	16,94	GIM	8939	
28)	16,21	GIM	8902	
29)	13,35	GIM	14416	Grandemaison Coll.
30)	16,10	GIM	8903	
31)	15,32	GIM	14417	Grandemaison Coll.
32)	17,98	GIM	8904	
33)	15,28	GIM	14418	Grandemaison Coll.
34)	15,59	GIM	8907	
35)	15,19	GIM	8910	
36)	7,21	GIM	12681	Kozievsky Coll.; imitation

In addition, a hoard of coins from Poljanka in the Kerch region discovered in 1985 contained 78 coins with the monogram  (18).

	Wt.	Mus.	Mus No.
1)	17,60	Kerch	260
2)	14,52	Kerch	409
3)	16,20	Kerch	523
4)	19,85	Kerch	552
5)	18,00	Kerch	581
6)	15,90	Kerch	591
7)	16,75	Kerch	597
8)	16,60	Kerch	601
9)	16,69	Kerch	602
10)	14,20	Kerch	608
11)	16,05	Kerch	617
12)	17,90	Kerch	956
13)	16,90	Kerch	957
14)	14,90	Kerch	958
15)	15,70	Kerch	959
16)	18,10	Kerch	960
17)	16,50	Kerch	961
18)	17,50	Kerch	963
19)	15,60	Kerch	964
20)	17,40	Kerch	965
21)	16,00	Kerch	966
22)	16,00	Kerch	967
23)	16,90	Kerch	968
24)	14,30	Kerch	969
25)	17,10	Kerch	970
26)	16,90	Kerch	971
27)	15,90	Kerch	972
28)	17,50	Kerch	973
29)	16,90	Kerch	974
30)	17,30	Kerch	975
31)	15,10	Kerch	976
32)	15,00	Kerch	978
33)	15,30	Kerch	979
34)	14,80	Kerch	980
35)	15,10	Kerch	981
36)	18,00	Kerch	982
37)	13,40	Kerch	983
38)	15,50	Kerch	984
39)	15,50	Kerch	985
40)	15,60	Kerch	986
41)	16,20	Kerch	987
42)	15,80	Kerch	988
43)	17,10	Kerch	989
44)	16,70	Kerch	990
45)	14,30	Kerch	991
46)	16,80	Kerch	992
47)	15,60	Kerch	993
48)	15,40	Kerch	994
49)	16,20	Kerch	995
50)	16,80	Kerch	996
51)	17,20	Kerch	997
52)	21,30	Kerch	998
53)	20,80	Kerch	999
54)	15,78	Kerch	1000
55)	15,20	Kerch	1001
56)	15,10	Kerch	1002
57)	14,50	Kerch	1003
58)	16,70	Kerch	1004
59)	17,70	Kerch	1005
60)	17,60	Kerch	1006
61)	18,20	Kerch	1007
62)	17,90	Kerch	1008
63)	15,70	Kerch	1009
64)	18,00	Kerch	1010
65)	13,60	Kerch	1011
66)	16,70	Kerch	1012
67)	17,30	Kerch	1013
68)	15,25	Kerch	1014
69)	13,24	Kerch	1015
70)	14,50	Kerch	1016
71)	17,25	Kerch	1017

72)	15,25	Kerch	1018	76)	15,60	Kerch	1022
73)	15,40	Kerch	1019	77)	16,60	Kerch	1023
74)	16,60	Kerch	1020	78)	16,70	Kerch	1024
75)	15,30	Kerch	1021				

II. Monogram  (19)

Krushkol, *VDI*, 1952, p.143, monogram №3.

Dies		Wt.	Dia.	Mus.	Mus. No.	Plate	Notes
A-H-a	1)		24 mm	OGAM	28604	pl.XIII,15a	
	2)	14,41	24 mm	GIM	8915	pl.XIII,15	Obv. only
B-J-b	1)	14,65	25 mm	GIM	8916	pl.XIII,16	
C-K c	1)	16,83	26 mm	GIM	8917	pl.XIII,17	
	2)	15,91	24 mm	GIM	14423		Grandemaison Coll.
	3)	17,55	26 mm	GIM	12670		Kozievsky Coll.
	4)	17,10	25 mm	GE	27563		
	5)	16,65	24 mm	GE	27562		
	6)	16,57	27 mm	GE	27564		
	7)	15,53	25 mm	Kerch	937		
	8)	16,70	25 mm	Kerch	938		

III. Monogram  (20)

Krushkol, *VDI*, 1952, p.143, monogram №8.

Dies		Wt.	Dia.	Mus.	Mus. No.	Plate	Notes
A-a	1)	16,46	26,5 mm	GIM	8918	pl.XIV,1	
B-b	1)	15,74	25 mm	GIM	8919	pl.XIV,2	
C-c	1)	17,94	25,5 mm	GIM	8920		
	2)	14,47	25 mm	Kr		pl.XIV,3	Private collection
	3)	18,04	28 mm	GIM	12674		Kozievsky Coll.
	4)	16,54	27 mm	GE	27565		
	5)	17,58	26 mm	GE	27567		
	6)	16,79	26 mm	GE	27569		
	7)	16,80	27 mm	GE	27571		
	8)	16,17	26 mm	GE	27567a		
	9)	16,17	26 mm	GE	27566		
	10)	17,13	25 mm	GE	27568		
	11)	17,00	25 mm	GE	27570		
	12)	17,38		Kerch	33		
	13)	15,40		Kerch	928		
	14)	15,80		Kerch	929		

IV. Monogram  (21)

	Wt.	Mus.	Mus. No.
1)	15,90	Kerch	761

V. Monogram  (22)

Krushkol, *VDI*, 1952, p.143, monogram №12.

Dies		Wt.	Dia.	Mus.	Mus. No.	Plate
A-a	1)	15,98	25 mm	GIM	8921	pl.XIV,4
B-b	1)	14,97	26 mm	GIM	8922	pl.XIV,5
B-c	1)	16,69	28 mm	GIM	8923	pl.XIV,6

VI. Monogram  (23)[100]

A-a	1)	11,84	24 mm	GIM	8924a		

VII. Monogram  (24)

Krushkol, *VDI*, 1952, p.143, monogram №7.

A-a	1)	16,90	25 mm	GIM	8925	pl.XIV,7	
	2)	15,92	25 mm	A		pl.XIV,8	

VII. Monogram  (25)[101]

A-a	1)	11,84	24 mm	GIM	8924b	pl.XIV,10	Rev. only
	2)	18,39	28 mm	GIM	8928	pl.XIV,9	Obv. only; poor condition

The dies on the following coins have not been linked:

	Wt.	Dia.	Mus.	Mus. No.	
1)	16,45	25 mm	GE	27538	
2)	14,47	25 mm	GE	27539	
3)	16,33	25 mm	GE	27540	
4)	16,50	25 mm	GE	27541	
5)	17,88	25 mm	GE	27542	
6)	17,13	25 mm	GIM	12667	Kozievsky Coll.
7)	15,65	24 mm	GIM	14422	Grandemaison Coll.
8)	17,25	23 mm	Kerch	950	
9)	17,43	24 mm	Kerch	952	
10)	17,71	24 mm	Kerch	953	
11)	17,30	23 mm	Kerch	954	
12)	15,70	23 mm	Kerch	955	

IX. Monogram  (26)

1)	16,79	23 mm	Kerch	949	
2)	14,85	20 mm	Kerch	432	

X. Monogram  (27)

1)	17,50		Kerch	563	
2)	16,70	20 mm	GIM	14420	Grandemaison Coll.

XI. Monogram  (28) with variants

	Wt.	Dia.	Mus.	Mus. No.	Plate	Notes
1)	18,07		GE	27582		
2)	17,52		GE	27583		
3)	15,45		GE	27584		
4)	18,45		GE	27585		
5)	17,30		GE	27586		
6)	16,97		GE	27587		
7)	17,03		GE	27888		
8)	14,93		GE	27589		
9)	15,33		GE	27590		
10)	17,67		GE	27591		
11)		24 mm	OGAM	23310	pl.XIV,11	
12)	16,90	24 mm	Kerch	1065		Monogram  (29)
13)	14,50	24 mm	Kerch	1066		
14)	16,97	27 mm	GIM	8945	pl.XIV,18	
15)	16,52	28 mm	GIM	8946	pl.XIV,19	Monogram  (30)

[100] As with other groupings of monograms it is doubtful if what Frolova sees as distinct instances (here 23-27, cf. below 28-33 and 39) are anything other than die variants of the same monogram. S.I.

[101] The distinguishing feature of this monogram is the absence of the semicircle above the horizontal bar. However, on pl. XIV,10 what appears to be a semicircle is clearly visible. S.I.

16)	15,45	26 mm	GIM	8948	pl.XIV,20	Monogram  (30)
17)	17,20	24 mm	Kerch	1043		Monogram  (31)
18)	16,80	25 mm	Kerch	877		Monogram  (32)
19)	16,90	25 mm	Kerch	888		
20)	14,40	23 mm	Kerch	1040		
21)	17,00	22 mm	Kerch	1051		
22)	14,70	24 mm	Kerch	1052		
23)	15,50	24 mm	Kerch	1056		
24)	17,24	22 mm	Kerch	1054		
25)	15.50	22 mm	Kerch	1055		
26)	13,81	25 mm	GIM	8947		Poor condition
27)	16,77	22 mm	GIM	8950		
28)	15,15	26 mm	GIM	8951		
29)	16,88	23 mm	GIM	12673		Monogram  (33) Kozievsky Coll.
30)	16,20	26 mm	BM	949	pl.XV,1	
31)	17,60	25 mm	Kerch	1048		
32)	14,60	23 mm	Kerch	1049		
33)	17,50	24 mm	Kerch	1050		
34)	15,90	23 mm	Kerch	668		
35)	15,80	24 mm	Kerch	712		
36)	13,60	24 mm	Kerch	659		
37)	17,60	24 mm	Kerch	933		
38)	17,20	24 mm	Kerch	1042		
39)	15,62	25 mm	Kerch	1044		

XII. Monogram  or  (34)

Krushkol, *VDI*, 1952, p.140, monogram №6.

	Wt.	Dia.	Mus.	Mus. No.	Plate	Notes
1)	15,98	25 mm	GIM	8929	pl.XIV,12a	
2)	16,25	26 mm	GIM	8930	pl.XIV,12	
3)	13,63	25 mm	GIM	8931		Poor condition
4)			OGAM	27476	pl.XIV,13	
5)	15,87	25 mm	GE	27578		Poor condition
6)	17,15	23 mm	Kerch	1030		

XIII. Monogram  (35)

1)	15,65	25 mm	GIM	8932	pl.XIV,14

XIV. Monogram  or  (36)

Krushkol, *VDI*, 1952, №3, monogram №5.

	Wt.	Dia.	Mus.	Mus. No.	Plate	Notes
1)	16,85	27 mm	OGAM	23613	pl.XIV,15	
2)	16,34	23 mm	GIM	8933		
3)	14,11	25 mm	GIM	8934	p.XIV,16	
4)	16,27	24 mm	GE	27577		
5)	18,60	25 mm	GE	25580		Poor condition
6)	18,60	25 mm	GE	25581		Poor condition
7)	18,10	25 mm	GE	27579		
8)	16,55	22 mm	Kerch	962		Poor condition
9)	16,83	22 mm	Kerch	1058		
10)	15,60	27 mm	Kerch	1059		
11)	14,48		Kerch	590		

XV. Monogram  or  (37)

1)	15,05	24 mm	GIM	8940
2)	18,47	27 mm	GIM	8944

XVI. Monogram  or  (38)

	Wt.	Dia.	Mus.	Mus. No.	Plate	Notes
1)	16,26	25 mm	GIM	8935	pl.XIV,17	
2)	16,34	26 mm	GIM	8936		Poor condition
3)	13,28	25 mm	GIM	8937		Poor condition
4)	17,02	25 mm	GIM	8938		Poor condition
5)	15,40	28 mm	GE	27592		
6)	17,80	27 mm	GE	27793		
7)	15,62	25 mm	GE	27794		
8)	15,43	26 mm	GE	27795		
9)	16,60	23 mm	Kerch	1028		
10)	17,70	24 mm	Kerch	1029		
11)	15,60	24 mm	Kerch	1031		
12)	15,70	24 mm	Kerch	1032		
13)	16,30	23 mm	Kerch	1033		
14)	13,70	22 mm	Kerch	1036		
15)	17,10	22 mm	Kerch	1034		
16)	15,40	23 mm	Kerch	1038		
17)	15,40	22 mm	Kerch	1039		

XVII. Monogram  (39)

1)	16,46	25 mm	GIM	8949

XVIII. Monogram  or  or  or  (40)

	Wt.	Dia.	Mus.	Mus. No.
1)	17,40	25 mm	GE	27572
2)	19,16	28 mm	GE	27573
3)	17,63	25 mm	GE	27574
4)	16,88	26 mm	GE	27575
5)	17,28		Kerch	943
6)	17,07		Kerch	944
7)	15,30	22 mm	Kerch	945
8)	18,06	26 mm	Kerch	946
9)	18,14	26 mm	Kerch	947
10)	16,74	26 mm	GIM	16669

XIX. Monogram  (41)

	Wt.	Dia.	Mus.	Mus. No.
1)	17,07	25 mm	Kerch	939

XX. Monogram  (42)

1)	13,20	20 mm	Kerch	940

XXI. Monogram  (43)

	Wt.	Dia.	Mus.	Mus. No.
1)	15,44		GE	27576
2)	17,00	25 mm	Kerch	936

XXII. Monogram  (44)

1)	9,95	27 mm	GE	27596	Cut on all sides
2)	21,15	25 mm	GIM	14421	Grandmaison Coll.

XXIII. Monogram  (45)

1)	20,95	30 mm	GE	27534
2)	19,95	26 mm	GE	27538
3)	19,88	27 mm	GE	27537
4)	19,64	25 mm	Kerch	948

XXIV. Monogram  or  (46)

1)	16,42	26 mm	GIM	8914
2)	16,46	27 mm	GIM	8927
3)	16,28	28 mm	GIM	8896

XXV. Monogram  (47)

1)	17,10	26 mm	Kerch	739

XXVI. Monogram  (48)

1)	15,95	25 mm	Kerch	1034

XXVII. Monogram  (49)

1)	17,40	24 mm	Kerch	1057

XXVIII. Monogram  (50)

1)	15,60	25 mm	Kerch	683
2)	16,12	27 mm	Kerch	689

XXIX. Monogram  (51)

1)	14,50	25 mm	Kerch	934

XXX. Monogram  (52)

1)	16,80	24 mm	Kerch	719

XXXI. Monogram  (53)

1)	16,20	24 mm	Kerch	1026
2)	16,90	25 mm	Kerch	1027

XXXII. Monogram  (54)

1)	16,30	24 mm	Kerch	1025

XXXIII. Monogram  (55)

1)	20,10	24 mm	Kerch	734

XXXIV. Monogram  (56)

1)	14,75	24 mm	Kerch	620

XXXV. Monogram  (57)

	Wt.	Dia.	Mus.	Mus. No.
1)	15,95	25 mm	Kerch	1034

There are numerous examples of anonymous coins in the Kerch hoard that show no monograms:

1)	17,00	23 mm	Kerch	935
2)	15,15	23 mm	Kerch	977
3)	16,40	23 mm	Kerch	1035
4)	16,75	25 mm	Kerch	1060
5)	16,50	21 mm	Kerch	1072

The number of monograms on Bosporan coins of the type: Dionysus / bowcase has grown since the 19th century. In 1884 Podshiwalov published a total of 8 monograms:

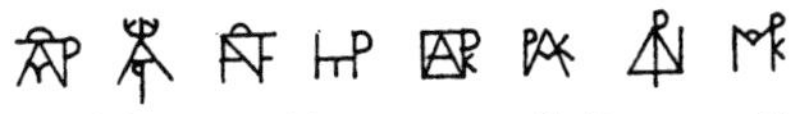

(*The Moscow Public and Rumijantzev Museum, Numismatic Collection, Catalogue of Coins*, Moscow,p.29-30, № 219-236).

In 1887 Podshivalow expanded the list of anonymous coins with the following:

('Monnaies des rois du Bosphore Cimmérien', Moscow 1887 p,13 = 'The Coins of the Cimmerian Bosporos Kings of the Spartocid and Achaemenid Dynasties', *ZOOID*, 15, 1889, p.14).

However, Zograph and Golenko claimed to know only 10 examples (K.V. Golenko, 'On the Coinage of Bosporan Anonymous Obols', *NSph*, 2, 1965, p.43). In 1952 Krushkol published 14 monograms:

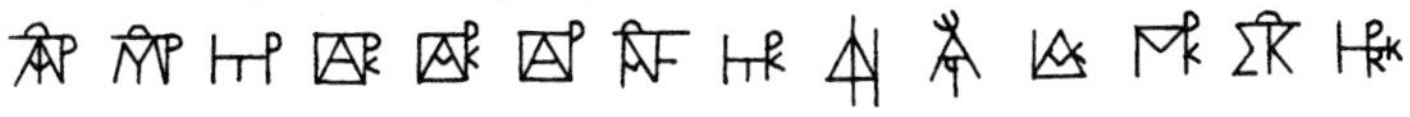

('Coins with Monograms from the Patraeus Hoard of 1950', *VDI*, 1952, 3, p.137-146).

In 1986 Anohin recorded 12 examples (Anohin, 1986, pl.40, №22-33)

(See further: S. Ireland, N. Frolova, 'Two Hoards of Bosporan Coins of the 1st Century B.C. from the Ancient Settlement of Poljanka (Kerch)', *Hermathena* 166 (1999) p.31-43)

Thus, we can distinguish more than 40 different monograms on the anonymous Bosporan coins. The material confirms the opinion that the monograms conceal the names of royal officials responsible of the mint of Bosporus. These anonymous obols can be dated to end of the 2nd century B.C. to 63 B.C..

§4 After 63 B.C.

The next type is - Obv. Laureate head of Apollo, Rev. Eagle on thunderbolt, ΠΑΝΤΙΚΑΠΑΙΤΩΝ, which points to the restoration of autonomous city mintage. Zograph dated this series to the last decade of Mithradates rule (1977 p.300). Golenko on the other hand ascribed it to Pharnaces, regarding the series typologically as a direct continuation of Mithradates' coinage (*NE*, 2, 1960, p.39, pl.III,5-11. However, coins of the Apollo / eagle type do not reveal any connection with Pharnaces.[102]

One should take into account that most of the 908 coins of the Apollo / eagle type from the 1985 Kerch hoard were overstruck on the the type of Dionysus / bowcase with monograms.

AE Obols

Obv. Head of Apollo r.

Rev. Eagle on thunderbolt, wings open; below, ΠΑΝΤΙΚΑΠΑΙΤΩΝ (in one or two lines); monogram 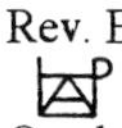 (58)[103]; star.

Oreshnikov, *Catalogue*..., p.56-61; Burachkov, XXI, 13, 8-143; Zograph, XLIII, 20; Anohin 214; *SNG BM* 945; Stancomb 605-6.

Like Golenko, Oreshnikov regarded obols of the Apollo / eagle type as belonging to the Pharnaces' coinage, as well as the tetrachalkoi type, Head of Apollo / tripod and thyrsus. While a dating to the time of Pharnaces is perfectly acceptable, to see them as royal issues is highly debatable.

Dies		Wt.	Dia.	Mus.	Mus. No.	Plate	Notes
A-a	1)	17,17	27 mm	GIM	8960	pl.XV,2	
	2)	11,15	26 mm	GIM	8976		Poor condition
B-b	1)	18,05	27 mm	GIM	8961		Overstruck on a coin Dionysus/bow in case
C-c	1)	18,05	27 mm	GIM	8962	pl.XV,3	
D-d	1)	16,30	25 mm	GIM	8963	pl.XV,4	
E-e	1)	15,87	26 mm	GIM	8964	pl.XV,5	
	2)	15,81	25 mm	GIM	8965		
G-g	1)	15,70	27,5 mm	GIM	8966	pl.XV,6	Overstruck
I-I	1)	15,57	26 mm	GIM	8967		Inscription in one line
J-j	1)	15,06	27 mm	GIM	8968	pl.XV,7	

---

[102] The fact that this type of coin is found overstruck on the Dionysus / bowcase type indates their order of production, and one can hypothesise that the change of type is significant. That they are city issues, just like the Dionysus / bowcase type (which bear unmistakable Mithradatic motifs) does not detract from the possibility that they were issued under the aegis of Pharnaces. S.I.

[103] On some coins, eg. pl. XV,16 and XVI,4, the monogram seems to be 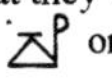 or  .

	2)	14,92	27 mm	GIM	8969		
	3)	14,67	27 mm	GIM	8970	pl.XV,8	
H-h	1)	14,66	27 mm	GIM	8971	pl.XV,9	
	2)	14,42	25 mm	GIM	8972	pl.XV,10	
	3)	15,63	25 mm	GIM	14197	pl.XV,11	Grandemaison Coll.
	4)	14,17	27 mm	GIM	8973	pl.XV,12	
	5)	14,12	27 mm	GIM	8974	pl.XV,13	
	6)	11,44	27 mm	GIM	8975		Poor condition
	7)	15,11	26 mm	GIM	14198		Grandemaison Coll.
G-g	1)	11,70	28 mm	GIM	8977	pl.XV,14	
F-f	1)	17,75	26 mm	GE	886	pl.XV,15	
	2)	16,58	28 mm	GE	887	pl.XV,16	
K-k	1)	17,75	28 mm	GIM	889	pl.XV,17	
L-l	1)	15,02	28 mm	GIM	890	pl.XV,18	
	2)	15,34	26 mm	GIM	892	pl.XV,19	
M-m	1)	18,10	28 mm	GIM	893	pl.XV,20	
	2)	14,87	28 mm	GIM	12665		Kozievsky Coll.; inscription in one line
	3)	17,56	28 mm	GIM	12666		Kozievsky Coll.; Overstruck on a coin: Dionysus/bowcase
N-n	1)	16,39	27 mm	GIM	894	pl.XVI,1	Overstruck on a coin: Dionysus/bowcase
O-o	1)	13,75	27 mm	GIM	896	pl.XVI,2	Overstruck on a coin Dionysus/bowcase
P-p	1)	14,57	27-28 mm	GIM	897	pl.XVI,3	Overstruck on a coin Dionysus/bowcase; monogram from undertype
N-r	1)	16,55	28 mm	GIM	898	pl.XVI,4	Overstruck on anonymous obol
S-t	1)	13,75	25 mm	GIM	899	pl.XVI,5	Overstruck on anonymous obol
	2)	14,25	25 mm	BM	945	pl.LXI,2	Enlarged

The dies of the following coins have not been investigated:

1)			OGAM	28239	pl.XVI,5a	Overstruck on a Sinope type coin
2)	7,00		OGAM	25353	pl.XVI,5b	Overstruck
3)	12,92	26 mm	GIM	12655		Kozievsky Coll.

The middle of the 1st century B.C.

AE Tetrachalkoi

Obv. Head of Apollo r.
Rev. Tripod, thyrsus leaning against; to r. ΠΑΝΤΙΚΑΠΑΙΤΩΝ; monogram 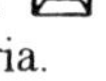 (58).
Overstruck on Pontic coins and early coins of Panticapaeum and Phanagoria.
Burachkov, XXI, 121; *SNG BM* 937.

Dies		Wt.	Dia.	Mus.	Mus. No.	Plate	Notes
A-a	1)	8,17	20,5 mm	GIM	8979	pl.XVI,6	Overstruck on a coin Sinope/Zeus-eagle, ΣΙΝΩΠΗΣ
B-b	1)	9,51	21 mm	GIM	8978	pl.XVI,7	Overstruck on a coin Sinope/Zeus-eagle, ΣΙΝΩΠΗΣ
C-c	1)	7,49	19 mm	GIM	8980	pl.XVI,8	Overstruck
D-d	1)	6,87	21 mm	GE	902	pl.XVI,9	Overstruck
D-e	1)	7,40	22 mm	GE	901	pl.XVI,10	Overstruck
E-j	1)			GE	903	pl.XVI,11	Overstruck
J-h	1)	7,39	20 mm	GE	904	pl.XVI,12	Overstruck
	2)	6,60	20 mm	GE	910	pl.XVI,13	Overstruck
H-f	1)	7,73	21 mm	GE	905	pl.XVI,14	Overstruck

F-?	1)	8,85	20 mm	GE	906	pl.XVI,15	Overstruck; Rev. - poor condition
F-l	1)	7,40	21 mm	GE	907	pl.XVI,16	Overstruck; on Rev. inscription [Φ]ΑΡΝΑΚΕ[ΙΑΣ](?) belonging to the original Pontic coin.
K-l	1)	8,60	20 mm	GE	908	pl.XVI,17	
L-m	1)	6,55	20 mm	GE	909	pl.XVI,18	Overstruck
	2)	6,73	20 mm	GIM	12660		Kozievsky Coll.

§ 5 Pharnaces (63 - 47 B.C.)

Gold coins

All known coins of the Bosporan King Pharnaces were published by Golenko and Karyszkovski in their article 'The Gold Coinage of King Pharnaces of the Bosporus', *NC*, 12 (1972), p.25-38, pl.1-2, from which we take our data.

The gold staters date to a short period of Pharnaces rule (55/54 - 51/50 B.C.).

Obv. Head of Pharnaces r. with diadem.

Rev. Half-naked Apollo l., seated on throne decorated with lion paws; laurel branch in outstretched right hand; left arm leaning upon lyre; in front, tripod; above and below, four-line legend **ΒΑΣΙΛΕΩΣ ΒΑΣΙΛΕΩΝ ΜΕΓΑΛΟΥ ΦΑΡΝΑΚΟΥ**; to r., date and sometimes monogram or symbol.

ΓΜΣ = Year 243 of the Pontic era (55/54 B.C.)[104]

Dies		Wt.	Mus.		Plate	
A-a	1)	8,25	P		pl.XVII,1	

ΔΜΣ = Year 244 of the Pontic era (54/53 B.C.)

A-a	1)	8,18	Jameson Collection pl.CXV	2146	pl.XVII, 2	Location unknown

ΕΜΣ = Year 245 of the Pontic era (53/52 B.C.)

A-g	1)	8,07	J.Friedländer und A. von Sallet, Das königlishe Münzkabinett. Berlin, 1877, p.136, №467		pl.XVII,3	
	2)	8,17	Vienna			'Bundcssamlung von Medaillen, Münzen, Geldzeichen', Golenko, Karyszkovski, *NC*, 1972, p.35, fig.1; Anohin 218
A-d	3)	8,12	P		pl.XVII,4	
B-e	4)	8,10	Oreshnikov, Catalogue of the Count A.S. Uvarov, Collection of Antiquities, VII, M., 1887, p.60, №437, pl.II		pl.XVII,5	Location unknown
B-e	1)	7,40	P		pl.XVII,6	Spasski, *The Cimmerian Bosporus*, p.62, pl.III,15

<u>ϛΜΣ = Year 246 of the Pontic era (52/51 B.C.)</u>

Dies		Wt.	Mus.	Plate	Notes
A-z	1)	8,15	Münich Staatliche Münzsammlung	pl.XVII,7	Monogram (61)
A-h	2)	8,14	Wien №15166	pl.XVII,8	Gajdukevich, *The Kingdom of Bosporus*, p.586, №53, pl.III. Monogram (61)
	3)	8,21		pl.XVII,9	*NC*, 1972, p.36, fig.2
A-I	4)	8,18		pl.XVII,10	Zograph, *Ancient Coinage*, pl.XLIV,3
A-n	5)	8,21		pl.XVII,14	*NC*, 1972, p.38, fig.3 – found near Trebizon; Addendum Sotheby's, 19, VI, 1990, 115

[104] The beginning of the Pontic era is believed to date from October 297 B.C. - See: Perl, 'The Eras of the Bithynian, Pontic and Bosporan Kingdom'. *VDI*, 1969, 3, p.40 f., 58 f.; Leschhorn, *Antike Ären*, p.86ff.

A-m	6)	8,14	Pieter Gorny Collection			München Auction, 20.X.1999 № 1031; on rev. 3 pellets and monogram 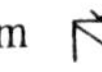 (63)

ZMΣ = Year 247 of the Pontic era (51/50 B.C.)

-f	1)	8,19	New York; Collection of the American Numismatic Society		pl.XVII,11	Giel, 'A new acquisition...', pl.VI,62; Minns, *Scythians and Greeks*, pl.VI,23; Anohin 220 A forgery of this coin is held by GIM, №389, 5,74 g.
-k	2)	8,07	Vienna 15167		pl.XVII,12	
	3)	8,10			pl.XVII,13	Location unknown
	1)	5,74	GIM	389	pl.XVII,15	Forgery
	2)		GE	198	pl.XVII,16	Forgery

§6 The coinage of Asander (49/48 - 21/20 B.C.)

Staters of Asander as Archon (49 - 45 B.C.)

The gold coins of Asander with the inscription ΑΡΧΟΝΤΟΣ ΑΣΑΝΔΡΟΥ ΒΟΣΠΟΡΟΥ (49/48 - c. 45/44 BC).

ET- A = year A 1

1. Obv_1 - Rev_1 Obv. Head of Asander r. Rev. Nike l. with downturned wings on prow; in field, ET- A; monogram  (60) and **Φ**. 8,16g., (pl.XVIII,1). Location unknown.

Giel, *Kleine Beiträge*, p.10, pl.II,22 = Grand Duke Alexander Michailovich; Bertier de la Garde, p.105, №12; Coll. Jameson, IV, p.61, №6541, pl.CXXXIV; Zograph, *AM*, pl.XLIV,4; Auction Bank Leu, 24.03.1959, №239; ibid., 04.04.1963, pl.III, №5; Auction Num. Fine Arts, 20/21.03.1975, №142 (8,12 g.). Karyszkovski, Frolova, 'The Reign of Asander in the Bosporus Based on Numismatic Data, p.89-112; Frolova, Karyszkowski, Delfs, 'Zu Chronologie der Herrschaft Asanders im Bosporos', p.63-81, pl.I-II; Nawotka, 'Asander', 1992, p.42, pl.III,1a.

ET- B = year 2

2. Obv_1-Rev_2 Obv. the same. Rev. Nike l. with upraised wings on prow; in field r., ΑΡΧΟΝΤΟΣ; l. ΑΣΑΝΔΡΟΥ ΒΟΣΠΟΡΟΥ; l. ET, r. B; unclear monogram and **Φ**. 8,17g., (pl.XVIII,2), Paris.

Mionnet, Suppl., IV. P.471, №27; Sestini, *Mus. Hederv.*, II, p.20, №1; Köhler, Serapis, II, p.71, №2; *Trésor de Num. et Gliptique*, Paris, 1849, p.51, pl.XXIV,11; Köhne, vol.II, p.160; Sibirskij, pl.IX,50; Bertier de la Garde, p.105, №13; Sallet, p.19,25, pl.I,1 (Rev.); Giel, *Kleine Beiträge*, pl.V,7; Bibl. Nation., Cab. De Méd., Guide (1929) №1026 (obv.); Waddington, *RN*, 1866, p.418; Burachkov, XXV, 41; Anohin 222; *RPC* I, 1843. This coin was sold by command of the People's Commissar for Education A.S. Bubnov, 15/16 June 1933, №1404, Moscow, through E.S. Weimarn (GIM) and A.V. Sosnovskij (Antiquariat), who placed it in auction.

ET- Γ = year 3

3. $Obv._2$-Rev_3 Obv. the same. Rev. Nike with upraised wings on prow l.; ΑΡΞΟΝΤΟΣ ΑΣΑΝΔΡΟΥ ΒΟΣΠΟΡΟΥ; l. TЭ, r. Γ; monogram A. 8,20g., (pl.XVIII,3), Vienna.

Sibirskij, pl.IX,51; Sallet, p.20,25; Burachkov, p.232, №48, pl.XXV, 42.; Giel, *Kleine Beiträge*, pl.5,8; Bertier de la Garde, p.105, №14, Gaidukevich, p.586, pl.III,55; Spasski, *Archaeological Numismatic Symposium*, Moscow, 1846, p.11, pl.II,3; Gaidukevich, *Bosp. Reich*, p.527, 586, pl.III,55; Anohin 223, *RPC* I, 1844. This coin, from the GIM Collection, was sold by command of the People's Commissar for Education A.S. Bubnov, 15/16 June1933, №1404 / Moscow, through E.S. Weimarn (GIM) and A.V. Sosnovskij (Antiquariat), who placed it in auction.

4. Weight unknown, as well as location. Sallet, p.19, 20, n. 33, p.25, pl.I,2 (rev.); Giel, *Kleine Beiträge*, p.11; Oreshnikov, *Catalogue of the Collection of Antiquities of Count A.S. Uvarov. VII*, p.62-63 with fig. in text.

ORDER NUMBER
PO NYAATP08

BOOK NUMBER
2291723

BAY NUMBER
2308-9

AUTHOR	Frolova, Nina
TITLE	The the Coinage of the Bosporan Kingdom: From the First Century Bc to the Middle of the First Century Ad (British Archaeological Reports International Series)

DESCRIPTION

This is an ex-library book and may have the usual library/used-book markings inside.This book has hardback covers. In good all round condition. No dust jacket. Re-bound by library.

ET- Δ = year 4

5. Obv$_3$-Rev$_4$ Obv. the same. Rev. Nike with upraised wings on prow l.; ΑΡΧΟΝΤΟΣ ΑΣΑΝΔΡΟΥ ΒΟΣΠΟΡΟΥ; l. ET , r. Δ; monogram (60). 8,08 - 8,10g., (pl.XVIII,4, cf. pl. LXI,3 enlarged), *SNG BM* №961.

Robinson - Walker - Jenkins - Carson, *The British Museum Quarterly*, 1952, p.49-50, pl.XIV,21. *A Guide to the Principal Coins of the Greeks*. London, 1959, p.98, pl.51,4. Anohin, 221. Anohin (followed by *SNG BM* 961 and *RPC* I, 1842) reads the date year as A, but year 1 coins have the wings of Nike pointing downwards, whereas in subsequent years they are raised; other differences between coins of year 1 and 4 are their monograms and the absence in year 4 of the monogram Φ present on the coin of years 1 and 2. Nawotka, 1992, p.31,41,43 №3a (pl.III, №.3a), dates the coin to year 4.[105]

Staters of Asander with the Title of King (c. 45/44 - 21 B.C.)[106]

Δ = year 4[107]

6. Obv$_4$-Rev$_5$ Obv. Diademed head of Asander r. Rev. Nike with upraised wings on prow l.; ΒΑΣΙΛΕΩΣ ΑΣΑΝΔΡΟΥ;[108] l. Δ (4). 8,19g., (pl.XVIII,5), Boston.

M. Comstock - C. Vermeule, *Museum of Fine Arts, Boston. Greek Coins 1950 - 1963*. Boston, 1964, p.36, №37, pl.XIII, №37; Anohin, 228.

7. Obv$_4$-Rev$_5$. 8,14g., pl. XVIII,6, Vienna.

Mionnet, Suppl., IV, p.473, №27; Köhler, Serapis, II, p.78, №14; Sibirskij, pl.IX,52; Waddington, *RN*, 1868, p.418; Sallet, p.25; Bertier de la Garde, p.105, №15; Nawotka, p.43, 5a.

8. Obv$_4$-Rev$_6$. 8,25g., (pl. XVIII,7), Temruk, private collection.

9. Obv$_5$-Rev$_7$. 8,14g., location unknown.

Auction Catalogue, Monnaies et Médailles, AG Basel, liste, 1979. Mai 1959. Basel, p.2,4, №8; Auction Lanz, München 42, 23.11.1987, 20, №207; Nawotka, pl.3,4a.

10. Obv$_4$- Rev$_8$. 8,20g. Pieter Gorny Auction 100 20.X.1999, München. Kat. II, №1032

The head of Asander placed on staters with the inscription ΒΑΣΙΛΕΩΣ ΑΣΑΝΔΡΟΥ is different from the head on those issued during his archonship. The diadem of Asander's head on staters with the title ΒΑΣΙΛΕΩΣ ΑΣΑΝΔΡΟΥ has its ends curling upwards; the head as archon is bare.

E = year 5 - coins with letter E are unknown.

ϛ = year 6

11. Obv$_6$-Rev$_8$. Obv. Diademed head of Asander r. Rev. Nike with upraised wings on prow l.; ΒΑΣΙΛΕΩΣ ΑΣΑΝΔΡΟΥ; l. ϛ and monogram (61).[109]

1) 8,11g., pl.XVIII,8, München.

Mionnet, Suppl., IV, 47, №28; Köhler, Serapis, II, p.73, №15; Sibirskij, pl.IX,58; Sallet, p.25; Imhoof-Blumer, *Porträtkopfe*, pl.V,6; Bertier de la Garde, p.105, №17; Nawotka, p.43, №6a. It seems that lead coins with the monogram (62) - Köhler, Serapis, II, p.75, №25, pl.VIII,12; Sibirskij, pl.IX,57 - are copies from a similar specimen, but not from the München copy.

Z = year 7

12. Obv$_6$-Rev$_9$. Obv. Diademed head of Asander r. Rev. Nike with upraised wings on prow l.; ΒΑΣΙΛΕΩΣ ΑΣΑΝΔΡΟΥ; l. Z and monogram (63)[110]. 8,23g., GE 637 (pl.XVIII,9).

Mionnet, *Descript.* II, p.362, №25; Köhler, p.73, №16; Sallet, p.25; Bertier de la Garde, p.105, №18; Anohin 230; Nawotka, p.43, №7a.

It seems that poorly preserved silver coins from Budapest Museum were minted from the same dies. 10,78g. (cast)

13. 8,08g., location unknown.

Münzen und Medaillen. AG. Basel Liste 454, April 1983, 2, №23.

---

[105] There is a potential problem here in that the head on the Archon year 4 coin is stylisitically tied to those of years 1 and 2, whereas that on the year 3 coin as illustrated is clearly closer to the head on coins showing Asander as king. Identification of the heads is discussed by Nawotka (1992). S.I.

[106] A listing of dates is given most recently in *RPC* I, 1847-63, following Bertier de la Garde. S.I.

[107] Most recently W. Leschhorn (*Antike Ären*, p.44-51) has discussed the problem of the dating of Asander and concludes that Asander began to coin with the title of King in 47/46 BC; cf. Introduction.

[108] On some issues the name is rendered as ΑΖΑΝΔΡΟΥ. S.I.

[109] The state of the coins makes it possible that monograms 61 and 63 are the same. S.I.

[110] Frolova mistakenly reads the letter N for what is clearly Λ in this indistinct monogram, suggesting that monogram 61 was intended. S.I.

H = year 8 - coins with letter H are unknown[111]

Θ = year 9

14. Obv_8-Rev_{10}. Obv. Diademed head of Asander r. Rev. Nike with upraised wings on prow l.; ΒΑΣΙΛΕΩΣ ΑΣΑΝΔΡΟΥ; l. Θ. 8,13g., Coll. Des Monnaies Grecques, H. De Nanteuil, 1925, p.230, №684; pl.XLII; Auction Hess/Leu 36, Lucerne, 17/18. 04.1968, p.36, №247; Nawotka, p.43, №9a.

15. Obv_8-Rev_{10}. 8,11g. (pl.XVIII, 10). From collections Prowe - Terlezkij - Private col. New York. Bertier de la Garde, p.105, №20 (8,12g.); Anohin 231; Nawotka, p.43, №9a, pl.III,9a.

16. 8,14g. *SNG BM*, 965.

17. 7,52g. (pl.XVIII,11). Moscow, private col. The coin is fragmentary.

I = year 10

18. $Obv._9$-$Rev._{11}$. Obv. Diademed head of Asander r. Rev. Nike with upraised wings on prow l.; ΒΑΣΙΛΕΩΣ ΑΣΑΝΔΡΟΥ; l. I. 8,17g. (pl.XVIII,12), Berlin.

Bertier de la Garde, p.105, №21 (1); *Das Königl. Münzkabinett*, Berlin, 1877, p.137, №469; Nawotka, p.44, №10a.

19. $Obv._9$-Rev_{11}. 8,15 g.

Köhne, II, p.163, №11, pl.IX,11; Sibirskij, pl.IX,54; Sallet, p.25; Bertie de la Garde, p.105, №21 (2); Coll Jameson, III, pl.CXV, 2147.

20. $Obv._9$-Rev_{12}. 8,13 g. (pl.XVIII, 13).

Auction Naville, XII, 1926, p.99, №1692; Nawotka, p.44, №10b.

AI = year 11

21. $Obv._{10}$-Rev_{13}. Obv. Diademed head of Asander r. Rev. Nike with upraised wings on prow l.; ΒΑΣΙΛΕΩΣ ΑΣΑΝΔΡΟΥ; l. AI. 8,17g., Tiflis, State Museum of Georgia (pl.XVIII,14). This year of coinage is absent from the Nawotka Catalogue.

BI = year 12

22. Obv_{10}-Rev_{14}. Obv. Diademed head of Asander r. Rev. Nike with upraised wings on prow l.; ΒΑΣΙΛΕΩΣ ΑΣΑΝΔΡΟΥ; l. BI. 8,17g., Tiflis, State Museum of Georgia (pl.XVIII,15). The same coins, but only obv., are recorded.

Sestini, D. *Cl. Gén.*, p.61; Sallet, p.25; Köhne, II, p.164; Bertier de la Garde, p.131, n. 33. This year of coinage is absent from the Nawotka Catalogue.

IΓ = year 13

23. Obv_{10}-Rev_{15} Obv. Diademed head of Asander r. Rev. Nike with upraised wings on prow l.; ΒΑΣΙΛΕΩΣ ΑΣΑΝΔΡΟΥ; l. IΓ . 8,00g, GE (pl.XVIII,16).

Spasski, Archaeological-Numismatic Symposium, p.12, pl.II,5; Anohin 233; Nawotka, p.44, №11a, pl.III,11a.

IΔ = year 14

24. Obv_{11}-Rev_{16}. Obv. Diademed head of Asander r. Rev. Nike with upraised wings on prow l.; ΒΑΣΙΛΕΩΣ ΑΣΑΝΔΡΟΥ; l. IΔ. 8,01g., GIM 391 (pl.XVIII,17).

Kazamanova L.N., pl.LIV,2.

25. Obv_{11}-Rev_{16}. 8,00g., Paris (pl.XVIII,18).

Mionnet, Suppl., II, p.363, №26; Köhler, p.74, №21; *Trésor*, p.52, №12, pl.XXIV,12; Sibirskij, pl.IX,55; Bertier de la Garde, p.105, T25; Spasski, *The Cimmerian Bosporus*, p.64, №2, pl.III,15; Anohin 234; Nawotka, p.44, №12a, pl.III,12a.

EI = year 15 - coins with letters EI are unknown.

ϛI = year 16

26. Obv_{11}-Rev_{17}. Obv. Diademed head of Asander r. Rev. Nike with upraised wings on prow l.; ΒΑΣΙΛΕΩΣ ΑΣΑΝΔΡΟΥ; l. Iϛ. 7,95g., Paris (pl.XVIII,19).

---

[111] Nawotka claims an issue for this year on the basis of a lead specimen in New York (Nawotka 1992, p.43, 8a). S.I.

Mionnet, *Description*, II, p.363, №27; Köhler, p.74, №23; Sallet, p.25; Bertier de la Garde, p.105, №27 (3); Anohin 235; Nawotka, p.43, №12b.

27. Obv_{12}-Rev_{18}. 8,03g., Prowe - Terlezkij collections (?) (pl.XVIII,20).

Bertier de la Garde, p.105, №27 (1); Auction Naville, XV, 1930, p.53, №858, pl.XXIX, 858; Ibid., XVI, 1933, p.81, №1327 pl.XLIV, 1327; Auction Numismatica Ars Classica, AG Zürich, 4. 27.02.1991. p.24, №130; Nawotka, pl.III, 13b.

28. Obv_{12}-Rev_{18}. 8,00g., (Giel) (pl.XVIII,21).

Giel, ZRAO, 1895, VII, p.11, №60; Bertier de la Garde, p.105, №27 (2); Auction Naville, XIII, 1928, p.56, №828, pl.XXVI, 828; Ibid., XVII, 1934, p.29, №522; Auction Hess-Leu 36,6/7.12.1966, pl.XVIII,584; Auction Münzen und Medaillen AG. Basel 41,18/19. 1970, p.18, №118; Nawotka, pl.II, 13a.

29. 8,00g., Tolmachev - Sosnovski collections (1929).

ZI = year 17

30. Obv_{13}-Rev_{19}. Obv. Diademed head of Asander r. Rev. Nike with upraised wings on prow l.; **ΒΑΣΙΛΕΩΣ ΑΣΑΝΔΡΟΥ**; l. **ZI**. 8,09g., *ANS*, 1944, 100, 40987 (pl. XIX,1).

Auction Schulmann. 26.09.1906; *Collection Joachim Jose dos Santos*, Amsterdam, 4786, pl.I,4786; Anohin, 236; Nawotka, №14a.

31. Obv_{14}-Rev_{20}.. Weight unknown, private collection (pl.XIX,2).

32. Obv_{14}-Rev_{20}. 7,93g., Berlin, 28675 (pl.XIX,3).

Bertier de la Garde, p.105, №28 (2); Köhler, p.75, №24; Mionnet, Suppl., IV, p.473, №39; Sallet, p.20; n. 34, p.25; Münz- Kabinette, 1877, S.137, №468 (7,15g.); Nawotka, №15a.

33. Obv_{14}-Rev_{20}. 7,90g.

Bertier de la Garde, p.105, №28 (3).

34. Obv_{14}-Rev_{20}. 8,22g.

Bertier de la Garde, p.105, №28 (1).

HI = year 18

35. Obv_{14}-Rev_{21}. Obv. Diademed head of Asander r. Rev. Nike with upraised wings on prow l.; **ΒΑΣΙΛΕΩΣ ΑΣΑΝΔΡΟΥ**; l. **HI**. 8,13g., GE 639 (pl.XIX,4).

Bertier de la Garde, p.105, №29 (1); Golenko, *NE*, X, p.107, №1 (pl.I,1).

36. Obv_{14}-Rev_{21}. 8,02g., Paris (pl.XIX,5).

Bertier de la Garde, p.105, №29 (2); Henning R., *Berliner Münzblätter*, 1908, p.92; Sallet, p.25; Anohin 237; Nawotka №13c.

ΘI = year 19

37. Obv_{15}-Rev_{22}. Obv. Diademed head of Asander r. Rev. Nike with upraised wings on prow l.; **ΒΑΣΙΛΕΩΣ ΑΣΑΝΔΡΟΥ**; l. **ΘI**. 7,93g., Pachomov Collection, Baku, 1959 (pl.XIX,6).

This year of coinage is absent from the Nawotka Catalogue.

K = year 20

38. Obv_{16}-Rev_{23}. Obv. Diademed head of Asander r. Rev. Nike with upraised wings on prow l.; **ΒΑΣΙΛΕΩΣ ΑΣΑΝΔΡΟΥ**; l. **K** . 8,06g., Prowe - Terlezkij Collection = GIM 390 (pl.XIX,7).

Bertier de la Garde, p.105, №31; Schlessinger, II, 26.02.1934, pl.VII,196; Gajdukevich, *The Kingdom of Bosporus*, pl.III, 56; Golenko, *NE*, X, 1972, p.107, №2, pl.II,2, p.105, n. 11; Anohin 238; Nawotka, №13d; Vienna, 37409, 8,54g.; *SNG Cop.*, №14, 8,12g.; Paul Nester, Coll. Lucien de Hirsch, 1405, 8,04g.; Sotheby 20.01.1898, №132, 8,78g.; GE, W, 8,17g. - Golenko, *NE*, X, 1972, pl.I,7; lead proof, *BMC Pontos*, 48, №4. Golenko considered all these to be modern counterfeits, though Nawotka, p.44 n.98, advances arguments to refute this.

AK = year 21

39. Obv_{16}-Rev_{24}. Obv. Diademed head of Asander r. Rev. Nike with upraised wings on prow l.; **ΒΑΣΙΛΕΩΣ ΑΣΑΝΔΡΟΥ**; l. **AK** (21). 8,06 g, GE 643 (pl.XIX,8).

Collection Roux: Monnaies grecques. Auction, Paris, 1911, pl.VI, 157 (31 mai 1911, p.18); Bertier de la Garde, p.105, №32 (1); Zograph, *Ancient Coinage*, pl.XLIV,6; Golenko, *NE*, X, p.107, №3, pl.I,3; Auction Bank Leu. Num. Fine Arts. The Garnett Collection II. 16/17.10. 1984, S.52, №237; Anohin 239; Nawotka, №18a - Nawotka's №19a, for which he cites Zograph; pl.XLIV,6 is in fact the same coin as his №18a.

40. Obv_{17}-Rev_{25}. 8,10g., Terlezkij Collection (pl.XIX,9).

Bertier de la Garde, p.105, №32 (3); Auction Hess, 208 (Dec. 1931), pl.IX,534; Auction Schlessinger, 11 (1934), pl.VII,196 (8,06g.); Nawotka №20b.

41. Obv_{17}-Rev_{25}. 8,10g., Giel (pl.XIX,10).

Bertier de la Garde, p.105, №32 (2); Giel, *Kleine Beiträge*, p.12; Auction Kraus, 1928, p.32, №726, pl.III,726; Auction Naville, XVII (1934), p.29, №521; Auction Hess-Leu, XVI, 1957, p.29, №249, pl.X,249; Auction E. Boudin, Paris, 1911, №157; Nawotka, №20a.

BK = year 22

42. Obv_{17}-Rev_{26}. Obv. Diademed head of Asander r. Rev. Nike with upraised wings on prow l.; ΒΑΣΙΛΕΩΣ ΑΣΑΝΔΡΟΥ; l. BK. 8,03g., Giel - Boston (pl.XIX,11).

Bertier de la Garde, p.105, №33; Giel, *Kleine Beiträge*, p.12; Auction Cahn, 75 (30 mai 1932), №353; Auction Naville, XVI, 1933, p.81, №1328, pl.XLIV,1328; Klawans Z.N., *An outline of Ancient Greek Coins* (Wisconsin, USA), 1959, №193; Anohin 240; Nawotka №20c.

ΓK = year 23

43. Obv_{18}-Rev_{27}. Obv. Diademed head of Asander r. Rev. Nike with upraised wings on prow l.; ΒΑΣΙΛΕΩΣ ΑΣΑΝΔΡΟΥ; l. ΓΚ. 8,14g., Uvarov, GIM 392 (pl.XIX,12).

Oreshnikov, *Catalogue of the Collection of Antiquities of Count A.S. Uvarov*. №VII. Moscow, 1887, p.66, №465, pl.II,465; Bertier de la Garde, p.105, №34 (1); Kazamanova, pl.LIV,3; Anohin, 241; Nawotka, №23a.

44. Obv_{18}-Rev_{27}. 8,08g., GE 640 (pl.XIX,13. Inscr. ΒΑΣΙΛΕΩΣ ΑΖΑΝΔΡΟΥ).

Bertier de la Garde, p.105, №34 (2); Sibirskij, pl.IX,56; Sallet, p.25.

45. Obv_{18}-Rev_{27}. 8,08g., Lemme - Berlin (pl.XIX,14. Inscr. ΒΑΣΙΛΕΩΣ ΑΖΑΝΔΡΟΥ).

Bertier de la Garde, p.105, №34 (3); Golenko, *NE*, X, p.107, №4, pl.I,4

46. Obv_{18}-Rev_{27}. 8,00g., Kerch, private collection (pl.XIX,15).

47. Obv_{18}-Rev_{27}. 8,07g.

Auction F. Sternberg, Zürich XX, 20.04.1988, p.62, №529.

48. Obv_{18}-Rev_{27}. 8,02g. (pl.XIX, 16).

Burachkov, p.233, №54, pl.XXV,43 - this coin was sold by the command of the People's Commissar for Education Bubnov in a 1933 Auction; Schlessinger, 11, 1934, №197; Auction Hess (5 mai 1935), Lucerno, p.2, №15, pl.I,15; Auction Hess-Leu, 45 (12/13 mai 1970), Lucerno, pl.IX, 234; Auction Hess 247, 29.06. 1978, p.22, №150; Nawotka, №22a.

49. Obv_{19}-Rev_{29}. 8,04g., Fogg Museum (pl.XIX,17).

Bertier de la Garde, p.105, №34 (4); *Arthur S. Dewing, Collection of Greek Coins*, L. Mildenberg - S. Hunter ed. (New York, 1985), p.124, №2105.

50. 8,02g., Anapa, private collection (pl.XX,16).

EK = year 25

51. 8,30g. The coin is overstruck (Terlezki Collection). Dies unknown.

Bertier de la Garde, p.105, №36, p.131, n. 34 (we have evidence that there is a lead coin with letters EK).

ZK = year 27

52. Obv_{20}-Rev_{30}. Obv. Diademed head of Asander r. Rev. Nike with upraised wings on prow l.; ΒΑΣΙΛΕΩΣ ΑΣΑΝΔΡΟΥ; l. ZK . 8,04g., (Perovskij) GE 641 (pl.XIX,18).

Bertier de la Garde, p.105, №38 (1); Köhne, II, p.163, №12; Sibirskij, pl.IX,58; Sallet, p.25.

53. Obv_{20}-Rev_{30}. 7,92g., Berlin (pl.XIX,19).

Bertier de la Garde, p.105, №38 (2); Nawotka №26a.

54. Obv_{21}-Rev_{31}. 8,05g., Weber, New York (pl.XIX,20).

Auction Sotheby-Wilkinson-Hodge, 20.04.1909, №15; L. Forrer, *The Collection of Weber*, 1926, vol.III, part 1, p.21, №4791, pl.174,1; Auction Helbing, München, 20.03.1928, p.34, №323, pl.XII,323; Anohin 243; Nawotka №24a.

55. Obv_{21}-Rev_{31}. 8,07g., New York (pl.XIX,21).

Auction Meyers R.J., 13.09.1976, New York, pl.VII, 159.

56. Obv_{21}-Rev_{31}. 8,04g..

Auction Lanz, Graz, I, 8/9.12.1972, S.10, №87; Auction Lanz, München, 23.07.1984, p.22, №244.

HK = year 28

57. Obv_{22}-Rev_{32}. Obv. Diademed head of Asander r. Rev. Nike with upraised wings on prow l.; **ΒΑΣΙΛΕΩΣ ΑΣΑΝΔΡΟΥ**; l. **HK**. 8,00g., Sotheby, 29.07.1844 (Thomas), 1741, London (pl.XX,1 and pl.LXI,5 enlarged).

Köhne, II, p.164; Bertier de la Garde, p.105, №39; Kazamanova, pl.LIV,4; Sibirskij, pl.IX,59; Sallet, p.25; Minns E., *Scythians and Greeks*, pl.VI,26; Anohin 244; Nawotka №27a; *SNG BM* 966; *RPC* I, 1862, which also records a specimen in Munich.

ΘΚ = year 29

58. Obv_{22}-Rev_{33}. Obv. Diademed head of Asander r. Rev. Nike with upraised wings on prow l.; **ΒΑΣΙΛΕΩΣ ΑΣΑΝΔΡΟΥ**; l. **ΘΚ**. 8,00g., Sotheby, 29.07.1844 (Thomas), London (pl.XX,2 and pl.LXI,6 enlarged).

Bertier de la Garde, p.105, №40 (1); Catalogue Thomas, p.241, №1741; Sallet, p.25; *BMC*, 1889, p.48, №3, pl.X,10 (coin №40 (2) was published by galvanic copy in the Leak Collection, 1856, p.47, but Bertier de la Garde was mistaken in regarding it as a different specimen); Anohin 245; *SNG BM* 967; Nawotka №29a.

59. Obv_{22}-Rev_{33}. 7,98g., GE 642 (pl.XX,3).

Bertier de la Garde, p.105, №40 (3).

60. Obv_{22}-Rev_{33}. 7,98g., Berlin (pl.XX,4).

Bertier de la Garde, p.105, №40 (4).

61. Obv_{22}-Rev_{34}. 7,98g., Meynerts - Sibirskij - Giel - Großfürst Collections (pl.XX,4a. Inscr. **ΒΑΣΙΛΕΩΣ ΑΖΑΝΔΡΟΥ**).

Köhne, II, p.157, n. 3; Giel, *Kleine Beiträge* p.11; Meynerts, *Revue Belge de Num.*, III, 1847, pl.I; Sibirskij, pl.IX,60; Burachkov, p.233, №55, pl.XXIV,44 - this coin was sold by the command of the People's Commissar for Education Bubnov, 15/16 June 1933, №1404/c; Bertier de la Garde, p.105, №40(5); Auction Hamburger, 11.06.1930, p.13, №290, pl.IX,290, 7,90g.; Nawotka №28a.

Imitations

These coins Golenko regarded as imitations; however, we think that they are original.

ZI = year 17

62. Obv_{24}-Rev_{35}. Obv. Diademed head of Asander r. Rev. Nike with upraised wings on prow l.; **ΒΑΣΙΛΕΩΣ ΑΣΑΝΔΡΟΥ**; l. 7,22g., GE 638 (pl.XX,5).

63. Obv_{24}-Rev_{36}. With the date ZO and blundered name.[112] 7,77g., New York (pl.XX,6.). Oreshnikov, *Numismatic Symposium*, III, 1915, p.62, pl.II,39; Auction Ratto, Lugano, 1927, p.122, №1696, pl.XLIII,1696.

K = year 20

Imitations of this year were published by Golenko, *NE*, X, p.103-107.

64. 8,54 g., Vienna (pl.XX,7).

65. 8,17 g., GE 645 (pl.XX,8). Golenko, *NE*, X, pl.I,7.

66. 10,95g., lead, London, *BMC*, 1889, X,11 (pl.XX,9; cf. pl.LXI,7, enlarged). Golenko, *NE*, X, p.107, №5, pl.I,5; in the Numismatic Department of the British Museum this coin is regarded as a modern imitation.

67. 8,12g., Copenhagen (pl.XX,11). Golenko, NE, X, p.107, №8.

68. 8,04g., Bruxelles, *Bibliotheque Royale de Belgique. Cabinet des Médailles* (pl.XX,10).

69. A. Gift of Evans (provenance - Kerch) (pl.XX,13).

70. 8,10 g, GE 1481 (pl.XX,14).

[112] The style of the head together with the blundering of both date and Asander's name (apparently ΑΙΧΙΝΝΛβV) must raise serious doubts as to the authenticity of the coin. S.I.

The Bronze Coins of Asander mid. 1st Century B.C.

Obols

Obv. Laureate head r.[113]
Rev. Prow l.; ΑΡΧΟΝΤΟΣ ΑΣΑΝΔΡΟΥ
Burachkov, XXV, 46-49; Zograph, XLIV,7; Anohin 224; *SNG BM* 964; *RPC* I, 1845[114]; Stancomb 608.

Dies		Wt.	Dia.	Mus.	Mus. No.	Plate	Notes
A-a	1)	16,56	28 mm	GE	27705	pl.XXI,1	
B-b	1)	16,19	29 mm	GE	27707	pl.XXI,2	
D-d	1)	15,89	27 mm	GE	27708	pl.XXI,3	
C-c	1)	18,26	31 mm	GE	27710	pl.XXI,4	
I-I	1)	16,09	26 mm	GE	27711	pl.XXI,5	
G-g	1)	16,30	28 mm	GE	27713	pl.XXI,6	
F-I	1)	16,90	28 mm	GE	27714	pl.XXI,7	Anohin 224
H-f	1)	17,72	27 mm	GE	27715	pl.XXI,8	
F-e	1)	13,90	28 mm	GE	27716	pl.XXI,9	Overstruck on a coin: Dionysus/bowcase; countermark: star on both sides
E-h	1)	15,91	28 mm	GE	27717	pl.XXI,10	Countermark: star on both sides
K-k	1)	15,50	27 mm	GE	27718	pl.XXI,11	Overstruck; countermark: star on both sides
L-l	1)	15,74	29 mm	GE	27719	pl.XXI,12	Overstruck; countermark: star on both sides
	2)	16,20	28 mm	OGAM	23617		
	3)	16,50	29 mm	OGAM	23607		
	4)	14,50	29 mm	OGAM	25320	pl.XXI,18	
	5)	16,02	30 mm	GIM	12658		
	6)	15,12	29 mm	GIM	12657		Kozievsky Coll.
M-m	1)	16,65	29 mm	GE	27720	pl.XXI,13	Overstruck on a Panticapaean or Sinope coin: Zeus/eagle on thunderbolt l.
N-m	1)	16,95	30 mm	GE	27721	pl.XXI,14	Overstruck on an Amastrian coin
O-o	1)	15,57	31 mm	GE	27722	pl.XXI,15	Overstruck on a coin: Zeus/eagle, before prow-trident
	2)	17,24		BM	964		Countermark: star on both sides
P-p	1)	15,40	25 mm	GE	27723	pl.XXI,16	Overstruck on a Sinope coin: Zeus/eagle
Q-q	1)	16,05	28 mm	GE	27724	pl.XXI,17	Overstruck on a Panticapaean coin: Dionysus/bowcase
R-r	1)	16,58	28 mm	GE	27725	pl.XXII,1	Overstruck on a Panticapaean coin:Zeus or Apollo/eagle, star
?-s	1)	14,90	30 mm	GE	27726	pl.XXII,2	Obv. Unknown; Rev. overstruck on a Panticapaeum coin: Dionysus/bowcase
T-t	1)	15,29	28 mm	GE	27727	pl.XXII,3	Overstruck on a Panticapaean coin: Dionysus/bowcase; on Rev. - trident
	2)	14,60	29 mm	OGAM	23610		
	3)	14,35	28 mm	GIM	12656		Kozievsky Coll.; overstruck on a coin: Apollo/eagle

---

[113] Frolova describes the head here as that of Nike in that some instances show wings, e.g. XXI, 18. Yet, as Nawotka (1992) observes, p.27, the head is undoubtedly male, and it may be that XXI, 18 is merely a heavy version of the tetrachalkoi below. S.I.

[114] In addition to *SNG BM* 964, *RPC* I, 1845 gives six further specimens, all with trident and bearing star countermarks: Copenhagen 13 (15.36g.), Oxford (18.70g., 15.76g.), Cambridge 1602-3 (13.46g., 13.13g.), Paris 89 (16.58g.). Frolova has (mistakenly) included the Ashmolean and one of the Fitzwilliam specimens in the next (lighter) Nike series. S.I.

Obv. Young head laureate, r.
Rev. Prow l.; ΑΡΧΟΝΤΟΣ ΑΣΑΝΔΡΟΥ.
(Often overstruck on coins: Dionysus/bowcase and often with countermark of a star on Obv. and Rev.).

Dies		Wt.	Dia.	Mus.	Mus No.	Plate	Notes
A-a	1)	14,41	28 mm	GIM	6771	pl.XXII,4	Overstruck on: Dionysus/ bowcase; countermarks
?-?	1)	16,87	30 mm	GIM	6773	pl.XXII,5	Unknown dies; overstruck twice on: 1) Apollo/eagle of Panticapaeum; 2) Dionysus/ bowcase of Panticapaeum
Ba-bb	1)	16,30	27mm	Odessa	23615	pl.XXII,6	
B-b	1)	15,29	29 mm	GIM	6774	pl.XXII,15	Countermarks
C-c	1)	13,06	28 mm	GIM	6776		Overstruck
Ca-ca	1)		27mm	Odessa	23544	pl.XXII,7	On rev. trident
D-d	1)	13,13	28 mm	GIM	6770	pl.XXII,8	Countermarks
E-e	1)	14,35	28 mm	GIM	6778a	pl.XXII,9	Overstruck on a Panticapaean coin: Dionysus/bowcase; Countermarks
G-g	1)	14,49	29 mm	GIM	6778	pl.XXII,10	Overstruck on a Panticapaeum coin: Dionysus/bowcase; countermarks
I-I	1)	14,26	29 mm	GIM	6779	pl.XXII,11	On Obv. – head of Nike?
H-h	1)	14,26	28 mm	GIM	6780	pl.XXII,12	
F-f	1)	14,39	28 mm	GIM	6781	pl.XXII,13	
K-k	1)	17,84	29 mm	GIM	6770a	pl.XXII,14	
L-l	1)	17,80	30 mm	GIM	6811	pl.XXII,18	Overstruck on Amisus coin: Head of Athena/Perseus; Countermarks; obv. only
M-m	1)	13,80	30 mm	GIM	6808	pl.XXII,16	Overstruck on Amisus coin: Head of Athena/Perseus; Countermarks
N-n	1)			OGAM	23608	pl.XXII,17	Rev. double struck
O-o	1)	13,12	26 mm	GIM	14199		Grandemaison Coll.
P-p	1)	13,03	26 mm	GIM	14200	pl.XXIII,2	Grandemaison Coll.
R-r	1)	14,73	26mm	GIM	6789		
S-s	1)	13,85	26mm	GIM	6772	pl.XXIII,3	
	2)	18,10	27 mm	OGAM	23614	pl.XXIII,1	
	3)	16,50	27 mm	OGAM	23725		

Tetrachalkoi

Obv. Bust of Nike r.
Rev. Prow, ΑΡΧΟΝΤΟΣ ΑΣΑΝΔΡΟΥ.
Anohin 225; *SNG BM* 962-3; *RPC* I, 1846[115]; Stancomb 609.

Dies		Wt.	Dia.	Mus.	Mus. No.	Plate	Notes
A-a	1)	6,36	21 mm	GE	27729	pl.XXIII,4	
B-b	1)	6,73	22 mm	GE	27730	pl.XXIII,5	
A-c	1)	8,08	22 mm	GE	27728	pl.XXIII,6	
A-d	1)	7,27	20 mm	GE	27733	pl.XXIII,7	
D-e	1)	8,28	22 mm	GE	26Γ	pl.XXIII,8	
C-f	1)	7,10	23 mm	GE	27750	pl.XXIII,9	Overstruck on a Panticapaean coin: Zeus = Apollo/eagle
E-h	1)	6,01	21 mm	GE	27751	pl.XXIII,10	Overstruck on a Sinope coin: Zeus/eagle on thunderbolt
A-I	1)	6,51	22 mm	GE	27752	pl.XXIII,11	Overstruck on a Sinope coin: Zeus/eagle

[115] *RPC* I, 1846 gives further specimens in Munich (1a), Oxford (7.96g., 8.04g., 11.43g., 9.57g), Paris 90 (7.07g.). S.I.

H-g	1)	7,47	22 mm	GE	27753	pl.XXIII,12	Overstruck on a Sinope coin: Zeus/eagle
G-I	1)	8,09	20 mm	GE	27754	pl.XXIII,13	Overstruck on a Sinope coin: Zeus/eagle
F-f	1)	7,60	24 mm	GE	27736	pl.XXIII,14	Overstruck on an Amisus coin: Zeus/eagle
K-k	1)	7,88	21 mm	GE	27737	pl.XXIII,15	Overstruck on an Amisus coin
L-l	1)	8,17	19 mm	GE	27738	pl.XXIII,16	Overstruck on an Amisus coin
M-m	1)	7,95	23 mm	GE	27739	pl.XXIII,17	
N-n	1)	8,05	24 mm	GE	27740	pl.XXIII,18	Overstruck on an Amisus coin: Ares/sword
	2)	8,07	24 mm	GIM	12659		Kozievsky Coll.; overstruck on an Amisus coin: Ares/sword
O-o	1)	6,49	25 mm	GE	27741	pl.XXIII,19	Overstruck on an Amisus coin: Aegis/Nike
A-p	1)	7,15	23 mm	GE	27743	pl.XXIII,20	Overstruck on an Amisus coin: Aegis/Nike
M-m	1)	5,96	23 mm	GE	27744	pl.XXIII,21	Overstruck on an Amisus coin: Aegis/Nike
	2)	5,78	23 mm	GE	27746	pl.XXIII,22	Overstruck
P-q	1)	6,02	25 mm	GE	27745		Overstruck on an Amisus coin: Aegis/Nike
R-r	1)	8,00	24 mm	GE	27747	pl.XXIII,23	Overstruck on an Amisus coin: Aegis/Nike
S-t	1)	6,40	24 mm	GIM	6769	pl.XXIII,24	Overstruck
M-s	1)	7,58	23 mm	GIM	6782	pl.XXIV,1	
B-m	1)	7,71	23 mm	GIM	6783	pl.XXIV,2	
A-x	1)	10,08	22 mm	GIM	6784	pl.XXIV,3	
S-ax	1)	8,26	22 mm	GIM	6786	pl.XXIV,4	
Aa-u	1)	8,52	22 mm	GIM	6804	pl.XXIV,5	Overstruck on an Amisus coin: Ares/sword
M-m	1)	8,25	22 mm	GIM	6797	pl.XXIV,6	Overstruck on an Amisus coin: Zeus/eagle
	2)	9,12	22 mm	GIM	6791	pl.XXIV,8	Overstruck on an Amisus coin: Zeus/eagle
	3)	8,87	20 mm	GIM	6795	pl.XXIV,7	Overstruck on a Sinope coin: Zeus/eagle
	4)	5,32	20 mm	GIM	6788	pl.XXIV,9	
	5)		20 mm	GIM	6788a	pl.XXIV,10[116]	

The dies on the following four coins are not clear:

	1)	7,70	22 mm	GIM	6792	pl.XXIV,11	Overstruck on a Sinope coin: Zeus/eagle
	2)	6,90	22 mm	GIM	6793	pl.XXIV,12	Overstruck on a Sinope coin: Zeus/eagle
	3)	8,77	22 mm	GIM	6794	pl.XXIV,13	Overstruck on a Sinope coin: Zeus/eagle
	4)	4,09	25 mm	GIM	12661		Kozievsky Coll.; overstruck on an uncertain type. Obv. has dolphin and spear
Ab-ab	1)	7,13	22 mm	GIM	6795a	pl.XXIV,14	Overstruck on a Sinope coin: Zeus/eagle

[116] This coin is very interesting specimen because it shows the type Apollo/Pegasus feeding, ΠΑΝΤΙΚΑΠΑΙΤΩΝ overstruck on an Asander coin type Head/prow, ΑΡΧΟΝΤΟΣ ΑΣΑΝΔΡΟΥ. This coin was published by Burachkov, pl.XXII,148. On it there were preserved the letters [ΑΡ]ΧΟΝΤ[ΟΣ] of the original inscription. Thus, bronze coins of Panticapaeum of the types Apollo/Pegasus, Apollo/quiver and bow and Apollo/prow, ΠΑΝΤΙΚΑΠΑΙΤΩΝ were minted after the bronze coins of Asander with his name ΑΡΧΟΝΤΟΣ ΑΣΑΝΔΡΟΥ or simultaneously with them.

Ac-ac	1)	7,92	21 mm	GIM	6798	pl.XXIV,15	Overstruck on a Sinope coin: Zeus/eagle
Ad-ad	1)	6,74	21 mm	GIM	6799	pl.XXIV,16	Overstruck on a Sinope coin: Zeus/eagle
Ae-ae	1)	6,37	21 mm	GIM	6800	pl.XXIV,17	Overstruck on a Sinope coin: Zeus/eagle
U-ux	1)	5,78	21 mm	GIM	6801	pl.XXIV,18	Overstruck on a Sinope coin: Zeus/eagle
Af-af	1)	7,47	21 mm	GIM	6803	pl.XXIV,19	Overstruck on a Sinope coin: Zeus/eagle
Ak-ak	1)	7,85	21 mm	GIM	6807	pl.XXIV,20	Overstruck on a Sinope coin: Zeus/eagle

The dies on the following coins are not clear:

1)	7,01	21 mm	GIM	6805	pl.XXIV,21	
2)	8,45	21 mm	GIM	6802	pl.XXIV,22	Overstruck on an Amastrian coin: Zeus/eagle
3)	7,78	20 mm	GIM	6811	pl.XXIV,23	Overstruck on an Amastrian coin
4)	6,34	21 mm	GIM	6812	pl.XXIV,24	Overstruck
5)	8,31	21 mm	GIM	6813	pl.XXIV,25	Overstruck
6)	6,54	21 mm	GIM	6790		
7)	7,08	21 mm	GIM	6797	pl.XXV,2	Overstruck on an Amisus coin: Dionysus/Cista; SNG BM 1199-1209
8)	7,33	21 mm	GIM	6815	pl.XXV,3	Overstruck on an Amisus coin: Aegis/Nike; SNG BM 1177-91
9)	6,30	21 mm	GIM	6816	pl.XXV,4	Overstruck on an Amisus coin: Aegis/Nike; SNG BM 1177-91
10)	4,81	20 mm	GIM	6861		Overstruck
11)	6,00	20 mm	GIM	6892		
12)	7,80	19 mm	GIM	6797[a]	pl.XXV,7	Overstruck on a Sinope coin: Zeus/eagle
13)	7,82	21 mm	GIM	6814	pl.XXV,8	Overstruck on a Sinope coin: Zeus/eagle
14)	7,21	20 mm	GIM	6810	pl.XXV,9	Overstruck
15)	7,21	21 mm	F	7391	pl.XXV,1	
16)	13,13	23 mm	F	1603	pl.XXV,5	Overstruck; countermark of star on each side[117]
17)	18,69	24 mm	A		pl.XXV,6	Overstruck
18)	4,81	20 mm	GIM	6861		Overstruck
19)	6,00	20 mm	GIM	6892		
20)	5,75	18 mm	BM	962		Overstruck on a Sinope coin: Zeus/eagle
21)	6,84	19 mm	BM	963		Overstruck on a Pontic coin: Aegis/Nike
22)	8,05	21 mm	OGAM	23642		
23)	7,65	23 mm	OGAM	25352		
24)	7,20	22 mm	OGAM	22937		
25)	6,65	23 mm	OGAM	23603		
26)	5,65	22 mm	OGAM	23621		

Bronze coins of Bosporan cities 49/48 - 21/20 BC

Three types of bronze coins have on the obv. Head of Apollo wearing a diadem with long ends. The head resembles that of Asander on gold staters with his name. This resemblance makes possible dating to 49/48 - 21/20 B.C. (the period of Asander's reign as the King of Bosporus) bronze coins of the following three types, all tetrachalkoi: 1) Apollo - Asander / quiver and bow; 2) Apollo - Asander / Pegasus feeding; 3) Apollo - Asander / prow, all with the inscription ΠΑΝΤΙΚΑΠΑΙΤΩΝ. The type, head of Heracles - Asander / club with lion's skin,

[117] This coin and the following one are to be assigned to the earlier series of obols.

ΠΑΝΤΙΚΑΠΑΙΤΩΝ is also an issue of Panticapaeum at the time of Asander's reign, as is a large obol issue: obv. Head of Apollo - Asander, rev. Lyre and palm branch.

Thus, the coinage of Bosporus of the mid. 1st century B.C. consisted of the king's issue of gold staters, two denominations of bronze coins with the legend ΑΡΧΟΝΤΟΣ ΑΣΑΝΔΡΟΥ (see above), three denominations of bronze coins of Panticapaeum (including three types of bronze tetrachalkoi), and, in addition, four types of bronze coins with the place-name ΦΑΝΑΓΟΡΙΤΩΝ: 1) head of Apollo - Asander / prow; 2) Head of Apollo - Asander / bow and arrow; 3) Head of Apollo - Asander / palm branch; 4) Head of Nike / palm branch.

The bronze coins with ΑΡΧΟΝΤΟΣ ΑΣΑΝΔΡΟΥ are clearly to be dated to years 1-4 of his rule in Bosporus, since we have on the Asander staters the letters Α, Β, Γ, Δ and the legend ΑΡΧΟΝΤΟΣ ΑΣΑΝΔΡΟΥ. But the four types of bronze coins with the names of ΠΑΝΤΙΚΑΠΑΙΤΩΝ and ΦΑΝΑΓΟΡΙΤΩΝ must be the very last issues of those cities. They may have been minted in the period from 49/48 to 21/20 B.C..

Tetrachalkoi

Type I

Obv. Head of Apollo - Asander r.
Rev. Quiver and bow, ΠΑΝΤΙΚΑ- ΠΑΙΤΩΝ.
Burachkov, XXI,132; Zograph, XLIV,10; Anohin 247; *SNG BM* 957; Stancomb 610.

Des		Wt.	Dia.	Mus.	Mus. No.	Plate	Notes
A-a	1)	6,80	20 mm	GIM	6839		
	2)	7,66	20 mm	GIM	6840	pl.XXV,11	
	3)	4,45	20 mm	GIM	14195	pl.XXV,12	Grandemaison Coll
	4)	7,50	20 mm	A		pl.XXV,10	
B-b	1)	7,25	20 mm	GIM	14193	pl.XXV,13	Grandemaison Coll.; on obv. countermark of caduceus
B-a	1)	6,15	19 mm	GIM	14194	pl.XXV,14	Grandemaison Coll.
	2)	7,40	20 mm	GIM	6841	pl.XXV,15	
C-c	1)	6,60	20 mm	GIM	6842	pl.XXV,16	
	2)	5,60	20 mm	GE	946	pl.XXV,17	
D-e	1)	6,07	19 mm	GIM	6830	pl.XXV,18	
C-d	1)	5,73	20 mm	GIM	6843	pl.XXV,19	
E-e	1)	5,01	19 mm	GIM	6844	pl.XXV,20	
	2)	4,77	19 mm	GIM	6849		
B-?	1)	4,59	20 mm	GIM	6845	pl.XXV,21	Poor condition; on obv. countermark of caduceus
	2)	7,09	20mm.	A		pl.XXV,23	
F-I	1)	6,61	20 mm	GIM	6848	pl.XXV,22	
	2)	4,60	20 mm	GE	944	pl.XXV,24	
A-d	1)	5,43	21 mm	GE	945	pl.XXV,25	
E-?	1)	7,10	20 mm	GE	940		Poor condition
	2)	5,59	20 mm	GE	943		Poor condition
	3)	4,15	19 mm	GIM	6846		Poor condition
A-e	1)	5,87	20 mm	GE	945		
	2)	4,72	19 mm	GIM	6851		
	3)	8,00		BM	957		
	4)	3,70	19 mm	OGAM	24852		
	5)	6,09	18 mm	OGAM	28006		
	6)	6,13	19mm	GIM	6852		

Type II

AE. Obv. Head of Apollo-Asander r.
Rev. Pegasus feeding l., ΠΑΝΤΙΚΑΠΑΙΤΩΝ.
Burachkov, XXII,148-149; Zograph, XLIV,9; Anohin 250; *SNG BM* 955-6; Stancomb 611-12[118]

Dies		Wt.	Dia.	Mus.	Mus.No.	Plate	Notes
A-a	1)	5,76	20 mm	GIM	6817	pl.XXVI,1	Anohin 250. Overstruck on a Pontic coin

[118] Nawotka (1992) p.48, 34a also records a coin of the type, obv. Head of Helios, rev. Pegasus r., Δ below, with the inscription ΒΑΣΙΛΕΩΣ ΑΣΑΝΔΡΟΥ, in the Fitzwilliam Museum, Cambridge (1604, wt. 2.12g.). S.I.

	2)	5,15	20 mm	A		pl.XXVI,2	
B-b	1)	6,76	22 mm	GIM	6818		Overstruck on a Pontic coin: Aegis/Nike
C-c	1)	5,03	22 mm	GIM	6819	pl.XXVI,3	Overstruck on a Sinope coin: Zeus/eagle; SNG BM 1543-9
D-d	1)	5,07	21 mm	GIM	6820	pl.XXVI,4	Overstruck on a Sinope coin: Zeus/eagle; SNG BM 1543-9
	2)	7,36	21 mm	GIM	6821	pl.XXVI,5	
A-i	1)	5,80	21 mm	GIM	6822	pl.XXVI,6	Overstruck on an Asander coin; on Rev. inscription
E-e	1)	6,00	22 mm	GIM	6823	pl.XXVI,7	Overstruck
F-f	1)	6,05	19 mm	GIM	6824	pl.XXVI,8	Overstruck, the original types illigible
G-g	1)	6,22	19 mm	GIM	6825	pl.XXVI,9	Overstruck, the original types illigible
	2)	4,86	20 mm	Hunterian		pl.XXVI,10	
?-?	1)	7,29	20 mm	GIM	6826	pl.XXVI,11	Dies unclear; overstruck
	2)	6,19	20 mm	GIM	6827		Dies unclear;overstruck on a Pontic coin: Aegis/Nike
B-?	1)	6,62	20 mm	GIM	6828	pl.XXVI,12	Rev.- poor condition; overstruck on a Pontic coin
I-I	1)	5,91	21 mm	GIM	6829	pl.XXVI,13	Overstruck on an Asander coin
	2)	5,81	20 mm	GIM	6831	pl.XXVI,14	
	3)	6,14	23 mm	GIM	12662		Kozievsky Coll.
K-k	1)	6,07	20 mm	GIM	6830	pl.XXVI,15	Overstruck
	2)	7,11	21 mm	GIM	12663		Kozievsky Coll.
	3)	6,92	22 mm	GIM	14196	pl.XXVI,16	Grandemaison Coll.
	4)	7,20	20 mm	GIM	6886		Poor condition
	5)	6,65	20 mm	GIM	6832		
	6)	7,42	20 mm	GIM	6834		
	7)	4,57	20 mm	GIM	6836		
	8)	8,30	20 mm	GIM	6885	pl.XXVI,21	
L-l	1)	6,79	19 mm	GIM	6833	pl.XXVI,17	Overstruck
	2)	7,33	20 mm	GIM	6835	pl.XXVI,18	Overstruck
A-?	1)	6,60	20 mm	GIM	6837	pl.XXVI,19	Rev.- poor condition; Overstruck
	2)	7,70	20 mm	GIM	6838	pl.XXVI,20	Rev.- poor condition; countermark caduceus
C-b	1)	7,39	21 mm	GE	913	pl.XXVI,22	Overstruck
A-f	1)	6,90	21 mm	GE	914	pl.XXVI,23	
A-af	1)	6,88	25 mm	GE	915	pl.XXVI,24	
M-m	1)	6,45	24 mm	GE	916	pl.XXVII,1	
M-n	1)	8,50	22 mm	GE	917	pl.XXVII,2	
M-o	1)	6,09	21 mm	GE	918	pl.XXVII,3	
?-?	1)	6,34	24 mm	GE	919	pl.XXVII,4	Dies poor; overstruck
M-?	1)	6,85	21 mm	GE	920	pl.XXVII,5	Countermark caduceus
N-	1)	6,53	21 mm	GE	921	pl.XXVII,6	Overstruck
?-?	1)	4,34	19 mm	GE	922	pl.XXVII,7	Dies poor
C-?	1)	7,00	21-23 mm	GE	924	pl.XXVII,8	Rev. die poor; overstruck on a Pontic coin
	2)	6,82	25 mm	GE	924[a]	pl.XXVII,9	Rev. die poor; overstruck on a Panticapaean coin: Dionysus/tripod
	3)	6,25		BM	956	pl.LXII,2	Enlarged
	4)	6,65		BM	955	pl.LXII,1	Enlarged
	1)	6,20	22 mm	OGAM	25346		
	2)	5,75	20 mm	OGAM	27911		
	3)	5,25	20 mm	OGAM	28696		
	4)	5,05	23 mm	OGAM	24715		

Type III

AE. Obv. Head of Apollo-Asander r.
Rev. Prow r., ΠΑΝΤΙΚΑΠΑΙΤΩΝ.
Burachkov, XXII,133-135; Zograph, XLIV,11; Anohin 251; *SNG BM* 958, Stancomb 613.

Dies		Wt.	Dia.	Mus.	Mus. No.	Plate	Notes
A-a	1)	5,75	19 mm	GIM	6857	pl.XXVII,10	
	2)	6,88	20 mm	GE	926	pl.XXVII,12	
A-b	1)	5,76	20 mm	GIM	6855	pl.XXVII,11	
	2)	5,68	19 mm	GE	927	pl.XXVII,13	
	3)	3,01	17 mm	Cop	58		
A-e	1)	6,91	24 mm	GE	929	pl.XXVII,14	Overstruck on a Pontic coin
	2)	6,65	20 mm	GIM	6859	pl.XXVII,14a	
?-?	1)	3,18	17 mm	GE	931	pl.XXVII,15	Poor condition
	2)	7,55	24 mm	GE	932	pl.XXVII,16	Overstruck
	3)	4,35	20 mm	GE	933	pl.XXVII,17	Overstruck
B-d	1)	3,28	15 mm	GE	934	pl.XXVII,18	
C-g	1)	3,23	16 mm	GE	935	pl.XXVII,19	
B-i	1)	2,32	16 mm	GE	936	pl.XXVII,20	
D-e	1)	2,00	15 mm	GE	937	pl.XXVIII,1	
	2)	3,24	15 mm	GIM	6860	pl.XXVIII,2	
C-f	1)	2,94	14 mm	GIM	6856	pl.XXVIII,3	
D-g	1)	7,52	19 mm	GIM	6853	pl.XXVIII,4	Overstruck
	2)	5,78	20 mm	GIM	6854	pl.XXVIII,5	
E-h	1)	7,33	19 mm	GIM	6858	pl.XXVIII,6	
G-f	1)	6,00	23 mm	GIM	14203	pl.XXVIII,7	Grandemaison Coll.
	2)	6,65	17 mm	GIM	14204	pl.XXVIII,8	Grandemaison Coll.
	3)	6,40		BM	958		
	4)	6,25	20 mm	GIM	14205		Grandemaison Coll.
	5)	7,18	21 mm	GIM	12628		Kozievsky Coll.

The end of Asander's rule (21/20 BC?)

Dichalkoi?

Obv. Diademed head of Heracles-Asander r.
Rev. Club and lion's skin, ΠΑΝΤΙΚΑΠΑΙΤΩΝ.
Köhne, I, p.378, №137; Burachkov, p.163, №181, pl.XXII,181; Anohin 248.

Dies		Wt.	Dia.	Mus.	Mus. No.		
A-a	1)		20 mm	GE	948	pl.XXVIII,10	
B-b	1)	3,55	19 mm	GE	949	pl.XXVIII,11	
	2)	4,57	19 mm	GE	950	pl.XXVIII,12	
C-c	1)	6,02	20 mm	GE	951	pl.XXVIII,13	
	2)	3,65	19 mm	GE	952	pl.XXVIII,14	
	3)	3,45	18 mm	GIM	12638		Kozievsky Coll.
	4)	4,42		Private collection, Moscow			Anohin, 248
	1)	3,58	17mm			pl.XXVIII,9	Coll. Bertier de la Garde

The time of Asander's reign (49/48 - 21/20 BC)

Obols

Obv. Head of Apollo - Asander r.
Rev. Lyre, r. - palm branch, ΠΑΝΤΙΚΑΠΑΙΤΩΝ.
Köhne, I, p.361, №86; Burachkov, p.153, №199, pl.XXI,118; Anohin 226.

Dies		Wt.	Dia.	Mus.	Mus. No.	Plate	Notes
A-a	1)	14,77	30 mm	GE	911/27273	pl.XXVIII,15	Anohin 226

	2)				Burachkov Collection		Countermark - 8-rayed star; overstruck on an unclear coin-type; Burachkov, p.153, №199, pl.XXI,118
	3)	9,32	26 mm	GE	912/27274		

The coinage of Phanagoria at the time of Asander's reign (49/48 - 21/20 B.C.)

Type I

Obv. Head of Apollo - Asander r.
Rev. Prow r., **ΦΑΝΑΓΟ ΡΙΤΩΝ**.
Burachkov, XXIII,13; Zograph, XLIV,12; Anohin 252, *SNG BM* 1004-5

Dies		Wt.	Dia	Mus.	Mus. No.	Plate	Notes
A-a	1)	5,56	19 mm	GE	104/27438	pl.XXVIII,16	Anohin 252
A-b	1)			GE	105/27439	pl.XXVIII,17	
B-c	1)	6,58	19 mm	GE	106/27440	pl.XXVIII,18	
C-d	1)	7,20	19 mm	GE	108/27442	pl.XXVIII,19	
D-e	1)	4,81	20 mm	GE	109/27443	pl.XXVIII,20	Overstruck on a coin of Asander: Apollo-Asander/ quiver and bow, ΠΑΝΤΙΚΑΠΑΙΤΩΝ.[119]
	2)	5,19	21 mm	GE	110/27444	pl.XXVIII,21	Overstruck on a coin: Apollo-Asander/prow, **ΠΑΝΤΙΚΑΠΑΙΤΩΝ**
	3)	5,91	21 mm	GIM	12714		Kozievsky Coll.
E-i	1)	7,31	25 mm	GE	111/27445	pl.XXIX,1	Overstruck on a coin: Apollo-Asander/prow, ΑΡΧΟΝΤΟΣ ΑΣΑΝΔΡΟΥ
	2)	5,78	19mm	BM	1004		
	3)	4,91	17mm	BM	1005		
		7,65	19mm	GIM	14592	pl.XXVIII,16a	Grandemaison Coll.
		6,27	19mm	A		pl.XXVIII,17a	

Type II

Obv. Head of Apollo-Asander r.
Rev. Bow and arrow, **ΦΑΝΑΤΟ ΡΙΤΩΝ**.
Burachkov, XXIII,14-15; Anohin 249; *SNG BM* 1006

Dies		Wt.	Dia.	Mus.	Mus. No.	Plate	Notes
A-a	1)	2,60	18 mm	GE	112	pl.XXIX,2	
	2)	5,59	19 mm	GE	113	pl.XXIX,3	
	3)	2,69	19 mm	GE	114/27448	pl.XXIX,4	Anohin 249
	4)	5,40	20 mm	GE	115	pl.XXIX,5	
B-b	1)	3,58	20 mm	GE	116	pl.XXIX,6	
	2)	3,48	18 mm	GIM	6693	pl.XXIX,7	
C-c	1)	2,20	19 mm	GIM	6691	pl.XXIX,8	
D-d	1)	4,14	19 mm	GIM	6685	pl.XXIX,9	
	2)	3,39	20 mm	GIM	12712		Kozievsky Coll.
	3)	2,96	17 mm	GIM	14536		Grandemaison Coll.
	4)	3,84	19mm	BM	1006		

[119] It is important to note from the evidence of overstriking here that this Phanagorean issue comes after the Panticapaean issues: quiver/bow, Apollo/prow and the ΑΡΧΟΝΤΟΣ ΑΣΑΝΔΡΟΥ issue: Apollo/prow.

Type III

Obv. Head of Apollo-Asander r.
Rev. Palm branch with bands,[120] ΦΑΝΑΓΟ ΡΙΤΩΝ.
Burachkov, XXIII,18

Dies		Wt.	Dia.	Mus.	Mus. No.	Plate	Notes
A-a	1)	3,32	20 mm	GIM	6670	pl.XXIX,10	Poor condition
	2)	4,37	20 mm	GIM	6681	pl.XXIX,11	Poor condition
B-b	1)	3,31	15 mm	GIM	6687	pl.XXIX,12	Poor condition
	2)	3,81	15 mm	GIM	6692	pl.XXIX,13	Poor condition
	3)	1,33	14 mm	GIM	6690	pl.XXIX,14	Poor condition

Type IV

Obv. Head on Nike r.; to l., 8-rayed star.
Rev. Palm branch,[121] **ΦΑΝΑΓΟ ΡΙΤΩΝ.**
Burachkov, XXIII,16-17; Zograph, XLIV,13; Anohin 227, *SNG BM* 995-6

Dies		Wt.	Dia.	Mus.	Mus No.	Plate	Notes
A-a	1)	8,10	15 mm	F		pl.XXIX,15	
	2)	6,18	20 mm	GE	91	pl.XXIX,16	
	3)	6,05	22 mm	GE	92	pl.XXIX,17	
B-b	1)	3,82	19 mm	GE	93	pl.XXIX,18	
C-c	1)	6,79	19 mm	GIM	6667	pl.XXIX,19	
D-d	1)	4,84	20 mm	GE	94	pl.XXIX,20	
D-e	1)	4,43	20 mm	GE	95	pl.XXIX,21	
E-f	1)	2,57	17 mm	GE	96	pl.XXIX,22	
F-i	1)	6,02	17 mm	GE	99	pl.XXIX,23	
I-k	1)	4,60	17 mm	GIM	6678	pl.XXIX,24	
	2)	4,23	17 mm	GIM	6684	pl.XXX,1	
K-l	1)	5,05	21 mm	GIM	6682	pl.XXX,2	Anohin 227
L-m	1)	2,59	15 mm	GE	97	pl.XXX,3	
	2)	5,32	15 mm	GE	98	pl.XXX,4	
M-n	1)	7,20	20 mm	GE	90	pl.XXX,5	
N-o	1)	2,37	15 mm	GIM	6689	pl.XXX,6	
M-p	1)	3,13	15 mm	GIM	6688	pl.XXX,7	
C-s	1)	3,17	15 mm	GIM	6686	pl.XXX,8	
E-t	1)	2,15	16 mm	GE	102	pl.XXX,9	
I-u	1)	4,85	16 mm	GE	101	pl.XXX,10	
L-x	1)	3,83	15 mm	F	4515	pl.XXX,11	
P-b	1)	3,83	7 mm	GIM	14537	pl.XXX,12	Grandemaison Coll.
	1)	5,70	17 mm	OGAM	25342		
	2)	4,60	20 mm	OGAM	28020		
	3)	2,75	15 mm	OGAM	27884		
	4)	6,25	20 mm	OGAM	27886		
T-e	1)	4,50	20 mm	GIM	6680	pl.LXII,4	Enlarged
	2)	6,24	16mm	BM	995		
		2.21	13mm	BM	996		

§ 7 Coinage of Queen Dynamis (21/20 - 17/16 B.C.)

Gold stater, ΖΟΣ = 277 B.e. = 21/20 BC.
Obv. Bust of Queen r.
Rev. Star and crescent, ΒΑΣΙΛΙΣΣΗΣ ΔΥΝΑΜΕΩΣ ΖΟΣ (277).

1)	8,07	20 mm	Yalta	pl.XX,12	Anohin, 253

[120] The poor quality of these coins makes their identification uncertain. The style of the head, for instance, is suggestive of the bow and arrow type.
[121] *SNG BM* interprets the type as an aplustre.

Gold stater, ΑΠΣ = 281 of the Bosporan era = 17/16 B.C..
Obv. Bust of Queen r.
Rev. Star and crescent, ΒΑΣΙΛΙΣΣΗΣ ΔΥΝΑΜΕΩΣ ΑΠΣ (281).

1)	8,05	20 mm	GIM	393	pl.XX,15	Frolova, 'Dating the Reign of Dynamis', *SA*, 1978, 2, p.49-61, pl.I,1; Anohin, 254; *RPC* I, 1864

§ 8 Coins of Kaisarea (Panticapaeum): end of the 1st century B.C.

Obv. Head of Aphrodite Urania r., wearing kalathos and veil; border of dots.
Rev. Sceptre; to l. & r., inscription in two lines - ΚΑΙ- ΣΑ- ΡΕ- ΩΝ; below right, Η; border of dots.
Burachkov, pl.XIII,1,e; Oreshnikov, Catalogue..., p.71, №501; Oreshnikov, *Excursus*..., pl.I,II; Zograph, XLV,12; Anohin 322a-б; Frolova, *NE*, XV, 1989, pl.I,1-29; II,1-7; *RPC* I, 1936; Stancomb 614-5.

Dies		Wt.	Dia.	Mus.	Mus No.	Plate	Notes
A-a	1)	9,25	23 mm	GIM	8661	pl.XXXI,1	
	2)	6,17		GIM	8662	pl.XXXI,2	
	3)	11,40	23 mm	GIM	12678		Kozievsky Coll.
A-ab	1)	5,48	21 mm	GE	27321	pl.XXXI,3	Anohin 322a
	2)	8,03	21 mm	GIM	12677		Kozievsky Coll.
A-b	1)	8,51	22 mm	GIM	8663	pl.XXXI,4	Rev. only
	2)	4,54	20 mm	GIM	8664		
	3)	7,42	20 mm	GIM	35		
A-c	1)	4,38	20 mm	GIM	5/8665	pl.XXXI,5	Rev. only
	2)	7,82	21 mm	GIM	6/8666		
A-d	1)	6,25	21 mm	GE	7/27322	pl.XXXI,6	Anohin 322б
A-i	1)	8,35	21 mm	GE	12/27327	pl.XXXI,7	
A-g	1)	6,84	22 mm	GE	13/27328	pl.XXXI,8	
A-f	1)	6,93	23 mm	GE	15/27330	pl.XXXI,9	
B-h	1)	8,55	21 mm	GIM	8667	pl.XXXI,10	
	2)	6,08	21 mm	GIM	4/8701		
B-e	1)	7,67	21,5 mm	GIM	8668	pl.XXXI,11	Rev. only
	2)	7,16	21 mm	GIM	8669		
B-j	1)	6,87	22 mm	GE	1/27316	pl.XXXI,13	
	2)	4,28	20 mm	GIM	36/8696		
B-k	1)	7,58	22,5 mm	GIM	8671	pl.XXXI,14	
	2)	5,50	26 mm	GIM	8672		
B-l	1)	6,76	22 mm	GIM	8673	pl.XXXI,12	Rev. only
	2)	5,70	23 mm	GIM	8679		
B-m	1)	4,12	20 mm	GIM	8674	pl.XXXI,15	Rev. only
B-n	1)	6,73	21 mm	GE	4/27319	pl.XXXI,17	
C-o	1)	6,61	21 mm	GIM	8675	pl.XXXI,18	
	2)	6,18	21,5 mm	GIM	8676		
C-p	1)	5,85	22 mm	GIM	8677	pl.XXXI,19	
C-s	1)	6,54	22 mm	GIM	8678	pl.XXXI,16	Rev. only
C-t	1)	6,50	21 mm	GIM	8680	pl.XXXI,20	Rev. only
C-u	1)	5,78	21 mm	GIM	8661	pl.XXXI,21	Rev. only
	2)	10,44			*NE*, IX, pl.II, №36		
	3)	6,50			*NE*, IX, p.50, №37		
	4)	5,05			*NE*, IX, p.50, №38		
	5)	5,51	22 mm	GIM	8682		
C-ph	1)	6,01	21 mm	GIM	8683		
	2)	4,92	21,5 mm	GIM	8684	pl.XXXI,22	Rev. only
	3)	5,70	22 mm	GIM	8700		
C-x	1)	4,80	21 mm	GIM	8692	pl.XXXI,23	Rev. only
D-r	1)	5,28	21 mm	GIM	8685	pl.XXXI,24	
	2)	6,76	22 mm	GIM	8686		
	3)	5,00	21 mm	GIM	8688		
	4)	6,70	21 ,5 mm	GIM	8702		
D-aa	1)	5,65	21,5 mm	GIM	8687	pl.XXXI,25	
	2)	6,13	20 mm	GE	9/27324	pl.XXXI,26	
	3)	9,04			*NE*, IX, p.50, №34		

	4)	8,36			*NE*, IX, p.50, №35		
D-ab	1)	4,90	21 mm	GIM	8693	pl.XXXII,1	Rev. only
	2)	5,02		Cop	9		
G-ac	1)	4,05	21 mm	GE	11/27326	pl.XXXI,27	
	2)	5,35	22 mm	GIM	8687	pl.XXXI,28	
	3)	5,52	22 mm	GIM	8689		
	4)	5,75	21, 5 mm	GIM	8690		
	5)	4,54	21 mm	GIM	8691		
	6)	2,88	21 mm	GIM	8697		
	7)	5,19	21 mm	GIM	8698		
	8)	9,37			*NE*, IX, pl.II, №39		
	9)	6,99			*NE*, IX, pl.II, №40		
	10)	5,20			*NE*, IX, pl.II, №41		
C-ad	1)	4,90	21 mm	GIM	8694	pl.XXXI,29	
	2)	6,26	21 mm	GIM	8699		
	3)	5,83	21 mm	GE	10/27325	pl.XXXII,2	
	4)	7,17	23 mm	GIM	8670	pl.XXXII,3	
G-ag	1)	4,66	18,5 mm	GIM	8703		
F-af	1)	7,13		A		pl.LXII,6[122]	

Obv. Head of Aphrodite Urania r., wearing kalathos and veil.
Rev. Inscription - **ΚΑΙCΑΡΕΩΝ**, sword (?).[123]
Anohin 322

Dies		Wt.	Dia.	Mus.		Plate	Notes
H-ak	1)			Phangoria Excavations		pl.XXXII,4a	Frolova, *VDI*, 1981, 1, №433; rev. only
	2)	11,78	25 mm	GE	16/27321	pl.XXXII,4	
	3)	6,90	25 mm	GE	17/27332	pl.XXXII,5	
H-al	1)	3,80	21 mm	GE	18/27333	pl.XXXII,6	
	2)	4,8	21 mm	GIM	8704	pl.XXXII,7	
	3)	7,45	21 mm	GIM	12676		Kozievsky Coll.

The dies of the following coins have not been determined:

	Wt.	Ref.
1)	5,96	*NSph*, I[124], №67
2)	7,58	*NSph*, I, №306
3)	6,54	*NSph*, I, №350
4)		*NSph*, I, №365
5)		*NSph*, I, №372
6)		*NSph*, I, №454
7)	4,28	*NSph*, I, №426
8)	5,15	*NSph*, I, №573
9)	7,47	*NSph*, I, №580
10)	6,61	*NSph*, I, №648
11)	6,82	*NSph*, I, №699

Coins of Agrippia (Phanagoria) H = 8

Obv. Head of Aphrodite Urania r., wearing diadem and veil; border of dots.
Rev. Prow l.; two-line inscription, **ΑΓΡΙΠ- ΠΕΩΝ**; below r., H.
Köhne, I, p.366, №103; Burachkov, XXIII,1f; Oreshnikov, *Excursus*..., pl.I,14; Zograph, pl.XLV,14; Anohin 323; Frolova, *NE*, XV, 1989, pl.II,8-25, pl.III,1-23; *SNG Cop*. 7-8; *RPC* I, 1935; Stancomb 631.

Dies		Wt.	Dia	Mus.	Mus. No.	Plate	Notes
A-a	1)	7,71	22 mm	GIM	8705	pl.XXXII,8	
A-b	1)	7,71	22 mm	GIM	8706	pl.XXXII,9	

[122] An instance of the type, obv. Head of Aphrodite wearing kalathos & veil r.; rev. Sceptre, ΒΑΣΙΛΕΩΣ; to r., ΒΑΡ; to l., H, is noted by Anohin 321 (cf. here pl.LXII,6a). However, the coin is generally regarded as false.

[123] Frolova tentatively interprets the type as a sword, but it is more likely that it is a variant on the sceptre of the previous series, with the additional difference in the lettering and the positioning of the inscription. S.I.

[124] Golenko K.V., Shelov D.B., 'Coins from the Excavation of Panticapaeum 1945 - 1961', *Numismatica i Sphragistika*, I, Kiev, 1963, p.13-65.

	2)	7,25	21 mm	GIM	8707		
	3)	9,46		*NE*, IX, p.50, №44, pl.II, 44			
B-c	1)	7,40	19,5 mm	GIM	8708	pl.XXXII,10	
B-d	1)	7,01	21 mm	GIM	8709	pl.XXXII,11	
	2)	5,73	18 mm	Phangoria			Frolova, *VDI*, 1981, 1, p.108, №117
B-e	1)	7,10	21 mm	GE	8/27458	pl.XXXII,12	
C-f	1)	7,44	22 mm	GIM	8710	pl.XXXII,13	
B-h	1)	9,27	23 mm	GIM	9/27459	pl.XXXII,14	
B-i	1)	7,12	22 mm	GIM	8712	pl.XXXII,15	
B-g	1)	4,93	21 mm	GIM	8713	pl.XXXII,16	
	2)			GE	7/27459		
C-k	1)	7,02	21 mm	GIM	8711	pl.XXXII,17	
	2)	6,97	23 mm	GE	1/27451	pl.XXXII,18	
	3)	6,16		*NE*, IX, p.50, №41, pl.II, 41			
	4)	6,36		*NE*, IX, p.50, №42, pl.II, 42			
	5)	4,60	19 mm	Cop	8		
C-l	1)	4,69	21 mm	GIM	8714	pl.XXXII,19	
D-m	1)	5,20	20,5 mm	GIM	8715	pl.XXXII,20	
D-n	1)	5,27	21,5 mm	GIM	8719	pl.XXXII,21	
D-o	1)	5,64	19,5 mm	GIM	8720	pl.XXXII,22	Rev. only
D-ap	1)	5,85		A		pl.LXII,7	
D-p	1)	6,04	20 mm	GIM	8721	pl.XXXII,23	Rev. only
E-r	1)	5,71	18 mm	GIM	8722	pl.XXXII,24	
F-s	1)	6,83	21 mm	GIM	8724	pl.XXXII,25	
	2)	6,28	21 mm	GIM	8725		
F-t	1)	5,24	22 mm	GIM	8726		
H-u	1)	6,49	20 mm	GIM	8727	pl.XXXIII,1	
A-ph	1)	6,03	20 mm	GIM	8728	pl.XXXIII,2	Rev. only
J-x	1)	6,38	20 mm	GIM	8729	pl.XXXIII,3	Rev. only
	2)	5,34	20 mm	GIM	8730		
G-w	1)	7,12	22 mm	GE	4/27454	pl.XXXIII,4	
	2)	7,67	20 mm	Cop	7		
	3)	4,14	22 mm	GIM	8731	pl.XXXIII,6	
	4)	5,24	22 mm	GIM	8733		
	5)	6,42		*NE*, IX, p.50, pl.II,46			
	6)	7,98	23 mm	GE	3/27458	pl.XXXIII,5	
	7)	5,56	22 mm	GIM	12679		Kozievsky Coll.
	8)	7,98	23 mm	GIM	12680		Kozievsky Coll.
G-z	1)	5,35	22 m	GIM	8732	pl.XXXIII,7	
	2)	5,59	22 mm	GIM	8733	pl.XXXIII,9	
	3)	5,54	21 mm	GE	5/27455	pl.XXXIII,8	
	4)	4,86	21 mm	GIM	8734	pl.XXXIII,10	
	5)	8,49		*NE*, IX, p.50, №45 pl.II,45			
K-aa	1)	6,46	22 mm	GIM	8735	pl.XXXIII,11	
K-ab	1)	3,34	18,5 mm	GIM	8736	pl.XXXIII,12	
K-ac	1)	5,58	21 mm	GIM	8737	pl.XXXIII,13	
	2)	6,86	21 mm	GIM	8738		
L-ad	1)		23 mm	GE	27457	pl.XXXIII,14	
L-ae	1)	5,38	21 mm	GIM	8739	pl.XXXIII,15	
M-af	1)	6,75	22 mm	GIM	8740	pl.XXXIII,16	
N-ag	1)	5,76	21 mm	GIM	8741	pl.XXXIII,17	
N-ah	1)	6,53	19 mm	GE	16/27466	pl.XXXIII,18	
	2)	5,65	18 mm	GIM	8744	pl.XXXIII,19	
	3)	6,08	19 mm	GIM	8742		
	4)	4,44	19 mm	GIM	8743		
	5)	7,63	21 mm	GIM	8745		
	6)	3,74	20 mm	GIM	8746		
D-ak	1)	5,10	20 mm	GIM	12/8716	pl.XXXIII,20	
D-al	1)	4,40	21 mm	GIM	8717	pl.XXXIII,21	
	2)	4,64	22 mm	GE	11/27461	pl.XXXIII,22	

D-am	1)	5,20	21 mm	GIM	8718	pl.XXXIII,23
	2)	9,65	23 mm	GE	27456	
	3)	7,89	23 mm	GE	12/27462	
	4)	5,45	21 mm	GE	13/27463	
	5)	4,27	20 mm	GE	15/27465	
	6)	4,29	16 mm	GE	17/27467	
	7)	5,59	20 mm	GE	18/27468	
Aa-an	1)	5,66		A		pl.LXII,8

The dies of the following coins have not been determined:

1)	6,59	*NSph*, I, №539
2)	5,38	*NE*, II[125], p.75, №14, 443

§9 The end of the 1st century B.C.

Coins with monogram BAE (64)

Series 1 - the monogram as a reverse

Type I

Obv. Winged head of Gorgon r.; under the chin, knot of two serpents; border of dots.
Rev. Monogram BAE (64) in centre; border of dots.
Köhne, vol.II, p.51, №7; Burachkov, p.228, №44; Giel, *Kleine Beirträge*, p.10, pl.II,20; Podshiwalov, 'The Coins of the Cimmerian Bosporus Kings of the Spartocid and Achaemenid Dynasties', p.17, №2, pl.II,19; Zograph, pl.XLIV,17; Anohin 256; Stancomb 961.

Dies		Wt.	Dia.	Mus.	Mus. No.	Plate	Notes
A-b	1)	9,65		B	6	pl.XXXIII,24	
B-a	1)	13,15	25 mm	GE	27758	pl.XXXIV,1	Anohin 256. Publ. by Oreshnikov, *Excursus*, p.27, pl.I,10
C-c	1)	6,99	21 mm	GE	27759		
D-d	1)	5,02	20 mm	GE	27760	pl.XXXIV,2	
E-e	1)	10,78	23	GE	27761	pl.XXXIV,3	Publ. by Podshiwalov, *ZOOID*, XV, pl.II,19
E-f	1)	10,50	22 mm	GE	27762	pl.XXXIV,4	
E-h	1)	7,89	22 mm		141/12704		Kozievsky Coll.; publ.: *NE*, XV, 1989, pl.IV,8
H-g	1)	6,41	21 mm	GE	27763	pl.XXXIV,5	
F-i	1)	10,57			NS, I, p.53, №554, pl.I,554		
G-k	1)	8,26	22 mm	New York, Private col.		pl.XXXIII,24a	
K-l	1)	9,17		Cop	15		
L-m	1)	8,72	22 mm	GIM	142/12705	*NE*, XV, 1989, pl.IV,8	Two countermarks

Type II

Obv. Lion running r.; above, star; border of dots.
Rev. Monogram BAE (64) in centre; border of dots.
Köhne, vol.II, p.51, №8; Zograph, pl.XLIV,18; BMC, 1889, pl..IX,5; Anohin 257[126]; Frolova, *NE*, XV, pl.IV,10-20; Stancomb 962-3.

Dies		Wt.	Dia.	Mus.	Mus. No.	Plate	Notes
A-a	1)	6,29	21 mm	GE	27764	pl.XXXIV,6	
	2)			BMC, 1889, pl.IX,5		pl.XXXIV,5a	
B-b	1)	6,23	20 mm	GE	27765	pl.XXXIV,7	Publ. by Podshiwalov, Coins..., pl.II,23 - Obv.
C-c	1)	5,88	20 mm	GE	27666	pl.XXXIV,8	Publ. by Podshiwalov, Coins..., pl.II,25 - Obv.
D-d	1)			GE	27767	pl.XXXIV,9	

[125] Golenko K.V., 'Coins from the Excavation at Nymphaeum 1939-1970', *NE*, II, 1960.
[126] Anohin's photograph is identical with Frolova's pl.XXXIV, 12, but is referred to as if Frolova XXXIV,6. S.I.

	2)	10,32	23 mm	GE	27768	pl.XXXIV,10	
E-e	1)	6,07	19 mm	GE	27769	pl.XXXIV,11	Publ. by Podshiwalov, Coins..., pl.II,24 - Obv., 25 -Rev.
I-i	1)	5,82	22 mm	GIM	6723	pl.XXXIV,12	
	2)			BMC, 1889, pl.IX,6		pl.XXXIV,14	
C-g	1)	3,63	18 mm	GIM	6724	pl.XXXIV,13	
H-h	1)	6,90	18 mm	GIM	138/*NE*, XV, 1989, pl.IV,20		
K-l	1)	10,69		Cop	16		

Type III

Obv. Dolphin r.; behind, trident; border of dots.

Rev. Monogram BAE (64) in centre; border of dots.

Giel, *Kleine Beiträge*, p.9, pl.II,19; Podshivalov, The Coins..., p.20, №12; Burachkov, p.227, №36, pl.XXIV,20; Zograph, pl.XLIV,19; Anohin 258; Frolova, *NE*, XV, pl.IV,21-24; Stancomb 964.

Dies		Wt.	Dia.	Mus.	Mus. No.	Plate	Notes
A-a	1)	3,32	16 mm	GE	27770	pl.XXXIV,15	
B-b	1)	2,93	16 mm	GE	27771	pl.XXXIV,16	
A-c	1)	5,29	16 mm	Antiken Münzen. Auction IX, F.Sternberg. Zürich, 1981, S.16, №95		pl.XXXIV,16a	Anohin 258
B-b	1)	3,79		*NE*, XI[127], p.66, №347, pl.II,347			
	1)	3,91	20 mm	Wells Coll.		pl.XXXIV,16b	

Type IV

Obv. Head of Helios l.; border of dots.

Rev. Monogram BAE (64) in centre.

Giel, 'A new acquisition in my collection', 1891, pl.VI,59; Frolova, *NE*, XV, pl.V,1.

A-a	1)					pl.XXXIV,17	The coin was not seen by Zograph

Series 2 - the monogram as a secondary element

Type V

Obv. Head of Helios, r.; border of dots.

Rev. Crescent moon; above, 8-rayed star; above l., monogram BAE (64).

Köhne, II, p.45, №1; Burachkov, pl.XXIV,17; Podshiwalov, Coins..., pl.II,18; Giel, *Kleine Beiträge*, pl.V,9; Bertier de la Garde, *ZOOID*, XXIX, 11; Zograph pl.XLIV, 20; Anohin 270; Frolova, *NE*, XV, pl.V,2.

Dies		Wt.	Dia.	Mus.	Mus. No.	Plate
A-a	1)	28,40	32 mm	GE	27772	pl.XXXIV,18

Type VI

Obv. Helmeted bust of Athena r.; border of dots.

Rev. Serpent with raised head, l.; below, monogram BAE (64); border of dots.

Podshiwalov, Coins..., p.19, №7, pl.II,21; Burachkov, p.226, №32; Anohin 271; Frolova, *NE*, XV, pl.V,3-5.

A-a	1)	13,40	26 mm	GE	27775	pl.XXXIV,19	Specimen of Podshiwalov, 'Coins...', p.29, №7
B-b	1)	12,96	26 mm	GE	27776	pl.XXXIV,20	
A-c	1)	12,05	25 mm	GIM	6725	pl.XXXIV,21	

[127] Golenko K.V., 'Coins from the Excavation of Nymphaeum 1939-1970', *NE*, XI, 1974.

Type VII

Obv. Head of Demeter r. wearing kalathos, within wreath; border of dots.

Rev. Protome of bull r.; to l., monogram BÂE (64); border of dots.

Podshiwalov, Coins..., p.19, №18, pl.II,26,27; Podshiwalov, *Beschreibung der unedirten und wenig bekannten Münzen*, p.10, №31, pl.I,18; Köhne, II, p.46, №2; Burachkov, p.227, №40, pl.XXIV,6; Anohin 272; Frolova, *NE*, XV, pl.V,6-14.

Dies		Wt.	Dia.	Mus.	Mus. No.	Plate	
A-a	1)	11,64	23 mm	GE	27777	pl.XXXV,1	
	2)	11,57	22 mm	GIM	6726	pl.XXXV,2	Anohin 272
A-b	1)	8,81	22 mm	GIM	6728	pl.XXXV,3	
A-c	1)	9,28	22 mm	GIM	6727	pl.XXXV,4	
A-d	1)	7,75	20 mm	GIM	6729	pl.XXXV,5	
B-e	1)	8,66	23 mm	GE	27778	pl.XXXV,6	
B-f	1)	7,34	20 mm	GE	27779	pl.XXXV,7	
C-h	1)	9,15	22 mm	GE	27780	pl.XXXV,8	

Dies not determined: 1 exp. from Gorgippia excavation - Frolova, 'Coins from the excavation of Gorgippia 1973-1977', *Symposium, Gorgippia*. Krasnodar, 1980, p.125, №7.

Type VIII

Obv. Helmeted bust of Athena r.; part of shield seen on left shoulder; border of dots.

Rev. Protome of horse r.; to l., monogram BÂE (64); border of dots.

Köhne, vol.II, p.52, №11 pl.VIII,2-3; Podshiwalov, Coins..., p.18, №6, pl.II,28; Burachkov, pl.XXIV,12; Anohin 273; Frolova, *NE*, XV, pl.V,15-23, pl.VI,1-7.

A-a	1)	8,08	21 mm	GE	24/27781	pl.XXXV,9	
B-b	10	8,22	20 mm	GE	25/27782	pl.XXXV,10	
C-c	1)	10,29	20 mm	GE	26/27783	pl.XXXV,11	
D-d	1)	8,32	21 mm	GE	27/27784	pl.XXXV,12	
E-e	1)	5,68	18 mm	GE	28/27785	pl.XXXV,13	
H-h	1)	6,54	20 mm	GIM	6730	pl.XXXV,14	
I-i	1)	7,48	20 mm	GIM	6731	pl.XXXV,15	
G-g	1)	6,74	20 mm	GIM	6732	pl.XXXV,16	
	2)	8,52	20 mm	GIM	6737	pl.XXXV,19	Anohin 273
C-a	1)	8,40	20 mm	GIM	6733	pl.XXXV,17	
	2)	8,84	21 mm	GIM	6734	pl.XXXV,18	
	3)			OGAM	25170	pl.XXXV,20	
	4)	8,80	21 mm	OGAM	25296	pl.XXXV,21	
	5)	7,20	20,5 mm	OGAM	25325	pl.XXXV,22	
	6)	6,40	20, 8 mm	OGAM	25329	pl.XXXV,23	
	7)	11,35	20 mm	GIM	129/12692		Kozievsky Coll.; Published by Frolova, *NE*, XV, 1989, pl.VI,7
F-f	1)	7,59		A		pl.LXII,9	

Dies of the following coins have not been determined:

1)	6,18	18 mm	Frolova, 'Coins from excavation of Phanagoria 1962-1975', p.108, №201		
2)	4,59		A		
3)	8,71		FM, Leak Coll.	1605	pl.LXII,10

Type IX

Obv. Head of Zeus Ammon r. within border of lines & dots.

Rev. Serpent wearing crown of Isis rising up, r.; to l., monogram BAE (64); border of dots.

Köhne, vol.II, p.49, №6; Podshiwalov, Coins..., p.3, №3; Burachkov, pl.XXIV,22; Oreshnikov, Catalogue..., p.57, №423; Brabitch, 'Motifs of Egypt in the Coinage of the Kingdom of Bosporus', *NE*, II, 1960, pl.I,1; Golenko, 'The Kerch Hoard of Bosporan Coins of the 1st Century BC, *NE*, IX, pl.I,2-4; Anohin 274; Frolova, *NE*, XV, pl.VI,7a-17.

Dies		Wt.	Dia.	Mus.	Mus. No.	Plate	Notes
A-a	1)	6,59	20 mm	GE	29/27786	pl.XXXV,24	Anohin 274
	2)	5,10	20 mm	GIM	6735	pl.XXXV,25	
	3)	5,00	19 mm	GE	31/27788	pl.XXXV,26	
	4)	6,15			*NE*, IX, p.49, №1, pl.I,1. Kerch		
	5)	5,44			*NE*, IX, p.49, №2. Kerch		
	6)	4,86			BMC, 1889, p.44, №9, pl.IX,4		
A-b	1)	6,11	20 mm	GIM	6736	pl.XXXVI,1	
	2)	5,50	19 mm	GIM	6738	pl.XXXVI,2	
A-c	1)	5,28	19 mm	GE	30/27787	pl.XXXVI,3	
	2)	5,78	20 mm	GE	32/27789	pl.XXXVI,4	
	3)	5,50	19 mm	GIM	6737	pl.XXXVI,5	
	4)	5,71			*NE*, IX, p.49, №3, pl.I,3 (Kerch)		
B-d	1)	6,36			*NE*, IX, p.49, №4, pl.I,4 (Kerch)		
	2)	5,80	19,1 mm	OGAM	27268	pl.XXXVI,6	
	3)			OGAM	27446	pl.XXXVI,7	
	4)	5,43	18 mm	GIM	125/12688		Kozievsky Coll.; *NE*, XV, p.14, pl.VI,17
	5)	4,98	18 mm	GIM	12689		Kozievsky Coll.
C-e	1)	4,78		F, general collection		pl.LXII,11	

Type X

Obv. Head of Artemis, r.; border of dots.

Rev. Dog seated, r., head turned to rear; to l., monogram BAE (64); border of dots.

Köhne, vol.II, p.47, №3; Burachkov, p.127, №37, pl.XXIV,18; Golenko, *NE*, IX, pl.I,5, №12; Golenko, Shelov, *NS*, I, p44, pl.II,352; Anohin 275; Frolova, NE, XV, pl.VI,18-24.

Dies		Wt.	Dia.	Mus.	Mus No.	Plate	Notes
A-a	1)	2,95	16 mm	GIM	6740	pl.XXXVI,8	Anohin 275
	2)	3,65	16 mm	GE	38/27790	pl.XXXVI,9	
	3)	3,17	16 mm	GE	35/27792	pl.XXXVI,10	
	4)	3,46	15 mm	GE	36/27793	pl.XXXVI,11	
	5)	3,55			*NS*, I, p.44, №352, pl.II,352		
	6)	3,39			*NS*, I, p.44, №353		
	7)	3,69		GIM	132		Kozievsky Coll.
	8)	3,63	15 mm	A		pl.XXXVI,14a	
A-b	1)	3,49	16 mm	GIM	6739	pl.XXXVI,12	
	2)	3,84	16 mm	GE	34/27791	pl.XXXVI,13	
	3)	4,99			*NE*, IX, p.49, №92, pl.I,5		
	4)	4,10			*NE*, IX, p.49		
	5)	3,76			*NE*, IX, p.49		
	6)	3,56			*NE*, IX, p.49		
	7)	2,85			*NE*, III[128], p.119, №1147		
	8)	3,95	15 mm	OGAM	27990		
	9)	3,55	14,7 mm	OGAM	28229		
	10)	2,75	14,8 mm	OGAM	25167		
	11)	2,55	14,7 mm	OGAM	25300		
A-c	1)	3,80	16 mm	GE	37/27794	pl.XXXVI,14	
	2)	4,67			*NE*, IX, p.49, №5		
	3)	4,52			*NE*, IX, p.49, №6		
	4)	4,11			*NE*, IX, p.49, №7		
	5)	4,11			*NE*, IX, p.49, №8		

---

[128] Shelov D.B., 'Coins from the Excavation of Phanagoria', *NE*, III, 1962 .

A-d	1)	3,69	14 mm	GIM	12695		Kozievsky Coll.

Series 3 - coins with monogram BAE (64) and sign of value

Type XI: I = 10

Obv. Head of Heracles r.

Rev. Lion's skin on club; to r., bow in case; to l., monogram BAE; below l., I (10); border of lines & wreath.

Bertier de la Garde, *ZOOID*, XXIX, Odessa, 1910, pl.I,12

Dies		Wt.	Dia.	Mus.	Mus. No	Plate	Notes
A-a	1)	27,07	32 mm	GE	33/27795	pl.XXXVI,15	

Bertier de la Garde remarked that the sign of value is absent on the reverse of several coins of this type. He supposed that two types of coins were minted - one with a sign of value and one without (*ZOOID*, 29, p.120, note 1).

Coins with monogram BAE (64) but without a sign of value

Zograph, pl.XLV,2; Anohin 276; Frolova, *NE*, XV, pl.VI,25-26, pl.VII,1.

A-b	1)	33,90	33 mm	Bertier de la Garde, *ZOOID*, XXIX, p.222, №12, pl.I,12			
	2)	28,63	34 mm	GE	39/27796	pl.XXXVI,16	Anohin 276
	3)	30,53	34 mm	GIM	8659	pl.XXXVI,17	Published by Frolova, 'Coins from the excavation of Gorgippia 1973-1977', p.125, №10

Type XII: Z = 7

Obv. Head of Hermes wearing petasos r.

Rev. Caduceus within wreath of laurel; to r. monogram BAE (64); to l. Z (7); border of dots.

Köhne, II, p.57, №18, Podshivalov, Coins..., p.23, №19; Burachkov, pl.XXIV,24; Anohin 277; Frolova, *NE*, XV, pl.VII,2-3.

A-a	1)	21,35	29 mm	GE	16//27773	pl.XXXVI,18	Anohin 277
	2)	21,65	30 mm	GE	17/27774		
A-b	1)	23,49	28 mm	GIM	6741	pl.XXXVI,19	Obv. only

Type XIII: ς = 6

Obv. Laureate head of Zeus r. within wreath; border of dots.

Rev. Eagle on thunderbolt r.; to r., monogram BAE (64); to l. ς (6). Border of dots.

Köhne, II, p.56, №17; Podshiwalov, Coins, p.22, №17; Burachkov, pl.XXIV,21; Zograph, pl.XLV,3; Anohin 278; Frolova, *NE*, XV, pl.VII,6-9.

Dies		Wt.	Dia.	Mus.	Mus. No.	Plate	Notes
A-a	1)	16,72	29 mm	GE	40/27797	pl.XXXVI,20	
	2)	15,17	28 mm	GIM	6742	pl.XXXVI,21	
A-b	1)	13,75	30 mm	GE	41/27798	pl.XXXVI,22	Anohin 278
	2)	7,00	24,5 mm	OGAM	23359	pl.XXXVI,23	
	3)	12,90	28 mm	GIM	6743	pl.XXXVII,1	
	4)	13,53	29 mm	GIM	140/12703		Kozievsky Coll.; *NE*, XV, p.15, pl.VII,9

Type XIV: E = 5

Obv. Diademed head of Poseidon r.; trident decorated with band over l. shoulder; border of dots.
Rev. Dolphin r.; above, monogram BAE (64), below, E (5); border of dots.
Köhne, vol.II, p.56, №16; Podshiwalov, Beschreibung..., S.10, №32, pl.III,53; Podshiwalov, Coins..., p.22, №16; Burachkov, pl.XXIV,19; Zograph pl.XLV, 4; Anohin 279; Frolova, *NE*, XV, pl.VII,10-17, pl.VIII,1-2.

Dies		Wt.	Dia	Mus.	Mus. No.	Plate	Notes
A-a	1)	13,75	26 mm	GE	42/27799	pl.XXXVII,2	Published by Giel, 'Description...', p.11, №58, pl.XIX,59; Zograph, pl.XLV,4, Anohin 279
B-b	1)	15,05	27 mm	GE	43/27800	pl.XXXVII,3	
C-c	1)	10,48	28 mm	GE	44/27801	pl.XXXVII,4	
	2)	9,28	22,5 mm	GIM	6744	pl.XXXVII,5	
	3)	10,05	22 mm	GIM	6745	pl.XXXVII,6	Burachkov Coll., pl.XXIV,19
	4)	10,40	20 mm	*NE*, IX, p.49, №13, pl.I,13 (Kerch)			

On the rev. of the following coins a sign of value was not seen

Dies		Wt.	Dia.	Mus.	Mus. No.	Plate	Notes
D-c	1)	6,40	21 mm	GE	45/27802	pl.XXXVII,7	Poor condition
	2)	7,49	21 mm	GIM	12698		Kozievsky Coll.
	3)	6,68	20 mm	GE	46/27803	pl.XXXVII,8	Poor condition; On Obv. countermarks: BAE (64) & capricorn; publ. by Golenko, *NE*, IX, pl.II
D-d	1)	6,00	20 mm	GE	47/27804	pl.XXXVII,9	Golenko, *NE*, IX, pl.II,2
E-e	1)	9,55	21 mm	GIM	8660	pl.XXXVII,10	
E-f	1)	12,21	26 mm	GIM	136/12699		Kozievsky Coll.; on Rev. - trident; *NE*, XV, pl.VIII,2

Dies of the following coins not determined:

1)	6,45			*NSph*, I, p.57, №651
2)	8,25	21,1 mm	OGAM	25294
3)	7,40	21,2 mm	OGAM	25291
4)	6,45	20,2 mm	OGAM	25299
5)	5,90	19,2 mm	OGAM	25297

Type XV: Δ = 4

Obv. Laureate head of Apollo r., within wreath; border of dots.
Rev. Tripod; to l. monogram BAE (64); to r., laurel branch; below, Δ (4); border of dots.
Köhne, vol.II, p.55, №15, pl.VIII,5; Burachkov, p.227, №39, pl.XXIV,15; Podshiwalov, Coins..., p.22, №16; BMC, 1889, p.45, №12; Zograph, pl.XLV,5; Anohin 280; Frolova, *NE*, XV, pl.VIII,3-14.

dies		Wt.	Dia.	Mus.	Mus. No.	Plate	Notes
A-a	1)	9,05	23 mm	GE	48/27805	pl.XXXVII,20	Anohin 280
	2)	7,85	22 mm	GE	49/27806	pl.XXXVII,11	
A-b	1)	9,47	23 mm	GE	50/27807	pl.XXXVII,12	
	2)	7,38	21 mm	GE	51/27808	pl.XXXVII,13	
	3)	6,83			*NE*, IX, pl.I,13		
A-c	1)	5,98	21 mm	GE	52/27809	pl.XXXVII,14	
A-d	1)	7,70	20 mm	GIM	6746	pl.XXXVII,15	
A-e	1)	7,73	21,5 mm	GIM	6747	pl.XXXVII,16	

A-f	1)	7,62	21 mm	GIM	6748	pl.XXXVII,17	
	2)	8,23	21 mm	GIM	6749	pl.XXXVII,18	
	3)	6,50	20,5 mm	GIM	6750	pl.XXXVII,19	
A-g	1)	8,50	20 mm	GIM	134/12697		Kozievsky Coll.; *NE*, XV, pl.VIII,13
A-h	1)	8,22		GIM	133/12696		Kozievsky Coll.; *NE*, XV, pl.VIII,14
	2)	8,98	20 mm	A		pl.LXII,12	
	3)	8,22	20 mm	F, Leak Coll.	1606	pl.LXII,13	

Dies of the following coins not determined:

1)	8,01			*NE*, III, p.87., №400
2)	5,82			*NS*, I, p.60, №725
3)	8,25	21,1 mm	OGAM	25294
4)	7,40	21,2 mm	OGAM	25291
5)	6,45	20,2 mm	OGAM	25299
6)	5,90	19,2 mm	OGAM	25297
7)	4,79			1982 Gorgippia excavation; Anapa
8)	4,01			1982 Gorgippia excavation; Anapa
9)	5,56			1984 Gorgippia excavation; Anapa

Type XVI: Γ = 3

Obv. Lion reclining r.; above, 8-rayed star; all within wreath; border of dots.

Rev. Palm branch and wreath; to r., monogram BÂE (64); below, Γ (3); border of dots.

Köhne, II, p.54, №14; Burachkov, p.226, №28, pl.XXIV,13; Podshiwalov, Coins..., p.21, №15; Zograph pl.XLV,6; Anohin 281; Frolova, *NE*, XV, pl.VIII,15-21.

Dies		Wt.	Dia.	Mus.	Mus. No.	Plate	Notes
A-a	1)	7,93	21 mm	GE	53/27810	pl.XXXVIII,1	Anohin 281
	2)	5,24	18,5 mm	GIM	6751	pl.XXXVIII,2	
	3)	6,82	20 mm	GIM	6752	pl.XXXVIII,3	
	4)	6,19	18 mm	GIM	6754	pl.XXXVIII,4	Poor condition
A-b	1)	6,43	20 mm	GE	54/27811	pl.XXXVIII,5	
B-c	1)	5,11			*NE*, IX, pl.I,18		
	2)	5,89			*NE*, IX, p.49, №19		
	3)	8,23	20 mm	GE	55/27812	pl.XXXVIII,6	
	4)	6,88	20 mm	GIM	139/12702		Kozievsky Coll.
B-d	1)	5,34	20 mm	GIM	6753	pl.XXXVIII,7	
C-c	1)	6,51			*NE*, IX, pl.I,15		
	2)	6,29			*NE*, IX, p49, №16		
	3)	4,73		A			On rev. sign of value l.
D-f	1)	4,33			*NE*, IX, pl.I,17		
A-c	1)	5,13			*NE*, IX, pl.I,20		
	2)	7,21			*NE*, IX, pl.I,21		

Dies of the following coin not determined:

1)	4,21	Frolova, 'Coins from excavation of Phanagoria', *VDI*, 1981, 1, p.111, №385

Type XVII: B = 2

Obv. Head of Dionysus r.; border of dots.

Rev. Cista with two thyrses ornamented with bands; to l., monogram BÂE (64); below cista, B (2); border of dots.

Burachkov, pl.XXIV,25; Podshiwalov, Coins..., p.21, №14, pl.II,29; Giel, *Kleine Beiträge*, pl.II,18; Zograph, pl.XLV,7; Anohin 282; Frolova, *NE*, XV, pl.VIII,22-27.

Dies		Wt.	Dia.	Mus.	Mus. No.	Plate	Notes
A-a	1)	5,35	19 mm	GE	56/27813	pl.XXXVIII,8	

	2)	4,44			*NE*, IX, pl.I,23		
	3)	4,13			*NE*, IX, p.50, №24		
	4)	3,97			*NE*, IX, №25		
	5)	6,10			*NE*, IX, №26		
	6)	4,68		GIM	12960		Kozievsky Coll.
A-b	1)	4,35	18 mm	GE	57/27814	pl.XXXVIII,9	Publ. by Podshiwalov, Coins..., pl.II,29
	2)	3,69			*NE*, IX, pl.I,22		
	3)	2,46	17 mm	GIM	6755	pl.XXXVIII,10	Poor condition
B-b	1)	4,53	16 mm	GE	58/27815	pl.XXXVIII,11	
	2)	4,26	17 mm	GIM	6756	pl.XXXVIII,12	
	3)			Countermark BAE (64) on obv.; publ. by Giel, 'A new asquisition...', p.353, №60, pl.III,60 (pl.XXXVIII,13)			
	1)	1,15			*NE*, III, p.119, №1134		

Type XVIII: A = 1

Obv. Head of Serapis r.; border of dots.

Rev. Cornucopia, lower end in the form of arrow, decorated with band; to l., monogram BAE (64); to r., A (1); border of dots.

Köhne, II p.53, №13, pl.VIII,6; Burachkov, p.227, №33, pl.XXIV,11; Zograph, pl.XLV, 8; Anohin 283; Frolova, *NE*, XV, pl.IX,1-6a.

Dies		Wt.	Dia.	Mus.	Mus. No.	Plate	Notes
A-a	1)	3,00	15 mm	GE	60/27817	pl.XXXVIII,14	
	2)	3,76	15 mm	GE	61/27818	pl.XXXVIII,15	
	3)	4,05	15 mm	GE	62/27819	pl.XXXVIII,16	
	4)	3,21	14 mm	GIM	6756a	pl.XXXVIII,17	
	5)	3,56	14 mm	GIM	6757	pl.XXXVIII,18	
	6)	4,40			*NE*, IX, pl.I,30		
	7)	4,04			*NE*, IX, №31		
	8)	3,74			*NE*, IX, №32		
	9)	4,03			*NE*, IX, №33		
B-a	1)	4,32			*NE*, IX, №27		
	2)	3,29			*NE*, IX, №28		
	3)	4,49			NE, IX, №29		
	4)	3,67	15 mm	GE	63/27820	pl.XXXVIII,19	
	5)	3,86	15 mm	GIM	12694		Kozievsky Coll.
	6)	4,34	15 mm	Private collection		pl.XXXVIII,19a	Obv. only

Series 4 - coins with monogram and sign of value, of lower weight

Type XIX: Z = 7

Obv. Head of Perseus l. with harpa; border of dots.

Rev. Herm r.; to l. monogram BAE (64); to r., palm branch decorated with band, Z (7). Border of dots.

Köhne, II, p.58, №19, pl.VIII,4; Burachkov, p.225, №25, pl.XXIV,23; Podshiwalov, Coins..., p.24, №21; BMC, 1889, p.45, №13-14, pl.IX,7; Zograph, pl.XLV, 10; Anohin 286; Frolova, *NE*, XV, pl.X,7-25; Stancomb 965.

Dies		Wt.	Dia.	Mus.	Mus. No.	Plate	Notes
A-a	1)	5,22	19 mm	GE	59/27816	pl.XXXVIII,20	
	2)	8,31	22 mm	GIM	6759	pl.XXXVIII,21	
	3)	5,36	20 mm	GIM	6761	pl.XXXVIII,22	Poor condition
B-b	1)	6,50	22 mm	GIM	6762	pl.XXXVIII,23	
	2)	6,80	22 mm	OGAM	23777	pl.XXXVIII,24	
	3)	5,33	22 mm	GE	67/27824	pl.XXXVIII,25	
	4)	5,32	22 mm	GIM	6766	pl.XXXVIII,26	
C-c	1)	6,65	21 mm	GE	64/27821	pl.XXXVIII,27	Anohin 286
	2)	8,58	21 mm	GE	65/27822	pl.XXXVIII,28	
	3)	4,39	21 mm	GIM	6760	pl.XXXIX,1	
A-d	1)	8,00	21 mm	GE	66/27828	pl.XXXIX,2	
	2)	8,61	21,5 mm	GIM	6765	pl.XXXIX,3	
	3)	5,32	22 mm	GIM	6766	pl.XXXIX,4	

D-d	1)	6,30	22 mm	GE	68/27825	pl.XXXIX,5	
	2)	7,29	21 mm	GIM	6768	pl.XXXIX,6	
	3)	8,89	22 mm	GIM	6667	pl.XXXIX,7	
	4)	6,87	21 mm	F		pl.LXII,14	
D-f	1)	6,38	21 mm	GIM	6764	pl.XXXIX,8	
B-e	1)	6,52	21 mm	A		pl.XXXIX,9	
D-g	1)	5,84	21 mm	GIM	137/12700		Kozievsky Coll.; *NE*, XV, pl.IX,25

Dies of the following coins not determined:

1)	3,91			*NSph*, III[129], p.181, №10
2)	9,50	22,7 mm	OGAM	25331
3)	7,85	21,2 mm	OGAM	27991
4)	7,10	21 mm	OGAM	25351
5)	6,85	22 mm	OGAM	25101
6)	6,60	21 mm	OGAM	25171
7)	5,65	21,2 mm	OGAM	23436
8)	4,95	21 mm	OGAM	28272
9)	9,85	21 mm	OGAM	28243
10)	7,25			NS, I, p.29, №37, pl.II,37
11)	6,70			*NSph*, I, p.57, №640
12)	3,13			*NE*, III, p.102, №758
13)	5,82			*NE*, III, p.102, №788
14)	5,85			*NE*, III, p.102, №1080

Series 5 - coins without monograms

Type XX: Z = 7

Obv. Head of Hermes in petasus r.; border of dots.
Rev. Caduceus; to l. Z (7); border of dots.
Podshiwalov, *Beschreibung...*, p.10, №30, pl.III,52; Burachkov, pl.XXIV,26; Zograph, pl.XLV,11; Anohin 290; Frolova, *NE*, XV, pl.X,1-4a.

Dies		Wt.	Dia.	Mus.	Mus. No.	Plate	Notes
A-a	1)	5,80	22 mm	GE	70/27827	pl.XXXIX,10	
	2)	4,59	20 mm	GE	71/27828	pl.XXXIX,11	Publ. by Burachkov, pl.XXIV,26
	3)	4,57	22 mm			pl.XXXIX,13	Publ. by Bertier de la Garde, *ZOOID*, XXIX, pl.II,21
	4)	3,72	22 mm	GIM	128/12691		Kozievsky Coll.; *NE*, XV, p.17, pl.X,4a
A-b	1)	5,95	20 mm	GIM	6768	pl.XXXIX,12	Anohin 290

Type XXI: B = 2

Obv. Head of Hermes, r.; border of dots.
Rev. Caduceus; to l., B (2); border of dots.
Bertier de la Garde, *ZOOID*, XXIX, pl.II,29; Anohin 291; Frolova, *NE*, XV, pl.X,5-6.

A-a	1)	2,75	15 mm	Private collection	pl.XXXIX,14	
	2)	2,67	15 mm		pl.XXXIX,15	Publ. by Bertier de la Garde, *ZOOID*, XXIX, pl.V,22

[129] Frolova N.A. Shelov D.B., Coins from the Excavation at Kepoi 1958-1963, *Numismatica i Sphragistica*, 3, 1965.

Type XXII: A = 1

Obv. Bust of Serapis; border of dots.

Rev. Cornucopia; to l., A (1); border of dots.

Bertier de la Garde, ZOOID, XXIX, p.223, №20, pl.II,20; Oreshnikov, *Zur Münzkunde des Cimmerischen Bosporus*, p.21, №XVI, pl.I,13; Burachkov, XXIV,11; Anohin 292; Frolova, *NE*, XV, pl.X,7-8.

Dies		Wt.	Dia.	Mus.	Mus. No.	Plate	
A-a	1)	1,52	14 mm	Private collection		pl.XXXIX,16	
	2)	2,21	13 mm	GIM	6769	pl.XXXIX,17	Anohin 292
	3)	1,73		1986 Gorgippia excavation; Anapa Museum			

Coins with monogram BAM (65): (12 B.C. - AD 14)

Type I: I = 10

Obv. Bust of Helios, r.; border of dots.

Rev. Halfmoon with 6-pointed star above; below, monogram BAM (65); to r., I (10); border of dots.

Giel, *Kleine Beiträge*, pl.V,10-11; Burachkov, pl.XXVI,92; Podshiwalov, *Beschreibung*..., p.13, №39, pl.I,22; Bertier de la Garde, *ZOOID*, XXIX, p.222, №17, pl.I,17; Zograph, pl.XLVI,4; Anohin 294; Frolova, *NE*, XV, pl.X,9-10a.

Dies		Wt.	Dia.	Mus.	Mus. No.	Plate	Notes
A-a	1)					pl.XXXIX,18	Giel, *Beiträge*,pl.V,10
	2)					pl.XXXIX,19	Giel, *Beiträge*, pl.V,11
	3)	7,20	23,5 mm	GIM	6782	pl.XXXIX,20	Anohin 294
	4)	7,41	24 mm	GE	3/27871	pl.XXXIX,21	
	5)					pl.XXXIX,22	Bertier de la Garde, *ZOOID*, XXIX, pl.I,17
B-b	1)	7,91	24 mm	GIM	144/12707		Kozievsky Coll.; *NE*, XV, p.18, pl.X, 10a

Type II: ς = 6

Obv. Helmeted head of Ares, r.; monogram, BAM (65); border of dots.

Rev. Trophy of weapons; to l., helmet; to r., ς (6); border of dots.

Bertier de la Garde, *ZOOID*, XXIX, p.222, №19, pl.I,19; Zograph, pl.XLVI,3; Anohin 295.

Dies		Wt.	Dia.	Mus.	Mus. No.	Plate	Notes
A-a	1)	5,14	20 mm	GE	27872	pl.XXXIX,23	Anohin 295
	2)	3,88	18 mm	GE	27878	pl.XXXIX,24	
	3)	4,82	18 mm	GIM	6788b	pl.XXXIX,25	
	4)	3,36	18 mm	USA, private collection (H.B. Wells)		pl.XXXIX,26	
	5)						Bertier de la Garde, *ZOOID*, XXIX, p.222, №19; *NE*, XV, p.18, pl.X,13

Type III: Δ = 4

Obv. Head of Heracles, r.; border of dots.

Rev. Tree with serpent entwined around; to r., monogram BAM (65); to l. Δ (4); border of dots.

Oreshnikov, Catalogue..., p.76; Bertier de la Garde, *ZOOID*, XXIX, pl.I,18; Anohin 296; Frolova, *NE* XV, pl.X,14-15a.

Dies		Wt.	Dia.	Mus.	Mus. No.	Plate	Notes
A-a	1)	3,23	18-20 mm	GIM	6784a	pl.XXXIX,27	Publ. by Oreshnikov, Catalogue..., p.76; Bertier de la Garde, *ZOOID*, XXIX, pl.I,18; Frolova, *NE* XV, pl.X,14-15a

2)	3,95	19 mm	GIM	6785a	pl.XXXIX,28	
3)	2,93	19 mm	GE	27874	pl.XXXIX,29	
4)	4,44	20 mm	GE	27875	pl.XXXIX,30	
5)	3,28	20 mm	GIM	143/12706		Kozievsky Coll.; *NE*, XV, pl.X,15a

§ 10 Gold staters with monogram (66) or (2)[130]

289 - 304 B.e. = 9/8 B.C. - AD 7/8

Obv. Roman bust l.
Rev. Roman bust r., monogram; below, date.

Recently a gold coin has appeared with the monogram (66) dated ϛΠΣ - 286 B.e. = 11 B.C.

1)	8,00	Private collection	May be false

ΘΠΣ - 289 B.e. - 9/8 B.C.

	Wt.	Mus.	Mus. No.	Plate	Notes
1)	7,92			pl.XL,1	*ZOOID*, XXIX, pl.II,35
2)	7,92	GE	646	pl.XL,2	Zograph, pl.XLIV,15, cf. Anohin 259

ϙΣ- 290 B.e. - 8/7 B.C.

1)	7,58			pl.XL,3	*ZOOID*, XXIX, pl.II,36
2)	7,24	GE	647	pl.XL,4	cf. Anohin 260

Αϙ Σ - 291 B.e. - 7/6 B.C.

1)	7,85	P		pl.XL,5	*ZOOID*, XXIX, pl.II,37

Γϙ Σ - 293 B.e. - 5/4 B.C.

1)	7,95			pl.XL,6	*ZOOID*, XXIX, pl.II,38; Naville,V, pl.LXV, 2338
2)	7,88	GIM	394	pl.XL,7	Anohin 262

Δϙ Σ - 294 B.e. - 4/3 B.C.

1)	7,99			pl.XL,8	*ZOOID*, XXIX, pl.II,39
2)	7,98	GE	648	pl.XL,9	Burachkov, pl.XXVI,65; Anohin 263

Εϙ Σ - 295 B.e. - 3/2 B.C.

1)	7,94	GMII	9657a	pl.XL,10	*NE*, III, p.68, №11; Golenko, 'Staters from new acquisitions of GMII', Reports of GMII, III, 1965, p.39, fig. 3

[130] *RPC* I 1865 records a gold stater: O. Bare head (Augustus) l.; R. Male head r.; to l. monogram BAE; below, A, Auktiones 6 (1976) lot 176, 8.05g. For a list of dates see *RPC* I 1866-80. A selection of specimens with the monogram is also given by Anohin 259-269a. S.I.

ϛϘΣ - 296 B.e. - 2/1 B.C.

1)	8,00	GMII	208063	pl.XL,11	Ibid. fig. 3,2

ΘϘΣ - 299 B.e.- AD 2/3

1)	7,95	BM		pl.XL,12	Wroth, BMC, 1889, p.49, №1 pl.X,12; *ZOOID*, XXIX, pl.II,40; Anohin 266; *RPC* I, 1873

T - 300 B.e. - AD 3/4

1)	7,80			pl.XL,13	*ZOOID*, XXIX, pl.III,41; Naville, V, pl.LXV,2339

BT - 302 B.e. - AD 5/6

1)	7,94			pl.XL,14	*ZOOID*, XXIX, pl.III,42
2)	7,90	GIM	395	pl.XL,15	Burachkov, pl.XXVI,67; Anohin 268

ΔT - 304 B.e. - AD 7/8

1)	7,92	GMII	208064	pl.XL,16	Reports of GMII, vol.III, p.39, drawing 3,3
2)	7,95	P		pl.XL,17	
3)	7,93	GIM	396	pl.XL,18	Burachkov, pl.XXV,58; Gajdukevich, pl.IV,60
4)	8,01	Lanz Graz, Auction I, 1972, pl.V,288			
5)	7,96				Weights given by Bertier de la Garde, *NS*, II, 1913, p.106, №64
6)	7,30				
7)	7,27				

Anohin, *Bosporus*, p.93, p.150, №293, published a gold stater with monogram  and the letters IT = 310 B.e. - AD 13 (*ANS*, New York, 7,93 g.), but this coin is false since the ends of the monogram, which on other coins consist of dots, are here formed from triangles. It is on the basis of this stater that Anohin founds his theory of a third reign for Dynamis.

Staters with monogram KNE (67)

305 - 306 B.e. = 8/9 - AD 9/10

ET - 305 Be - AD 8/9

	Wt.	Mus.	Mus. No.	Plate	Notes
1)	7,96			pl.XL,19	*ZOOID*, XXIX, pl.III,44; Naville, V, №2340
2)	7,88	GIM	397	pl.XL,20	Oreshnikov, Catalogue, pl.III, 536; Zograph, pl.XLIV,16; Gajdukevich, pl.IV,61
3)	7,92	GIM	398	pl.XL,21	Anohin 284
4)	7,95				Bertier de la Garde, *NSph*, II, 1913, p.106, №65
5)	7,89				

ϚT - 306 B.e. - AD 9/10

1)	7,92			pl.XL,23	*ZOOID*, XXIX, pl.III,45
2)				pl.XL,22	Sotheby, Auction Catalogue, Collection of Russian Noble, pl.VII,258; cf. Anohin 285
3)	7,88				Bertier de la Garde, *NSph*, II, 1913, p.106, №66
4)	7,82				

Staters with monogram  or  (68)

307 - 310 B.e. = 10/11 - AD 13/14

ZT - 307 B.e. - AD 10/11

1)	7,19	München, State Mus.		pl.XL,24	
2)	7,92			pl.XLI,1	*ZOOID*, XXIX, pl.III,46
3)	7,80	BM		pl.XLI,2	BMC, 1889, pl.X,13; Anohin 288; *RPC* I, 1879

IT - 310 B.e. - AD 13

1)	8,02			pl.XLI,3	Giel, 'A new Acquisition...', pl.VI,64; *ZOOID*, XXIX, pl.III,47; Anohin 289

§11 Staters of Aspurgus with monogram BÂP (69)

311 - 334 B.e. = AD 14/15 - 37/38[131]

AIT - 311 Be = AD 14/15

	Wt.	Mus.	Mus. No.	Plate	Notes
1)	6,71			pl.XLI,4	Giel, 'A New Acquisition...', pl.VI,64; *ZOOID*, XXIX, pl.III,48; cf. Anohin 297

ΓIT - 313 B.e. = AD 16/17

1)	7,96	München, State Mus.	177	pl.XLI,5	*ZOOID*, XXIX, pl.III,49
2)	7,92	Cop	22	pl.XLI,6	Anohin 298

ΔIT - 314 B.e. = AD 17/18

1)	7,85	Moscow, Private collection		pl.LXII,5	Enlarged; cf. Anohin 299

EIT - 315 B.e. = AD 18/19

1)	7,98			pl.XLI,7	ZOOID, XXIX, pl.III,50; Anohin 300

ϚIT - 316 B.e. = AD 19/20

1)	7,96			pl.XLI,8	Burachkov, pl.XXVI,73; *ZOOID*, XXIX, pl.III,51; Minns, *Scythians and Greeks*, pl.VII,4; Schlessinger, 11, pl.VII,199; Anohin 301

ZIT - 317 B.e. = AD 20/21

1)	8,00	GE	651	pl.XLI,9	*ZOOID*, XXIX, pl.III,52
2)	7,99	GIM	399	pl.XLI,10	Anohin 302

[131] See further *RPC* I 1881-1901. The issue with the date BIT - 312 B.e. = AD 15/16 does not occur in the current catalogue. S.I.

HIT - 318 B.e. = AD 21/22

1)	7,95	GE	652	pl.XLI,11	Anohin 303
2)	8,00			pl.XLI,12	Burachkov, pl.XXVI,74; Schlessinger, 11, pl.VII,200

KT - 320 B.e. = AD 23/24

1)	7,90			pl.XLI,13	*ZOOID*, XXIX, pl.III,54
2)	7,91	GIM	400	pl.XLI,14	Gajdukevich, pl.IV,62; Anohin 304

AKT - 321 B.e. = AD 24/25

1)	7,98	BM		pl.XLI,15	W. Wroth, BMC, 1889, pl.XI,1; Anohin 305

ΓKT - 323 B.e. = AD 26/27

1)	7,92	Location unknown		pl.XLI,16	Sotheby, 1924, Property of Russian Nobles, pl.VII,261
2)	7,94			pl.XLI,17	*ZOOID*, XXIX, pl.III,56; Naville, V, №2341; cf. Anohin 306

ΔKT- 324 B.e. = AD 27/28

1)	7,36	GE	653	pl.XLI,18	*ZOOID*, XXIX, pl.III,57
2)	7,92	GIM	401	pl.XLI,19	Anohin 307
3)	7,97				Bertier de la Garde, *NS*, II,
4)	7,98				1913, p.61, №84

EKT - 325 B.e. = AD 28/29

1)	7,94	BM		pl.XLI,20	BMC, 1889, pl.XI,2; *ZOOID*, XXIX, pl.III,58; Anohin 308; *RPC* I, 1892
2)	7,95	GIM	402	pl.XLI,21	
3)	7,97				Bertier de la Garde, *NS*, II, 1913, p.107, №85

ϚKT - 326 B.e. = AD 29/30

1)	7,90			pl.XLI,22	*ZOOID*, XXIX, pl.III,59; Naville, V, №234; Naville XVI, №21329; cf. Anohin 309
2)	6,80	P			Bertier de la Garde, *NS*, II, 1913, p.107, №86

ZKT - 327 B.e. = AD 30/31

1)	7,89			pl.XLI,23	*ZOOID*, XXIX, pl.III,60
2)	7,90	GE	654		Zograph, pl.XLV,15; cf. Anohin 310
3)		Location unknown		pl.XLI,24	Sotheby, 1924, Property of Russian Nobles, pl.VII,260

HKT - 328 B.e. = AD 31/32

1)	7,91	P		pl.XLII,1	Anohin 311
2)	7,92				Bertier de la Garde, *NS*, II,
3)	7,90				1913, p.61, №88
4)	7,90				Helbing, München, 1928, №324

ΘΚΤ - 329 B.e. = AD 32/33

1)	7,89	GE	655	pl.XLII,2	*ZOOID*, XXIX, pl.III,62; Anohin 312
2)	7,915	GMII	5185	pl.XLII,3	*NS*, I, p.51, №517a, pl.II, 517a
3)	7,88	BM		pl.XLII,4	BMC, p.50, №3

ΛΤ - 330 B.e. = AD 33/34

1)	7,90			pl.XLII,5	*ZOOID*, XXIX, pl.III,63; Anohin 313

ΑΛΤ - 331 B.e. = AD 34/35

1)	7,96	GIM	403	pl.XLII,6	
2)	7,85	GE	656	pl.XLII,7	
2^{a})				pl.XLII,8	Sotheby, 1924, pl.VII,259
3)	7,76	BM		pl.XLII,9	BMC, 1889, pl.XI,3; *RPC* I, 1898; cf. Anohin 314
4)	7,96	Berlin Mus.		pl.XLII,10	
5)	7,94	Berlin Mus.		pl.XLII,11	
6)	7,98				Bertier de la Garde, *NS*, II, 1913, p.108
7)	7,91				

ΒΛΤ - 332 B.e. = AD 35/36

1)	7,92	GIM	404	pl.XLII,12	Burachkov, pl.XXVI,80; Anohin 315
2)	7,95			pl.XLII,13	*ZOOID*, XXIX, pl.IV,65
3)	8,00				Bertier de la Garde, *NS*, II, 1913, p.108, №92
4)	7,86				

ΓΛΤ - 333 B.e. = AD 36/37

1)	7,84	GIM	405	pl.XLII,14	Anohin 316
2)	7,83			pl.XLII,15	*ZOOID*, XXIX, pl.IV,66

ΔΛΤ - 334 B.e. = AD 37/38

1)	7,87	GE	657	pl.XLII,16	Anohin 317
2)	7,90			pl.XLII,17	*ZOOID*, XXIX, pl.IV,67, but it is possible that pl.XLII,16 and 17are one and the same example

Bronze coins of Aspurgus

Type I

Variation I

Obv. ΚΑΙΣΑΡΟΣ·ΤΙΒΕΡΙΟΥ. Head of Tiberius r; border of dots.
Rev. Head of Aspurgus r.; to l., monogram ΒΑΡ (69) to r., ΙΒ (12); border of dots.
Zograph, pl.XLV,16; Anohin 319; Stancomb 966-7.

Dies		Wt.	Dia.	Mus.	Mus. No.	Plate	Notes
A-a	1)	7,08	23 mm	GIM	6787	pl.XLIII,1	Anohin 319
	2)	4,97	23 mm	GIM	6789		
A-b	1)	5,60	23 mm	GE	27844	pl.XLIII,2	
A-c	1)	8,97	23 mm	GIM	6788c	pl.XLIII,3	
B-d	1)	5,58	21 mm	GIM	6970	pl.XLIII,4	
C-e	1)	6,25	20 mm	GE	27841	pl.XLIII,5	
D-f	1)	6,98	21 mm	GE	27842	pl.XLIII,6	
F-g	1)	8,54	21 mm	GE	27843	pl.XLIII,7	

H-a	1)	9,55	25 mm	GE	27845	pl.XLIII,8	
I-a	1)	8,12	24 mm	GE	27846	pl.XLIII,9	
	2)	3,74	21 mm	GIM	12731		Kozievsky Coll.
	3)	12,28	24 mm	GIM	12733		Kozievsky Coll

Variation II

Obv. **ΚΑΙΣΑΡΟΣ ΤΙΒΕΡΙΟΥ**. Laureate head of Tiberius, r.; border of dots.
Rev. Head of Aspurgus r.; to l., monogram **BAP** (69); to r., **IB** (12); border of dots.
RPC I, 1903.[132]

Dies		Wt.	Dia.	Mus.	Mus. No.	Plate	Notes
A-a	1)	10,96	24 mm	GE	10/27833	pl.XLIII,10	
	2)	7,18	23 mm	GIM	6794	pl.XLIII,11	
	3)	9,95				pl.XLII,18	BMC, 1889, pl.XI,5
	4)	7,49	21 mm	GIM	12732		Kozievsky Coll.
B-b	1)	7,99	23 mm	GIM	6791	pl.XLIII,12	
C-c	1)	6,23	24 mm	GIM	6792	pl.XLIII,13	
D-d	1)	7,25	23 mm	GIM	6793	pl.XLIII,14	
	2)	6,82	23 mm	GIM	6795		
E-c	1)	8,11	24 mm	GE	11/27834	pl.XLIII,15	
	2)	8,00	21 mm	GIM	6796		
	3)	8,04	22 mm	GIM	6797		
	4)	7,34	22 mm	GIM	6798	pl.XLIII,16	
H-h	1)	7,85	21 mm	GIM	6799		
	2)	7,58	22 mm	GIM	6800		
	3)	7,37	22 mm	GIM	6801	pl.XLIII,17	
G-g	1)	9,71	22,5 mm	GIM	6802	pl.XLIII,18	
	2)			OGAM	23766	pl.XLIII,19	
C-i	1)	8,24	20 mm	GIM	6804		
	2)	8,87	23 mm	GE	27835	pl.XLIII,20	
	3)	6,88	22 mm	GIM	6806		

Coins in poor condition:

1)	8,82	22 mm	GIM	6803	pl.XLIII,21
2)	5,79	21 mm	GIM	6805	pl.XLII,20
3)	6,08	21 mm	GIM	12730	

Variation III

Obv. As previous.
Rev. As previous, but monogram written as **BAΓ** (70) and sign of value r. **BI**; border of dots.

Dies		Wt.	Dia.	Mus.	Mus. No.	Plate	Notes
A-a	1)	6,27	20 mm	GIM	6807	pl.XLIV,1	
	2)	6,41	21 mm	GIM	6808	pl.XLIV,2	
	3)	7,55	21 mm	GIM	6617		
A-b	1)	6,90	21 mm	GIM	6809	pl.XLII,21	
	2)	7,58	21 mm	GIM	6810		
	3)	8,56	23 mm	GIM	6813	pl.XLIV,3	
	4)	6,32	21,5 mm	GIM	6618		
A-c	1)	7,94	23 mm	GIM	6811	pl.XLIV,4	
	2)	5,09	22 mm	GIM	12734		Kozievsky Coll.
A-d	1)	5,67	22 mm	GIM	6812		
	2)	7,72	23 mm	GIM	6817		
	3)	6,44	21 mm	GIM	6818		
A-e	1)	6,41	20 mm	GIM	6814	pl.XLIV,5	
A-f	1)	6,50	21 mm	GE	27837	pl.XLIV,6	Value mark IB
B-h	1)	8,47	24 mm	GE	27838	pl.XLIV,7	
B-g	1)	10,54	23 mm	GE	27839	pl.XLIV,8	

[132] *RPC* I 1903 records 14 other specimens. S.I.

Variation IV

Obv. As previous.
Rev. As previous, but head of Aspurgus l.; to r., monogram ΙΑΒ (70a); to l., **BI**; border of dots.

A-a	1)	8,66	21 mm	GIM	6815	pl.XLIV,9
A-b	1)	5,69	20 mm	GIM	6816	pl.XLIV,10
A-c	1)	6,68	21 mm	GE	27847	pl.XLIV,11
A-d	1)	8,12	21 mm	GE	27848	pl.XLIV,12
B-d	1)	7,92	22 mm	GE	27849	pl.XLIV,13[133]

Coins in poor condition:

1)	6,71	GIM	6819
2)	8,84	GIM	6820
3)	6,65	GIM	6821
4)	5,42	GIM	6822
5)	6,23	GIM	6823
6)	5,45	GIM	6824
7)	7,46	GIM	6825
8)	6,87	GIM	6839
9)	5,73	GIM	6840

Type II

Obv. **ΓΑΙΟΥ ΚΑΙΣΑΡΟС ΓΕΡΜΑΝΙΚΟΥ**. Head of Caligula r.; border of dots.
Rev. Head of Aspurgus r.; to l., monogram **ΒΑΡ** (69), to r. **IB** (12). Border of dots.
Zograph, pl.XLV,17; Anohin 320; *RPC* I, 1904.[134]

Dies		Wt.	Dia.	Mus.	Mus. No.	Plate	Notes
A-a	1)	8,11	21 mm	GIM	6826	pl.XLIV,14	
	2)	8,81	22 mm	GIM	6827		
	3)	7,09	20 mm	GIM	6855		
	4)	7,48	27 mm	GIM	6829	pl.XLIV,15	
B-b	1)	7,52	23 mm	GIM	6828	pl.XLIV,16	
	2)	9,95	26 mm	GIM	6867	pl.XLIV,17	Anohin 320[135]
	3)	7,27	27 mm	GE	46/27866	pl.XLIV,18	
	4)	5,56	23 mm	GIM	6861		
	5)	6,62	23 mm	GIM	6870		
C-c	1)	7,86	21 mm	GIM	6837	pl.XLIV,19	
	2)	7,70	21 mm	GIM	6831		
	3)	8,12	23 mm	GE	42/27862	pl.XLIV,20	
	4)	7,09	20 mm	GIM	6865		
D-d	1)	4,80	21 mm	GIM	6832		
	2)	7,15	20 mm	GIM	6836	pl.XLV,1	
	3)	6,70	21 mm	GIM	6835		
	4)	8,19	20,5 mm	GIM	6838		
A-j	1)	8,28	22,5 mm	GIM	6842	pl.XLV,2	
	2)	6,11	22 mm	F 62 Gen. Coll.			
D-h	1)	8,28	23 mm	GE	27861	pl.XLV,3	
E-e	1)	7,23	22 mm	GIM	6843	pl.XLV,4	
H-e	1)	5,06	22 mm	GIM	6844	pl.XLV,5	
	2)	6,93	21 mm	GIM	6845		
	3)	7,43	20 mm	GIM	6846		
G-g	1)	7,27	20 mm	GIM	6847		
E-g	1)	8,48	25 mm	GE	27863	pl.XLV,6	
F-i	1)	7,54	21 mm	GIM	6834	pl.XLV,7	
I-k	1)	9,79	22 mm	GIM	6830	pl.XLV,8	

[133] The monogram on this coin is clearly the more normal ΒΑΙ. S.I.
[134] *RPC* I 1904 records 14 other specimens. S.I.
[135] Anohin's reference would equate his coin 320 with GIM 6828. S.I.

K-l	1)			GIM	6834	pl.XLV,9	
L-m	1)	6,79	24 mm	GE	27864	pl.XLV,10	
M-n	1)	10,50	24 mm	GE	27865	pl.XLV,11	
N-o	1)	10,85	21 mm	GIM	6854	pl.XLV,12	
	2)	8,50	22 mm	GIM	6856		
P-p	1)	7,81	19,5 mm	GIM	6855	pl.XLV,13	
	2)	9,70	23 mm	GE	27952	pl.XLV,14	
	3)	5,96	23 mm	GIM	6856	pl.XLV,15	
O-r	1)	4,49	22 mm	GIM	6858		
	2)	10,65	24 mm	GE	27954	pl.XLV,16	
	3)	6,60	21 mm	GIM	6859		
	4)	10,99	22,5 mm	GIM	6868a		
	5)	8,39	21,5 mm	GIM	6864		
R-r	1)	8,03	24 mm	GE	33/27858	pl.XLV,17	
	2)	8,13	21 mm	GIM	6860	pl.XLV,18	
S-s	1)	7,60	21 mm	GIM	6862	pl.XLV,19	
T-t	1)	8,96	23 mm	GE	31/27851	pl.XLV,20	
	2)	8,01	22 mm	GIM	6857		
U-u	1)	6,35	22 mm	GE	27855	pl.XLV,21	
	2)	8,01	22 mm	GIM	6876		
X-z	1)	6,16	23 mm	GE	27857	pl.XLVI,1	
	2)	8,63	22 mm	GIM	6877		
X-w	1)	9,00		OGAM	22016	pl.XLVI,2	
AB-w	1)	8,03	24 mm	GE	27850	pl.XLVI,3	
	2)	7,62	22 mm	A			
Z-t	1)	8,60	22 mm	GE	27858	pl.XLVI,4	
Z-ph	1)	7,67	24 mm	GE	27859	pl.XLVI,5	
W-ph	1)	7,60	23 mm	GE	27860	pl.XLVI,6	
AC-ab	1)	8,07	25 mm	GE	27868	pl.XLVI,7	
	2)	7,55	23 mm	F Gen. Coll.			
	3)	9,07	25 mm	GIM	12735		Kozievsky Coll.

Coins in poor condition:

1)	5,51	20 mm	GIM	6868
2)	4,99	19 mm	GIM	6869
3)	7,79	20 mm	GIM	6871
4)	7,68	21 mm	GIM	6872
5)	9,97	24 mm	GIM	6873
6)	8,03	22 mm	GIM	6874

Type III

Obv. Helmeted head of Ares, r.; to l.,  (71).
Rev. Trophy of weapons; to l., monogram BAP (69); to r., ϛ (6); border of dots.
Anohin 318; *RPC* I, 1902.

A-a	1)	6,36	16 mm	GIM	6878	pl.XLVI,8	
	2)	5,46	16 mm	GIM	6879	pl.XLVI,9	
	3)	5,11	18 mm	GIM	6880	pl.XLVI,10	
	4)	4,46	15 mm	GIM	6881	pl.XLVI,11	
	5)	5,17	15 mm	GE	27830	pl.XLVI,12	
	6)	5,09	20 mm	GE	27831	pl.XLVI,13	Anohin 318; *RPC* I, 1902
	7)	6,03	18 mm	GE	27838	pl.XLVI,14	
	8)	5,86	18 mm		*NS*, I, p.52, №520, pl.II,520		
	9)	5,76	18 mm		Gorelij private collection		
	10)	5,06	18 mm	GIM	12728		

§12 Gold staters of Gepaipyris

ΔΛΤ - 334 B.e. = AD 37/38

Obv. Head of Emperor r.; line border.
Rev. Roman head r.; to l. monogram (72); below, ΔΛΤ; line border.
Anohin 324

	Wt.	Dia.	Mus.	Mus No.	Plate	Notes
1)	7,80		München		pl.XLVI,15	Bertier de la Garde, *ZOOID*, XXIX, pl.IV,68
2)	7,88		BM		pl.XLVI,16	BMC. 1889, p.50, №5, pl.XI,4; *RPC* I, 1905
3)	7,87	20 mm	GE	658	pl.XLVI,17	Anohin 324

ΕΛΤ - 335 B.e. = AD 38/39

Obv. As previous.
Rev. As previous; to l. (72); below, ΕΛΤ.
Anohin 325

1)	7,56	20 mm	OGAM	52304	pl.XLVI,18	Minns, pl.VII,6; Bertier de la Garde, *ZOOID*, XXIX, pl.IV,69; cf. *RPC* I, 1906
2)	7,88	20 mm	GE	659	pl.XLVI,19	Anohin 325

Bronze coins of Gepaipyris

AD 37 - 38

Type I

Obv. **ΒΑCΙΛΙCCΗC ΓΗΠΑΙΠΥΡΕΩC**. Diademed bust of Queen Gepaipyris r.; border of dots.
Rev. Head of Aphrodite Urania wearing kalathos and veil, r.; to r. or l. **IB** (12); border of dots.
Köhne, II, p.216, №8; Burachkov, XXVI,94; Zograph, pl.XLVI,7; Anohin 326; *RPC* I, 1907.[136]

Dies		Wt.	Dia.	Mus.	Mus. No.	Plate	Notes
A-a	1)	6,65	24 mm	GIM	6992	pl.XLVII,1	
	2)	8,05	24 mm	GIM	6993		
	3)	6,68	21 mm	GIM	6994		
	4)	7,74	23 mm	GE	27912	pl.XLVII,2	**IB** r.
	5)	7,31	23 mm	GIM	6995		
	6)	8,48	23 mm	A			
A-b	1)	10,71	24 mm	GIM	6996	pl.XLVII,3	**IB** r.
	2)	8,69	24 mm	A			
B-c	1)	6,84	23 mm	GIM	6997	pl.XLVII,4	
	2)	7,80	24 mm	GIM	6704		
C-d	1)	11,73	23 mm	GIM	6898	pl.XLVII,5	**IB** l.
	2)	8,37	24 mm	GIM	6999		
	3)	4,97	23 mm	GIM	6719		
	4)	10,15	25 mm	GE	27916	pl.XLVII,6	**IB** l.
	5)	7,57	25 mm	GIM	6723	pl.XLVII,7	**IB** l.
B-b	1)	7,96	25 mm	GE	27918	pl.XLVII,8	**IB** l.
D-a	1)	6,63	21 mm	GIM	6700	pl.XLVII,9	
	2)	6,32	21 mm	GIM	6701		
D-e	1)			OGAM	23629	pl.XLVII,10	**IB** l.
D-c	1)	8,27	24 mm	GE	27914	pl.XLVII,11	**IB** l.
	2)	8,25	22 mm	GIM	6716	pl.XLVII,13	Obv. only
E-f	1)	8,13	23 mm	GIM	6702	pl.XLVII,12	**IB** l.
	2)	5,71	24 mm	GIM	6715		

---

[136] *RPC* I 1907 records 14 specimens not recorded here. S.I.

E-h	1)	7,01	23 mm	GIM	6703	pl.XLVII,14	IB l.
H-g	1)	8,00	24 mm	GE	27915	pl.XLVII,15	IB l.
G-I	1)	10,84	21 mm	GIM	6706	pl.XLVII,16	IB l.; Anohin 326
	2)	7,73	22 mm	GIM	6710		Poor condition
	3)	7,82	23 mm	GE	27917	pl.XLVII,17	IB l.
	4)	7,70	23 mm	FM Minns,64, Gen Coll.			
	5)	8,01	23 mm	GIM	12726		Kozievsky Coll.
G-k	1)	9,95	23 mm	GIM	6707	pl.XLVII,18	IB l.
	2)	8,40	23 mm	GIM	6708	pl.XLVIII,1	
	3)	8,87	23 mm	GIM	6709	pl.XLVIII,2	Poor condition
	4)	6,86	22 mm	GIM	6711		
K-l	1)	7,80	24 mm	GIM	6704	pl.XLVIII,3	IB l.
	2)	10,55	23 mm	GIM	6705		

Type II, brockage[137]

Obv. ΒΑϹΙΛΙϹϹΗϹ ΓΗΠΑΙΠΥΡΕΩϹ. Bust of Gepaipyris r; border of dots.
Rev. The same image of Gepaipyris in intaglio.

Dies		Wt.	Dia.	Mus.	Mus. No.	Plate
A-a	1)	9,62	25 mm	GE	27919	pl.XLVIII,4

Coins in poor condition:

1)	6,91	23 mm	GIM	6717
2)	10,00	23,5 mm	GIM	6718
3)	4,97	22 mm	GIM	6719
4)	8,36	23 mm	GIM	6720
5)	5,00	21,5 mm	GIM	6721
6)	5,55	22,5 mm	GIM	6722a
7)	7,98	24 mm	GIM	6722b

Type III

Obv. ΒΑϹΙΛΙϹϹΗϹ ΓΗΠΑΙΠΥΡΕΩϹ. Bust of Gepaipyris r.; border of dots.
Rev. ΒΑϹΙΛΕΩϹ ΜΙΘΡΑΔΑΤΟΥ. Diademed head of Mithradates r.; border of dots.
RPC I. 1911; Stancomb 968.[138]

Dies		Wt.	Dia.	Mus.	Mus. No.	Plate
A-a	1)			GE	27902	
	2)	8,60	26 mm	GE	27903	pl.XLVIII,5
	3)	11,26	25 mm	GIM	6724	pl.XLVIII,6
B-b	1)	6,57	23 mm	GE	27905	pl.XLVIII,7
	2)	8,67	25 mm	GE	27904	pl.XLVIII,8

[137] One might question whether such mistakes in minting are to be classed as a separate type. S.I.
[138] There is a potential problem in assigning these coins. Frolova gives them to Gepaipyris, while assigning similar issues below to Mithradates (Bronze coins of Mithradates, Type I). The two issues differ in that the coins illustrated on pl. XLVIII, 5-8 have no mark of value, while those at pl.XLVIII, 9-18 do (IB), and the inscription on the Mithradatic side is differently positioned on the two issues. The coins illustrated by *RPC* I ostensibly belongs to the series listed here, while Stancomb's appears to combine the two in having a mark of value (IB) but the Mithradatic inscription positioned as here. However, whether this is enough to assign the coins to different issuers is open to argument. S.I.

§13 Coins of Mithradates (AD 39 - 45)

Gold staters 336 B.e. = AD 39/40

Obv. Laureate head of Caligula r.; border of dots.
Rev. **ΒΑCΙΛΕΩC ΜΙΤΗΡΙΔΑΤΟΥ**; Nike advancing l., holding palm branch in l. hand, wreath in r.; in field, **ς - ΛΤ** (336 B.e.); border of dots.
Anohin 327.

Dies		Wt.	Mus.	Plate	Notes
A-a	1)	7,85	Location unknown	pl.XLVI,21	Giel, *ZRAO*, VII, p.225, №62, pl.XX,62; Minns, pl.VII,10
	2)	6,45	BM, acquired 1931	pl.XLVI,20	This specimen may have been published by Bertier de la Garde, *ZOOID*, XXIX, p.229, №70, pl.IV,70; *RPC* I, 1908
	3)	7,86	GIM 406	pl.XLVI,22	Presented by Th.P. Prowe to the Moscow State History Museum 28 August 1917; Anohin 327

Staters 337 B.e. = AD 40/41

Obv. As previous.
Rev. As previous, **Ζ - ΛΤ**.
Anohin 328.

	Wt.	Mus.	Mus. No.	Notes
1)	7,85	Yalta	27818	Anohin 328
2)	7,87	Yalta	27819	Frolova, 'The gold coin 338 B.e. = AD 41 of Mithradates III from GIM', *VDI*,1986, 4, pl,1, №5-6

Staters 338 B.e. = AD 41/42

Obv. Laureate head of Claudius r.; border of dots.
Rev. **ΒΑCΙΛΕΩC ΜΙΤΗΡΙΔΑΤΟΥ.** Nike advancing l., holding palm branch in l. hand, wreath in r.; in field, **Η - ΛΤ** (338 B.e.); border of dots.
Anohin 329; *RPC* I, 1909.

A-a	1)	7,91		Location unknown		pl.XLVI,23	Giel, *ZRAO*, V, pl.VI,67; Bertier de la Garde, *ZOOID*, XXIX, p.229, №71, pl.IV,71; Ratto, Lugano, 1926, p.121, №1687 = XLVI,24; Anohin 329
	2)	7,88	20 mm	GIM	10164	pl.XLVI,25	Received by GIM from A.V. Gorelij in 1981

Bronze coins of Mithradates

Type I

Obv. **ΒΑCΙΛΕΩC ΜΙΤΗΡΑΔΑΤΟΥ**. Diademed bust of Mithradates r.; border of dots.
Rev. **ΒΑCΙΛΙCCΗC ΓΗΠΑΙΠΥΡΕΩC**. Bust of Queen Gepaipyris r.; to r., **ΙΒ** (12); border of dots.
Anohin 331.

Dies		Wt.	Dia.	Mus.	Mus. No.	Plate	Notes
A-a	1)	8,33	23 mm	GE	27911	pl.XLVIII,9	
B-b	1)	8,95	25 mm	GIM	6725	pl.XLVIII,10	
	2)	7,55	23 mm	GE	27909	pl.XLVIII,11	
C-c	1)	7,51	25 mm	GIM	6728	pl.XLVIII,12	Anohin 331
D-d	1)	9,03	24 mm	GIM	6729	pl.XLVIII,13	
E-e	1)	9,65	27 mm	GE	27908	pl.XLVIII,14	
A-e	1)	11,05	25 mm	GE	27910	pl.XLVIII,15	
H-f	1)	9,17	24 mm	GIM	6726	pl.XLVIII,16	
	2)	6,59	21 mm	GIM	6727		
	3)	8,41	22 mm	GIM	6730	pl.XLVIII,17	
F-g	1)			OGAM	23932	pl.XLVIII,18	
	2)	10,13	22 mm	GIM	12727		Kozievsky Coll.

Type II-brockage[139]

Obv. ΒΑCΙΛΕΩC ΜΙΘΡΑΔΑΤΟΥ. Diademed bust of Mithradates r. Border of dots.
Rev. Bust of Mithradates in intaglio; [ ]ΔΑΤΟΥ; border of dots.

A-a	1)	7,45	25 mm	GE	27896	pl.XLIX,1

Type III

Obv. ΒΑCΙΛΕΩC ΜΙΘΡΑΔΑΤΟΥ. Diademed bust of Mithradates r.; border of dots.
Rev. Club of Heracles; skin draped over; to l.; bow in case; to r., trident; below, ΙΒ; border of dots.
Anohin 330; *RPC* I, 1910[140]; Stancomb 969.

Dies		Wt.	Dia.	Mus.	Mus. No.	Plate.	Notes
A-a	1)	11,41	27 mm	GIM	6731	pl.XLIX,2	
A-b	1)	5,36	23 mm	GIM	6732	pl.XLIX,3	
B-d	1)	8,85	24 mm	GIM	6733	pl.XLIX,4	
C-c	1)	7,01	21 mm	GIM	6734	pl.XLIX,5	
D-e	1)	8,33	23 mm	GIM	6735	pl.XLIX,6	
D-f	1)	9,06	21 mm	GIM	6736	pl.XLIX,7	
E-g	1)	9,62	23,5 mm	GIM	6737	pl.XLIX,8	
F-h	1)	9,72	24,5 mm	GIM	6738	pl.XLIX,9	
H-i	1)	8,68	24 mm	GIM	6739	pl.XLIX,10	
I-k	1)	8,57	25 mm	GIM	6740	pl.XLIX,11	
K-l	1)	8,74	24 mm	GIM	6741	pl.XLIX,12	
L-m	1)	6,24	22 mm	GIM	6742	pl.XLIX,13	
	2)	5,85	23 mm	GIM	6759		
N-n	1)	7,11	22 mm	GIM	6743	pl.XLIX,14	
	2)	7,32	22 mm	GIM	12734		Kozievsky Coll.
N-o	1)	8,12	23 mm	GIM	6744	pl.XLIX,15	
N-p	1)	8,58	23 mm	GIM	6745	pl.XLIX,16	
N-r	1)	8,55	23 mm	GIM	6746	pl.XLIX,17	
N-s	1)	7,55	23 mm	GIM	6747		
O-t	1)	8,12	22 mm	GIM	6758	pl.XLIX,18	Rev. only
	2)	8,30	22 mm	GIM	12736		Kozievsky Coll.
P-u	1)	7,19	23 mm	GE	6748	pl.L,1	
P-x	1)	7,05	23 mm	GE	27881	pl.L,2	
	2)	7,32	23 mm	GE	27891	pl.L,3	
	3)	5,50	20 mm	GE	27892	pl.L,4	
	4)	7,18	23 mm	GIM	6776		
	5)	9,45	23 mm	A			
R-z	1)	9,38	24 mm	GIM	6749		
	2)	8,87	23 mm	GIM	6750	pl.L,5	Anohin 330[141]
	3)	8,15	25 mm	GE	27889	pl.L,6	
	4)	8,65	24 mm	A			
S-w	1)	8,10	24 mm	GIM	6751	pl.L,7	
S-ab	1)	8,11	21 mm	GIM	6752		
	2)	9,40	25 mm	GE	27883	pl.L,8	
T-ph	1)	7,96	21 mm	GIM	6756	pl.L,9	
	2)	8,73	23 mm	GIM	6757		
U-ad	1)			OGAM	23602	pl.L,10	
W-ac	1)	13,00	25 mm	GIM	6760	pl.L,11	
W-ae	1)	8,22	23 mm	GE	27894	pl.L,12	
	2)	6,68	22 mm	GIM	6762		
Z-af	1)	9,02	25 m	GE	27895	pl.L,13	
Z-ag	1)	5,42	23 mm	GIM	6768		
	2)	9,04	23 mm	GIM	6761		
Z-ah	1)	8,84	23 mm	GIM	6764	pl.L,14	
	2)	8,73	25 mm	GE	27886	pl.L,15	
Ab-ap	1)	10,47	26 mm	GIM	6766	pl.L,16	

[139] As with the brockage coins of Gepaipyris, it is doubtful if such coins represent a separate type. The positioning of the inscription associates the coin with Type III of Gepaipyris or Type III of Mithradates S.I.
[140] *RPC* I records 22 specimens not recorded here. S.I.
[141] Anohin's coin-image is the same as that of GIM 6750, though the museum number he gives is 6744 = pl.XLIX, 15. S.I.

Ab-ak	1)	11,16	27 mm	GE	27878	pl.L,17
Ac-al	1)	9,10	25 mm	GE	27876	pl.LI,1
Ad-am	1)	7,22	27 mm	GE	27879	pl.LI,2
Ah-an	1)	5,79	21 mm	GE	27880	pl.LI,3
Af-aa	1)	6,80	24 mm	GE	27882	pl.LI,4
Ae-bb	1)	8,16	25 mm	GE	27884	pl.LI,5
Ag-dd	1)	8,88	24 mm	GE	27885	pl.LI,6
Ak-cc	1)	6,78	25 mm	GE	27888	pl.LI,7
Al-kk	1)	10,18	25 mm	GE	27893	pl.LI,8
Am-ss	1)	7,32	23 mm	GE	27891	pl.LI,9
An-tt	1)			OGAM	23867	pl.LI,10
As-gg	1)	10,88	23 mm	GE	27899	pl.LI,11
At-tt	1)	8,86	20 mm	A		pl.LI,12

Coins in poor condition:

1)	5,63	20 mm	GIM	6753
2)	5,94	21 mm	GIM	6754
3)	8,12	21 mm	GIM	6755
4)	6,94	20 mm	GIM	6765

§14 Coins of Kotys I

Gold coins of Kotys I

BMT - 342 B.e. = AD 45

Obv. Laureate head of Claudius r.; line border.
Rev. Head of Britannicus r.; to l. BAK (73); below, BMT; line border.
Burachkov, p.249, drawing in text; BMC, 1889, pl.XI,9; Bertier de la Garde, *ZOOID*, XXIX, p.229, №72, pl.IV,72; Karyszkovski, *VDI*, 1953, 3, pl.I,1, Anohin 332; *RPC* I, 1912.

Dies		Wt.	Dia.	Mus.	Mus. No.	Plate	Notes
A-a	1)	7,84	20 mm	GIM	407	pl.LI,13	Schlessinger, 11, Berlin, 1934, II, №201, pl.VII,201; Anohin 332
	2)	7,85	19 mm	BM		pl.LI,14	BMC, 1889, pl.XI,9; Bertier de la Garde, *ZOOID*, XXIX, pl.IV,72; *RPC* I, 1912
	3)	7,84	20 mm	GE	665		
	4)	7,86		Berlin State Museum		pl.LI,15	

EMT - 345 B.e. = AD 48

Obv. Laureate head of Claudius, r.; line border.
Rev. Head of Britannicus r., to l. BAK (73), below, EMT; line border.
Burachkov, pl.XXVI,95; Anohin 333; *RPC* I, 1913.

Dies		Wt.	Dia.	Mus.	Mus. No.	Plate	Notes
A-a	1)	7,86	20 mm	GIM	408	pl.LI,16	Oreshnikov, Catalogue..., pl.III,554; Anohin 333
	2)	7,82	20 mm	Berlin State Museum		pl.LI,17	Bertier de la Garde, *ZOOID*, XXIX, pl.IV,73
	3)	7,80	19 mm			pl.LI,18	A. Hess, Lucerne, 1935, pl.I,17; this specimen is from the Burachkov Coll. - pl.XXVI,95; Schlessinger, 11, pl.VII,202
	4)	One coin of this year was found at a village in the Krasnodar region. It is kept in the Krasnodar Museum of History. Weight unknown.					

ϚMT - 346 Be = AD 49

Obv. Laureate head of Claudius r.; line border.
Rev. Head of Britannicus r.; to l. BΑ̂Κ (73); below ϚMT; line border.
Anohin 334; *RPC* I, 1914.

Dies		Wt.	Dia.	Mus.	Mus. No.	Plate	Notes
A-a	1)	7,94	21 mm	GE	660	pl.LI,19	cf.Anohin 334
	2)	7,91	20 mm			pl.LI,20	Bertier de la Garde, *ZOOID*, XXIX, p.230, №74, pl.IV,74
	2)	7,91		NM	4318	pl.LI,21	Found in the Mischako necropolis

ΘMT - 349 B.e. = AD 52

Obv. Laureate head of Claudius r.; line border.
Rev. Laureate bust of Nero r.; to l., BΑ̂Κ (73); below, ΘMT; line border.
Burachov, XXVI,96; Anohin 335; *RPC* I, 1915.

Dies		Wt.	Dia.	Mus.	Mus. No	Plate	Notes
A-a	1)	7,90	21 mm	GIM	409	pl.LI,22	
	2)	7,89	21 mm	GE	661		
A-b	1)	7,79	21 mm	GIM	410	pl.LI,23	Anohin 335
A-c	1)	7,796	20 mm	München State Museum		pl.LI,24	
A-d	1)	7,88	20 mm	BM		pl.LII,1	BMC, 1889, pl.XI,10; Bertier de la Garde, *ZOOID*, XXIX, p.230, №75, pl.IV,75; *RPC* I, 1915

NT - 350 B.e. = AD 53

Obv. Laureate head of Claudius r.; line border.
Rev. Laureate bust of Nero r.; to l., BΑ̂Κ (73); below, NT; line border.
Anohin 336; *RPC* I, 1916.

Dies		Wt.	Dia.	Mus.	Mus. No	Plate	Notes
A-a	1)	7,89	20 mm	Berlin State Museum		pl.LII,2	Bertier de la Garde, *ZOOID*, XXIX, p.230, №76, pl.IV,76; Anohin 336
	2)	7,91	20 mm	P	127	pl.LII,3	

BNT - 352 B.e. = AD 55

Obv. Bust of Agrippina, r.; line border.
Rev. Laureate bust of Nero l.; to r. BΑ̂Κ (73); below, BNT; line border.
Anohin 337a; *RPC* I, 1917.

Dies		Wt.	Dia.	Mus.	Mus No.	Plate	Notes
A-a	1)	7,92	20 mm	München State Museum	178	pl.LII,4	
	2)	7,85	20 mm	GIM	411	pl.LII,5	Anohin 337a
	3)	7,80	19 mm			pl.LII,6	A.Hess, Lucerne, 1935, p.2, №18, pl.I,18; Schlessinger, 11, pl.VII,203; Burachkov, pl.XXVI,98

Obv. As previous.
Rev. As previous, but bust of Nero r. and to l. monogram BΑ̂Κ - Burachkov, XXVI,98, Anohin 337.

	Wt.	Dia.	Mus.	Mus. No.	Plate	Notes
1)	7,87	19 mm	GE	662	pl.LII,7	Bertier de la Garde, *ZOOID*, XXIX, p.230, №77, pl.IV,77

ΓNT - 353 B.e. = AD 56

Obv. Laureate head of Claudius r.; line border.
Rev. Laureate bust of Nero r.; to l., BAK (73); below, ΓNT; line border.
RPC I, 1918.

A-a	1)	7,94	20 mm	Location unknown	pl.LII,8	

The coins of this year are very rare. Bertier de la Garde knew only one specimen from 353 B.e. (*NS*, II, p.109, №114; *ZOOID*, XXIX, p.230, №78, pl.IV,78). Karyszkovski (*VDI*, 1953, 3, p.189, pl.I,9) regarded this coin as being in the Hermitage Collection, but this is not so.

ΔNT - 354 B.e. = AD 57

Obv. Laureate head of Claudius r.; line border.
Rev. Laureate bust of Nero r.; to l., BAK(73); below, •ΔNT. Line border.
Anohin 339; *RPC* I, 1919.

Dies		Wt.	Dia.	Mus.	Plate	Notes
A-a	1)	7,89	20 mm	BM	pl.LII,9	BMC,1889, pl.XI,11; Bertier de la Garde, *ZOOID*, XXIX, p.230, №79, pl.IV,79; Anohin 339
	2)	7,80	21 mm	Location unknown	pl.LII,10	The coin was in the Burachkov Coll., pl.XXVI,99; Schlessinger, 11, pl.VIII,204

ENT - 355 B.e. = AD 58

Obv. Laureate head of Claudius r.; line border.
Rev. Laureate bust of Nero r.; to l., BAK (73); below •ENT; line border.
Burachkov, XXVI,100; Anohin 340; *RPC* I, 1920.

Dies		Wt.	Dia.	Mus.	Mus. No.	Plate	Notes
A-a	1)	7,91	20 mm	München State Museum		pl.LII,11	
	2)	7,91	20 mm	BM		pl.LII,12	BMC,1889, pl.XI,12; Bertier de la Garde, *ZOOID*, XXIX, p.230, №80, pl.IV,80; Anohin 340
	3)	7,87	20 mm	GE	663	pl.LII,13	

ϚNT - 356 B.e. = AD 59

Obv. Laureate head of Claudius r.; line border.
Rev. Laureate bust of Nero r.; to l., BAK (73); below, •ϚNT; line border.
Burachkov, pl.XXVI,101; *RPC* I, 1921.

A-a	1)	7,88	Gaidukevich, *Bosp. Reich*, p.588, №68, pl.IV,68. He said that this is a cast from GMII			
	2)	7,86	20 mm	Location unknown	pl.LII,14	Bertier de la Garde, *ZOOID*, XXIX, p.231, №81, pl.IV,81
	3)	7,95		Vienna		

ZNT - 357 B.e. = AD 60

Obv. Laureate head of Claudius r.; line border.
Rev. Laureate head of Nero r.; to l., BAK (73), below, •ZNT; line border.
Burachkov, pl.XXVII,102; Anohin 342; *RPC* I, 1922.

Dies		Wt.	Dia.	Mus.	Mus. No.	Plate	Notes
A-a	1)	7,93	20 mm	P	129	pl.LII,15	
	2)	7.92	21 mm	P	130	pl.LII,16	Bertier de la Garde, *ZOOID*, XXIX, p.231, №82, pl.IV,82

3)	7,94	20 mm	GIM	412	pl.LII,17	Oreshnikov, Catalogue..., vol.III, 560
4)	7,91	20 mm	GIM	413	pl.LII,18	
5)	7,90	20 mm	GE	664		Anohin 342
6)	7,88	20 mm	Berlin State Museum		pl.LII,19	
7)	7,89				pl.LII,20	Sotheby, Property of Russian Nobles, pl.VII,262

ΘNT - 359 B.e. = AD 62

Obv. Laureate head of Claudius r.; line border.
Rev. Laureate head of Nero r.; to l., [monogram] (74); below, •ΘNT; line border.
Burachkov, pl.XXVII,103, Anohin 343; *RPC* I, 1923.

Dies		Wt.	Dia.	Mus.	Mus. No.	Plate	Notes
A-a	1)	7,93	20 mm	P	131	pl.LII,21	*RPC* I, 1923
	2)	7,96	21 mm			pl.LII,22	Bertier de la Garde, *ZOOID*, XXIX, p.231, №83, pl.IV,83
	3)	7,87	20 mm	GE	666	pl.LII,23	Zograph, pl.XLVI,13
	4)	7,03	19 mm				Auction catalogue, XVI, Geneve, 1933
	5)	7,04	19 mm				Auction Katalog, Cahn, Fr.A.M., 1932, №354
	6)	7,96				pl.LII,24	Minns, pl.VII, obv 23, rev 22

Bronze coins of Kotys I

Series I (AD 45 - 50)

Denomination Δ = 4

Obv. Female head r.; to monogram [monogram] (72); border of dots.
Rev. Head of Aphrodite Urania wearing kalathos and veil r.; to l., monogram [monogram] (73); to r. Δ.
Burachkov, pl.XXVII,113; *RPC* I, 1928.[142]

	Wt.	Dia.	Plate	Notes
1)	5,12	20 mm	pl.LIII,1	Bertier de la Garde, p.162, drawing in text, p.224, №31, pl.II,31

Denomination ϛ = 6

Obv. Diademed head of Aspurgus, father of Kotys I, r.; to r., monogram [monogram] (69); border of dots.
Rev. Diademed head of Kotys I r.; to r.; monogram [monogram] (73); above, part of bow, below ϛ (6); border of dots.

Anohin 346; *RPC* I, 1927.

	Wt.	Dia.	Mus.	Mus. No.	Plate	Notes
1)	3,73	17 mm	GIM	6914	pl.LIII,2	Burachkov, pl.XXVII,106; *RPC* I, 1927
2)	3,46	17 mm	GE	67/27980	pl.LIII,3	Bertier de la Garde, *ZOOID*, XXIX, p.224, №30, pl.II,30; Zograph, pl.XLVI,12; Karyszkovskij, VDI, 1953, 3, pl.I,16; cf.Anohin 346
3)	3,65	17 mm	GIM	12738		Kozievsky Coll.

142 *RPC* I Suppl. 1928 records a further specimen in Paris (wt. 5.48g). S.I.

Denomination H = 8

Obv. BRITANNIKOY KAICAPOC. Head of Britannicus r.; border of dots.
Rev. Diademed head of young Kotys I r.; to l., monogram BΛK (73); to r., H (8); border of dots.
Burachkov, pl.XXVII,105; Zograph, pl.XLVI,11, Anohin 345; *RPC* I, 1926.[143]

Dies		Wt.	Dia.	Mus.	Mus.No.	Plate	Notes
A-a	1)	4,95	20 mm	GIM	6911	pl.LIII,4	
	2)	4,75	21 mm	GE	27977	pl.LIII,5	
	3)	5,70	20 mm	GE	27970	pl.LIII,6	
A-b	1)	4,07	20 mm	GIM	6912	pl.LIII,7	
	2)	5,39	20 mm	GE	27978	pl.LIII,8	
A-c	1)	5,37	20 mm	GIM	6913	pl.LIII,9	Anohin 345
	2)	4,93	20 mm	GE	27979	pl.LIII,10	
	3)	5,58	20 mm	GIM	12739		Kozievsky Coll.

Dies of the following coins not determined:

1)	4,70	19,6 mm	OGAM	24350
2)	3,10	18,8 mm	OGAM	23304

Series II (AD 49 - 54)

Denomination IB = 12 - asses

Type I

Obv. TI · KΛAYΔIOY KAICAPOC. Laureate head of Claudius r.; below, IB; border of dots.
Rev. IOYΛIAN AΓPIΠΠINAN KAICAPOC. Head of Agrippina l.; to l., monogram BΛK (73); border of dots.

BMC, 1889, pl.XI,14; Anohin 344; *RPC* I, 1924.[144]

Dies		Wt.	Dia.	Mus.	Mus. No.	Plate	Notes
A-a	1)	8,52	24 mm	GIM	6871	pl.LIII,11	
	2)	7,45	25 mm	GIM	6872		
B-b	1)	7,94	24 mm	GIM	6873	pl.LIII,12	
	2)	7,40	24 mm	GIM	6899		
	3)	9,04	25 mm	GE	45/27958	pl.LIII,13	
C-c	1)	7,15	24 mm	GIM	6874	pl.LIII,14	
	2)	8,91	25 mm	GE	27955	pl.LIII,15	
	3)	7,00	24 mm	GE	27954	pl.LIII,16	
	4)	6,50	24 mm	A			
D-d	1)	9,12	23 mm	GIM	6875	pl.LIII,17	
D-e	1)	7,95	25 mm	GE	27953	pl.LIII,18	
E-f	1)	6,20	23 mm	GIM	6876	pl.LIII,19	
	2)	5,82	23 mm	F			Minns, 66
F-h	1)	9,88	24 mm	GIM	6877	pl.LIII,20	
	2)	9,67	24 mm	GE	28941		
	3)	9,55	25 mm	GE	28942	pl.LIII,21	
H-g	1)	10,45	25 mm	GE	28956	pl.LIII,22	
	2)	5,92	25 mm	GE	27960		
	3)	7,22	25 mm	GE	27961		
G-I	1)	8,36	24 mm	GE	28959	pl.LIII,23	Obv. only

[143] *RPC* I records specimens also in London. S.I.
[144] *RPC* I 1924 records specimens also in Munich, Vienna and New York. S.I.

Type II

Obv. ΤΙ · ΚΛΑΥΔΙΟΥ ΚΑΙCΑΡΟC. Laureate head of Claudius r.; below, ΙΒ; border of dots.
Rev. ΙΟΥΛΙΑΝ ΑΓΡΙΠΠΙΝΑΝ ΚΑΙCΑΡΟC. Head of Agrippina r.; to r., monogram ΒΑΚ (73); border of dots.

Burachkov, pl.XXVII,107; *RPC* I Suppl 1925A.[145]

A-a	1)	7,85	24 mm	GIM	6879	pl.LIII,24	
B-b	1)	5,92	25 mm	GE	27960	pl.LIV,1	
B-c	1)	7,22	24 mm	GE	27961	pl.LIV,2	
C-d	1)	5,22	20 mm	GE	27962	pl.LIV,3	
D-e	1)	9,32	20 mm	GIM	12746		Kozievsky Coll.

Type III

Obv. ΤΙ · ΚΛΑΥΔΙΟΥ ΚΑΙCΑΡΟC. Laureate head of Claudius r.; below, ΙΒ; border of dots.
Rev. ΙΟΥΛΙΑΝ ΑΓΡΙΠΠΙΝΑΝ CΕΒΑCΤΗΝ. Head of Agrippina l.; to l., monogram ΒΑΚ (73); border of dots.

Burachkov, pl.XXVII,109., Anohin 348[146]; *RPC* I, 1925.[147]

A-a	1)	7,93	25 mm	GIM	6882	pl.LIV,4	
	2)	7,52	25 mm	GIM	6888	pl.LIV,5	
	3)	8,74	25 mm	GE	28938		
	4)	10,87	25 mm	GIM	6905		
	5)	8,17	24 mm	GE	27939	pl.LIV,6	Obv. only
	6)	9,13	24 mm	F			
A-b	1)	9,70	25 mm	GIM	6891	pl.LIV,7	
B-c	1)	5,01	25 mm	GIM	6884	pl.LIV,8	
B-d	1)	5,20	23 mm	GE	27947	pl.LIV,9	
	2)	5,24	25 mm	GIM	6883	pl.LIV,10	
	3)	4,86	23 mm	GIM	6908		
	4)	8,08	23 mm	GIM	12747		Kozievsky Coll.
B-e	1)	7,80	24 mm	GE	27946	pl.LIV,11	
	2)	5,64	22 mm	A			
B-f	1)	7,11	23 mm	GIM	6892	pl.LIV,12	
B-h	1)	10,05	23 mm	GIM	6895	pl.LIV,13	
B-g	1)	7,62	25 mm	GIM	6896	pl.LIV,14	
C-I	1)	6,04	25 mm	GIM	6848		
	2)	9,80	25 mm	GE	27933	pl.LIV,15	
	3)	8,38	23 mm	GIM	6887	pl.LIV,16	
	4)	10,21	26 mm	GIM	6878		
	5)	6,03	25 mm	GE	28934	pl.LIV,17	
A-k	1)	8,31	25 mm	GIM	6625		
	2)	6,27	23 mm	GIM	6899	pl.LIV,18	
	3)	5,97	22 mm	F			
A-l	1)	11,27	25 mm	GE	27937	pl.LIV,19	
D-m	1)	8,20	25 mm	GE	27944	pl.LIV,20	
B-n	1)	4,86	25 mm	GE	27945	pl.LIV,21	
	2)	5,37	22 mm	GIM	6626		
E-o	1)	6,05	24 mm	GE	27940	pl.LV,1	
F-r	1)	6,46	25 mm	GIM	6889	pl.LV,2	
F-s	1)	6,63	24 mm	GIM	6902	pl.LV,3	
H-t	1)	6,75	24 mm	GIM	6893	pl.LV,4	
G-u	1)	6,97	24 mm	GE	27941	pl.LV,5	
	2)	9,75	25 mm	GIM	6901		
F-ph	1)	6,08	24 mm	GIM	6890	pl.LV,6	
	2)	8,67	25 mm	GIM	6908a		
	3)	6,35	24 mm	GIM	6904		
Fa-fa	1)	7,90	23 mm	A			
I-x	1)	7,01	23 mm	OGAM	24364	pl.LV,7	

[145] *RPC* I wrongly interprets the reverse inscription, suggesting that the coin in Samsun museum, Turkey belongs to Type III. S.I.
[146] Anohin's ref., GE 27967 is recorded by Frolova as a Type IV coin. S.I.
[147] *RPC* I records numerous other specimens. S.I.

K-z	1)	6,80	24 mm	OGAM	22117	pl.LV,8	
A-w	1)	8,75	23 mm	GIM	6886	pl.LV,9	
Z-f	1)	5,62	22 mm	GE	27950	pl.LV,10	
	2)	3,66	21 mm	GIM	6897		
	3)	4,90	24 mm	GIM	6910		
	4)	6,88	21 mm	GIM	6881		
	5)	8,91	21 mm	GIM	12744		Kozievsky Coll.
Z-aa	1)	4,43	20 mm	GE	27952	pl.LV,11	
	2)	6,10	20 mm	OGAM	24334	pl.LV,12	
M-ab	1)	5,93	21 mm	GIM	6907	pl.LV,13	
	2)			GE	28906	pl.LV,14	
	3)	9,33	20 mm	GIM	6900		

Dies of the following coins not determined:

1)	5,89	23 mm	GIM	6880	
2)	6,79	26 mm	GIM	6909	
3)	8,43	25 mm	GIM	6894	
4)	8,38	24 mm	GIM	6885	
5)	6,89	24 mm	GIM	6883a	
6)	6,86	21 mm	GIM	6951	
7)	9,09	24 mm	GIM	12745	Kozievsky Coll.

Type IV

Obv. **TI · ΚΛΑΥΔΙΟΥ CEBACTOY KAICAPOC**. Laureate head of Claudius r.; below, **IB**; border of dots.

Rev. **ΙΟΥΛΙΑΝ ΑΓΡΙΠΠΙΝΑΝ CEBACTHN**. Head of Agrippina l.; to l., monogram **BΆK** (73).; border of dots.

Burachkov, pl.XXVII,110. Anohin 349.[148]

Dies		Wt.	Dia.	Mus.	Mus. No.	Plate	Notes
A-a	1)	5,25	22 mm	GE	27963	pl.LV,15	
	2)	6,98	22 mm	GE	27964	pl.LV,16	
	3)	5,46	22 mm	GIM	12745		Kozievsky Coll.
A-b	1)	7,02	23 mm	GE	27965	pl.LV,17	
A-c	1)	6,77	23 mm	GE	27966	pl.LV,18	Anohin 349
	2)	4,67	22 mm	GIM	6921	pl.LV,19	
A-d	1)	4,88	22 mm	GIM	6918		
B-e	1)	8,35	22 mm	GE	27967	pl.LV,20	

Dies of the following coins not determined:

	Wt.	Dia.	Mus.	Mus. No.
1)	9,20	24,5 mm	OGAM	24343
2)	8,70	23,5 mm	OGAM	22112
3)	8,25	24,6 mm	OGAM	24340
4)	8,20	24,9 mm	OGAM	24338
5)	7,50	22,5 mm	OGAM	25121
6)	7,30	25,6 mm	OGAM	24342
7)	6,60	22 mm	OGAM	24337
8)	6,30	26 mm	OGAM	22102
9)	5,80	25 mm	OGAM	24336
10)	5,75	23 mm	OGAM	24385
11)	5,70	24,6 mm	OGAM	22101
12)	5,40	23 mm	OGAM	24326
13)	5,50	21,7 mm	OGAM	24329
14)	5,50	25,1 mm	OGAM	24351
15)	5,40	21,5 mm	OGAM	24367

[148] The type is absent from *RPC* I. S.I.

Series III (AD 54 - 59)

Denomination IB = 12 asses

Obv. NEPWNOC ΚΛΑΥΔΙΟΥ CEBACTOY KAICAPOC. Laureate head of Nero r.; border of dots.
Rev. ΑΓΡΙΠΠΙΝΗC CEBACTHC. Head of Agrippina, l.; to l.; monogram BÂK (73); below, IB (12); border of dots.
Zograph, pl.XLVI, 10; Anohin 350; *RPC* I, 1929[149]; Stancomb 972

Dies		Wt.	Dia.	Mus.	Mus. No.	Plate	Notes
A-a	1)	5,92	25 mm	GIM	6915	pl.LV,21	
	2)	5,74	23 mm	GE	27970a	pl.LV,22	
A-b	1)	8,30	22 mm	GE	27969	pl.LV,23	
	2)	4,45	21 mm	GIM	6922		Poor condition
A-c	1)	6,90	21 mm	GE	27968	pl.LV,24	Cf. Anohin 350
	2)	7,90	21 mm	GIM	12746		Kozievsky Coll.
	3)	5,18	21 mm	GIM	6917		
	4)	5,60	21 mm	GIM	6916		
	5)	6,35	23 mm	GIM	6955		
B-d	1)	5,48	22 mm	GE	27971	pl.LVI,1	
	2)	6,48	23 mm	GE	27972	pl.LVI,2	
A-e	1)	5,89	22 mm	GIM	6952	pl.LVI,3	
A-h	1)	4,91	22 mm	GIM	6953	pl.LVI,4	
B-f	1)	5,70	23 mm	GIM	6954	pl.LVI,5	

Dies of the following coins not determined:

	Wt.	Dia	Mus.	Mus. No.		Wt.	Dia	Mus.	Mus. No.
					5)	5,90	22,3 mm	OGAM	24325
1)	4,60	22,4 mm	OGAM	24388	6)	5,19	21 mm	OGAM	24352
2)	3,40	21,5 mm	OGAM	24386	7)	4,80	21 mm	OGAM	23310
3)	7,90	24,2 mm	OGAM	24323	8)	4,30	20,5 mm	OGAM	24327
4)	6,15	23,7 mm	OGAM	23308	9)	4,15	20,5 mm	OGAM	24348

Series IV (AD 63)

Denomination IB = 12 - asses

Obv. NEPWNOC ΚΛΑΥΔΙΟΥ CEBACTOY KAICAPOC. Laureate bust of Nero r.; border of dots.
Rev. ΠΟΠΠΗΙΑC CEBACTHC. Bust of Poppaea, l.; to l. BÂK (73); below, IB; border of dots.
Burachkov, pl.XXVII,111; Anohin 351. (See, however, *RPC* I p..334)

Dies		Wt.	Dia.	Mus.	Mus. No.	Plate	Notes
A-a	1)	7,59	24 mm	GIM	6920		
	2)	7,82	22 mm	GE	27973	pl.LVI,6	Anohin 351
	3)	5,28	22 mm	GE	27974	pl.LVI,7	
	4)	5,98	22 mm	GE	27975		
B-b	1)	8,98	20 mm	GIM	12740		Kozievsky Coll.

Series V (AD 63 - 68)

Denomination MH = 48 - sestertii

Obv. NEPWNOC ΚΛΑΥΔΙΟΥ KAICAPOC CEBACTOY. Laureate head of Nero r.; border of dots.
Rev. Wreath; in centre, MH; border of dots.
Burachkov, pl.XXVII,114; Anohin 352; *RPC* I, 1932 & Suppl.

Dies		Wt.	Dia.	Mus.	Mus. No.	Plate	Notes
A-a	1)	14,42	30 mm	GIM	6923		
	2)	14,33	30 mm	GIM	6930	pl.LVI,8	
	3)	10,85	28 mm	GIM	6927		
	4)	13,54	30 mm	GE	27983	pl.LVI,9	

[149] *RPC* I records specimens in Copenhagen, Vienna, Oxford and Paris. S.I.

	5)	12.93	30 mm	GIM	12747		Kozievsky Coll.
A-b	1)	14,91	28 mm	GIM	6924		
	2)	17,79	30 mm	GIM	6928	pl.LVI,10	
A-c	1)	15,28	31 mm	GIM	6926		
	2)	11,39	32 mm	GIM	6925		
	3)	8,74	30 mm	GIM	6623	pl.LVI,11	
	4)	14,66	30 mm	GE	27982	pl.LVI,12	
	5)	14,58	30 mm	GE	27984	pl.LVI,13	
	6)			OGAM	25130	pl.LVI,14	Anohin 352
A-d	1)	15,06	31 mm	GIM	6929	pl.LVI,15	
	2)	14,85	32 mm	GE	27981	pl.LVI,16	
	3)	9,90	28,2 mm	OGAM	22771		
	4)			Anapa, Archaeological Museum		pl.LVI,17	
	5)			Kerch, Archaeological Museum		pl.LVII,1	

Denomination KΔ = 24 - dupondii

Type I

Obv. NEPWNOC KAICAPOC. Bust of Nero r.; border of dots.
Rev. Nike holding wreath and palm branch; K- Δ; border of dots.
Burachkov, pl.XXVII,115; Anohin 353; *RPC* I, 1933.

Dies		Wt.	Dia.	Mus.	Mus. No.	Plate	Notes
A-a	1)	9,90	28 mm	GIM	6932	pl.LVII,2	
A-b	1)	11,50	28 mm	GE	27985	pl.LVII,3	Obv. only
	2)	10,40	27 mm	GE	27986	pl.LVII,4	
A-d	1)	11,86	26 mm	GE	27987	pl.LVII,5	
A-c	1)	12,80	27 mm	GE	27988	pl.LVII,6	
	2)	9,26	26 mm	GE	27989	pl.LVII,7	
	3)	9,36	26 mm	GIM	12748		Kozievsky Coll.
A-i	1)	9,06	26 mm	GIM	6931	pl.LVII,8	
	2)	14,02	28 mm	GIM	6935	pl.LVII,9	Anohin 353
	3)			Kerch, Archaeological Museum		pl.LVII,10	
A-e	1)	10,50	27mm	A			

Type II

Obv. Temple of five columns; KA- ΠE; border of dots.
Rev. Wreath; in centre, monogram BΔK (73); below, KΔ; border of dots.
Burachkov, pl.XXIX,117; Anohin 370; *RPC* I, 1930; Stancomb 973.

Dies		Wt.	Dia.	Mus.	Mus No.	Plate	Notes
A-a	1)	6,55	22 mm	GIM	6936	pl.LVII,11	Anohin 370; *RPC* I, 1930
	2)	7,81	22 mm	GIM	4034	pl.LVII,12	
	3)	7,26	22 mm	GIM	12749		Kozievsky Coll.
B-b	1)	9,39	24 mm	GIM	6944		
A-c	1)	6,78	25 mm	GIM	6947	pl.LVII,13	
B-d	1)	4,42	21 mm	GIM	6941	pl.LVII,14	
D-e	1)	5,90	22 mm	GIM	6940	pl.LVII,15	
E-f	1)	5,36	22 mm	GIM	6988	pl.LVII,16	
H-h	1)	8,19	22 mm	GIM	6937	pl.LVII,17	
	2)	6,25	22 mm	Cop	53	pl.LVIII,1a	
B-g	1)	4,24	21 mm	GIM	6043	pl.LVII,18	
J-I	1)	5,81		Gorelij private collection		pl.LVIII,1	Temple of six columns

Dies of the following coins not determined:

1)	8,22	25 mm	GE	28407	
2)	7,80	23 mm	GE	28411	

3)	4,60	22 mm	GE	28413	
4)	9,80	22 mm	GE	28414	
5)	7,05	23 mm	GE	28415	
6)	6,20	23 mm	GE	28416	
7)	8,52	25 mm	GE	28417	
8)	6,45	21 mm	GIM	6973	
9)	4,77	21 mm	GIM	6948	
10)	4,81	23 mm	GIM	6950	
11)	5,10	22 mm	GIM	6974	
12)	6,70	23 mm	OGAM	23317	
13)	7,60	23 mm	OGAM	23326	
14)	6,35	24 mm	OGAM	24331	
15)	6,70	21,2 mm	OGAM	23642	
16)	4,30	21,5 mm	OGAM	23305	
17)			GIM		pl.LVII,19

Type III

Obv. Temple of five columns; KA- ΠE; border of dots.
Rev. Wreath; in centre, monogram BAΣY (75); above, NO; below, KΔ; border of dots.
Burachkov, pl.XXIX,201, Anohin 371; *RPC* I, 1931; Stancomb 974.

Dies		Wt.	Dia.	Mus.	Mus. No.	Plate	Notes
A-a	1)	11,34	25 mm	GIM	6939		
	2)	9,34	25 mm	GIM	6942	pl.LVIII,2	
B-b	1)	10,76	24 mm	GIM	6971	pl.LVIII,3	
C-c	1)	7,99	26 mm	GIM	6972		
D-d	1)	9,03	26 mm	GIM	6949		
E-e	1)	6,94	25 mm	GIM	6984	pl.LVIII,4	Obv. only
H-h	1)	8,83	25 mm	GIM	6975	pl.LVIII,5	
	2)	9,77	25 mm	GIM	12750		Kozievsky Coll.
F-f	1)	5,06	20 mm	GIM	6976	pl.LVIII,6	
I-i	1)	6,41	20 mm	GIM	6977	pl.LVIII,7	
K-k	1)	8,92	24 mm	GIM	6982	pl.LVIII,8	Obv. only
L-l	1)	3,20	21 mm	GIM	6980	pl.LVIII,9	
M-m	1)	6,78	20 mm	GIM	6981	pl.LVIII,10	
N-n	1)	5,92	23 mm	GIM	6983	pl.LVIII,11	
O-o	1)	6,26	22 mm	GIM	6985	pl.LVIII,12	
P-p	1)	8,80	26 mm	GIM	6990	pl.LVIII,13	Obv. only

Dies of the following poor quality coins not determined:

1)	4,40	20 mm	GIM	6978		
2)	9,23	23 mm	GIM	6979		
3)	5,43	21 mm	GIM	6986		
4)	7,28	23 mm	GIM	6987		
5)	7,03	25 mm	GIM	6988		
6)	8,22	24 mm	GIM	6989		
7)	8,23	25 mm	GE	28522		
8)	9,85	25 mm	GE	28525		
9)	8,45	25 mm	GE	28528	pl.LVIII,14	Obv. only
10)	6,99	24 mm	GE	28530		
11)	8,62	25 mm	GE	28531		
12)	7,72	23 mm	GE	28532		
13)	7,42	24 mm	GE	28535		
14)	4,24	20 mm	GE	28533	pl.LVIII,15	
15)	5,42	21 mm	GE	28529		
16)	5,86	21 mm	GE	28534		
17)	6,15	21 mm	GE	28536		
18)	8,20	24 mm	GE	28523		
19)	12,56	28 mm	GE	28524		
20)	6,94	23 mm	GIM	6984		
21)	11,20	26 mm	OGAM	23315		
22)	8,03	24 mm	OGAM	5849		

	23)	7,50	24 mm	OGAM	24155		
	24)	7,92	22mm	BM		pl.LVIII,16	BMC, 1889, pl.XV,10; *RPC* I, 1931
	25)			1980 Gorgippia excavation - №212			
	26)	6,44		1982 Gorgippia excavation - №598			
	27)	7,85		1982 Gorgippia excavation - №655			
	28)	7,14		1986 Gorgippia excavation - №1013			
	29)	7,70	24 mm	OGAM	24333		
	30)	6,00	22 mm	OGAM	24261		
	31)	5,70	22 mm	OGAM	23313		
	32)	3,80	21 mm	OGAM	24370		
	33)	8,57		F		pl.LVIII,17	
	34)	10,40		1983 Gorgippia excavation		pl.LVIII,19	
	35)			Cop	62	pl.LVIII,18	

Type IV

Obv. Temple of five columns, ΚΑ- ΠΕ; border of dots.
Rev. Wreath; in centre, monogram ΒΑΕΙΥ (76); below ΚΔ; border of dots.
Burachkov, pl.XXIX,202; Anohin 372.

Dies		Wt.	Dia.	Mus.	Mus. No.	Plate	Notes
A-a	1)	7,41	23 mm	GIM	6991	pl.LVIII,20	Anohin 372
	2)	8,95	25 mm	GE	28537		
	3)	12,52	25 mm	GE	28538		
	4)	5,94	25 mm	1983 Gorgippia excavation - №714			
	5)	7,58	24 mm	Gorelij private collection		pl.LVIII,21	Poor condition

Appendix

Proofs of gold staters from the GIM Collection

	Inventory №	Bosporan era	Modern chronology	Weight	Proof
			Dynamis		
1	393	281	17/16 B.C.	8,05	800
			Uncertain Rulers		
			Monogram  (2)		
2	394	293	4 B.C.	7,88	800
3	395	302	AD 5	7,90	750
4	396	304	AD 7	7,93	750
			monogram  (67)		
5	397	305	AD 8	7,88	750
6	398	305	AD 8	7,92	750
			Aspurgus		
7	399	317	AD 20	7,99	800
8	400	320	AD 23	7,91	800
9	401	324	AD 27	7,92	800
10	402	324	AD 27	7,95	800
11	403	331	AD 34	7,96	800
12	404	332	AD 35	7,92	800
13	405	333	AD 36	7,84	800
			Gepaipyris		
			Monogram 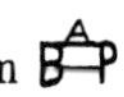 (72)		
15	52304	335	AD 38	7,56	9,18
			Mithradates		
14	406	336	AD 39	7.86	800
			Kotys I		
			Monogram  (73)		
16	407	342	AD 45	7,84	800
17	408	345	AD 48	7,86	800
18	409	349	AD 52	7,90	800
19	410	349	AD 52	7,79	800
20	411	352	AD 55	7,85	800
21	412	357	AD 60	7,94	800
22	413	357	AD 60	7,91	800

Abbrevations

AJA	—	American Journal of Archaeology
AJN	—	American Journal of Numismatics
BMC	—	A Catalogue of the Greek Coins in the British Museum, London
CIRB	—	Corpus Inscriptionum Regni Bosporani
Drevnosti	—	Drevnosti (Antiquities), published by the Moscow Archaeological Society
IAK	—	Izvestiya Arkheologicheskoi Komissii = Reports of the Archaeological Comission, Moscow – St Petersburg
ITUAK	—	Izvestiya Tavricheskoi Uchonoi Arkhivnoi Komissii = Reports of the Tauric Comission for Scholarly Records, Simpheropol
Klio	—	Beitrage zur alten Geschichte, München
KSIIMK	—	Kratkie Soobshchenia Instituta Istorii Material'noi Kulturi = Brief Communications of the Institute of History of Material Culture, Moscow
KSOGAM	—	Kratkie Soobshchenia Odesskogo Gosudarstvennogo Arkheologicheskogo Musea = Brief Communications of the Odessa Archaeological Museum, Odessa
MIA	—	Materiali i issledovaniya po Arkheologii SSSR = Materials and Research Inquiries on USSR Archaeology, Moscow - Leningrad
NC	—	Numismatic Chronicle, London
NE	—	Numismatica i Epigrafica = Numismatics and Epigraphy, Moscow
NS	—	Numismaticheskij Sbornik = Numismatic Symposium, Moscow, 1918
NSph	—	Numismatica i Sphragistica, Kiev
NZ	—	Numismatische Zeitschrift, Wien
RN	—	Revue Numismatique, Paris
RPC	—	Roman Provincial Coins I & Supplement
VDI	—	Vestnik Drevnei Istorii = Ancient History Herald, Moscow
SNG, Copenhagen	—	The Royal Collection of Coins and Medals. Danish National Museum. Vol.IV, Bosporus - Bythynia, 1982
SA	—	Sovietskaya Arckheologia = Soviet Archaeology, Moscow
ZOOID	—	Zapiski Odesskogo Obshestva Istorii i Drevnostei = Proceedings of the Odessa Society for History and Antiquity
ZRAO	—	Zapiski Russkogo Arkheologicheskogo Obshestva = Records of the Russian Archaeological Society

Abbrevations for the Catalogue of Coins

Anohin	— V.A. Anohin, *The Coinage of the Bosporus*, Kiev, 1986.
Bertier de la Garde	— A. Bertier de la Garde, 'Materials for Metrological Study of the Monetary Standards of the Ancient Greek Cities and Kings of Sarmatia and Taurus', *NS*, II, Moscow, 1913.
Burachkov	— P.O. Burachkov, *General Catalogue of Coins Pertaining to the Hellenic Colonies which Existed in Antiquity on the Northern Coast of the Black Sea*. Odessa, 1884.
Giel, *Kleine Beiträge*	— Chr. Giel, *Kleine Beiträge zur antiken Numismatik Südrusslands*, Moscow, 1886.
Giel, 'Description'	— Chr. Giel, 'Description of Coins which have entered my Collection in 1892 and 1893', *ZRAO*, VII, 1895, separate offprint.
Giel, 'A new acquisition'	— Chr. Giel, 'A New Acquisition in my Collection, *ZRAO*, V, 1892.
Imhoof-Blumer	— F. Imhoof-Blumer, *Portraitköpfe auf antiken Münzen hellenischer und hellenisierter Völker*, Leipzig, 1885.
Kazamanova	— L.N. Kazamanova, *Einführung in die antike Numismatik*. Moscow, 1969.
Köhler	— H.K.E. Köhler, 'Suite des médailles d'Asander, d'abord de archont, après roi du Bosphore Cimmérien'. *Serapis*, II, St Petersburg 1850.
Köhne	— B.V. Köhne, 'Description of the Museum of Prince V.V. Kochubei', St Petersburg, 1857.
Minns	— H.E. Minns. Scythians and Greeks. Cambridge, 1913.
Mionnet, Description	— T.E. Mionnet, *Description des médailles antiques grecques et romaines. Suppl. II*, Paris, 1822.
Mionnet, suppl. IV	— Mionnet T.E. *Description des médailles antiques grecques et romaines. Suppl. IV*, Paris, 1829.
Nanteuil	— H. de. Nanteuil, *Collection des monnaies grecques*. Paris, 1925.
Oreshnikov, Catalogue	— A.W. Oreshnikov, *Catalogue of the Collection of Antiquities of Count A.S. Uvarov. VII*, Moscow, 1887.
Podshiwalov, Beschreiburg	— A. Podshiwalov. *Beschreiburg der unedirten und wenig bekannnten Münzen von Sarmatia Europaea, Chersonesus Taurica und Bosphorus Cimmerius aus der Sammlung A.M. Podshiwalov*, Moscow, 1882.
Podshiwalov,	— A.M. Podshiwalov. *The Moscow Public and Rumijanzev Museum. Numismatic Department. Vol.I*, Moscow, 1884.
Sallet	— A. von Sallet, *Beiträge zur Geschihchte und Numismatik der Könige des Cimmerischen Bosporus und des Pontus*, Berlin, 1886.
Sestini, Cl. Gen.	— D. Sestini, Classes Générales, Firenze, 1821.
Sestini, Hederv.	— D. Sestini, *Descrizione delle medaglie antiche del Museo Hedervariano del Bosfore Cimmerio fino all'Armenia Romana*. P. II. Firenze, 1838.
Sibirskij	— Prince A. Sibirskij, *Catalogue des médailles du Bosphore Cimmérien précédé d'études sur l'histoire et les antiquités de ce pays*. St Petersburg, 1859.
Spasski, Arch. Num. Symp.	— G. Spasski, *Archaeological Numismatic Symposium*, Moscow, 1846.
Spasski, Cimmerian Bosphorus	— G. Spasski, *The Cimmerian Bosporus*, Moscow, 1848.
Stancomb	— *Sylloge Nummorum Graecorum, volume XI, The William Stancomb Collection of Coins of the Black Sea Region*, Oxford 2000.
Trésor	— *Trésor de Numismatique et de Glyptique ou Recueil Général de Medailles, Monnaies, Pierrres Gravées, Bas Reliefs etc.* Paris, 1849.
Waddington	— W.H. Waddington, 'Sur la chronologie des rois du Pont et du Bosphore et des princes d'Olbia', *Rev. Num.* 1886.
Zograph	— A.N. Zograph, *Ancient Coinage*. Part II, BAR. Supplementary Series 33. Oxford, 1933.

Collections

A	—	Ashmolean Museum, Oxford
Anapa -	—	Anapa Region Museum
ANS	—	The Collection of the American Numismatic Society
Baku	—	Pachomov Collection
Brussells	—	Bibliotheque Royale Albert 1. Cabinet des Medailles
Cop	—	The Royal Collection of Coins and Medals, Danish National Museum. Copenhagen
B	—	Staatliche Museen zu Berlin, Münzkabinett. Berlin
BM	—	British Museum
SNG BM	—	Sylloge Nummorum Graecorum, IX. British Museum, pt.1. Black Sea. London,1993
F	—	Fitzwilliam Museum, Cambridge
FMC	—	Fitzwilliam – Macmillan Collection
GE	—	Gosudarstvenny Ermitazh = State Hermitage, St Petersburg
GIM	—	Gosudarstvenny Istorichesky Musei = State Historical Museum, Moscow
GMII	—	Gosudarstvenny Musei Izobrazitelnykh Iskusstv im. A.S. Pushkina = Pushkin State Museum of Fine Arts, Moscow
Kerch	—	Kerch Historical-Archaeological Museum
Kr	—	Krasnodar Museum
Münich	—	Staatliche Münzsammlung, Münich
NM		Novorossijski Museum
OGAM	—	Odessa State Archaeological Museum
P	—	Bibliotheque Nationale, Paris
Vienna	—	Bundessammlung von Medaillen und Münzen, Geldzeichen
Yalta	—	Yalta Regional Museum

Auction Catalogues

Ars Classica, XI	—	Catalogue Monnaies Antique, Geneva, 1930
Ars Classica AG	—	Zürich. 27.02.1991
Boudin	—	Auction Boudin Collection, Paris, 1911
Cahn, 60	—	A.E. Cahn. Auction-Katalog, Fr. a. M., 1928
Cahn, 75	—	A.E. Cahn. Auctions-Katalog, 30.0.9. Fr. a. M., 1930
Egger 1904	—	Brüder Egger. Auctions-Katalog, Wien, 1904
Hamburger, 1930	—	Leo Hamburger. Auctions-Katalog. Alte Ausländische Sammlung. Fr. a. M., 1930
Helbing, 1928	—	O. Helbing, Nacht. Auctions-Katalog. München, 1928
Hess, 1931	—	A. Hess, Nacht. Auction-Katalog, 208. Griechische Münzen aus dem Besitz eines Ausländischen Museums. Fr. a. M., 1931
Hess, 1935	—	A. Hess. Auctions-Katalog. Monnaies Grecques. Lucerne, 1935
Hess, 1957	—	A. Hess-Leu. Auctions-Katalog, XVI, 1957
Hess, 1966	—	A. Hess-Leu. Auctions-Katalog, 136, 1966
Hess 1968	—	A. Hess-Leu. Auctions-Katalog, 1968. Lucerne, 17/18.04.1968
Hess 1970	—	A. Hess-Leu. Auctions-Katalog, 11979, Lucerne, 12/13.05 1970
Hess 1978	—	Auction Hess 247. 20.06.1978
Jameson	—	Collection R. Jameson. Monnaies grecques antiques. Paris, 1924
Kraus	—	Auction Kraus, 1928
Lanz Graz 1	—	Auction Lanz Graz, 1. München, 8/9.12.1972
Lanz Graz 28	—	Auction Lanz Graz, 28. München, 07.05.1984
Lanz Graz 42	—	Auction Lanz Graz, 42. München, 23.11.1987
Leu	—	Auction Bank Leu, 29.03.1959
Leu	—	Auction Bank Leu. Num. Fine Art. The Garret Col., 1984
Myers	—	Auction R. Myers, N.Y., 13.09.1976
Naville, V	—	Catalogue de monnaies Grecques Antiques. Geneva, 1923
Naville, XII	—	Catalogue de monnaies Grecques, XII. Geneva, 1926
Naville, XIII	—	Catalogue de monnaies Grecques, XIII. Geneva, 1928
Naville, XV	—	Catalogue de monnaies Grecques, XV. Geneva, 1930
Naville, XVI	—	Catalogue de monnaies Grecques, XVI. Geneva, 1933
Naville, XVII	—	Catalogue de monnaies Grecques, XVII. Geneva, 1934
Ratto	—	Auction Ratto. Lugano, 1927
Roux	—	Auction Collection Roux. Monnaies Grecques. Paris, 31.5.1911
Schlessinger. 11	—	F. Schlessinger. Münz-Auction, 11, Sammlung aus ausländischen Museumbesitz. Berlin, 1934
Sotheby 1844	—	Sotheby 29.07.1844 (Thomas Collection)
Sotheby 1898	—	Sotheby 20.01.1898
Soheby 1909	—	Sotheby-Wilkinson-Hodge 20.04.1909
Sotheby	—	Sotheby, Wilkinson, Hodge. Catalogue of rare coins. The property of Russian Nobleman. Auction 2-3 June 1924
Sotheby 1990	—	Sotheby's Addendum 19.06.1990
Schulman	—	Auction Schulman. 26.09.1906
Sternberg	—	Auction F. Sternberg, XX, Zurich 20.04.1988

BIBLIOGRAPHY

A guide to the Principal Coins of the Greeks. London, 1959.
Alföldi A. 'Hasta-Summa Imperii', *AJA*, 63.1, (1959), pp.1-27.
Anohin V.A. *Coinage of Bosporus*. Kiev, 1986.
Baldus H.R. 'Die Daten von Münzprägung und Tod der Königin Pythodoris von Pontos', *Chiron*, 13, (1983) pp.537-43.
Bertier de la Garde A.L. 'The Coins of the Kings of the Cimmerian Bosporus Determined by Monograms', *ZOOID*, 29 (1910) pp.117-232.
Bertier de la Garde A.L. 'Materials for the Metrological Study of the Monetary Standards of the Ancient Greek Cities and Kings of Sarmatia and Tauris', *Num. Sbornik*, II. Moscow, 1913, pp.19-134.
Bibliotheque Nationale Cabinet de Médailles. Guide. Paris, 1929.
Blavatskaya T.V. 'Aspurgus and Bosporus in AD 15', *SA*, 3 (1965) pp.26-37.
Blavatskaya T.V. 'Inscriptions of King Aspurgos', *SA*, 2 (1965) pp.197-209.
Blavatski V.D. *Panticapaeum*. Moscow, 1964.
Blavatski V.D. 'On Rhescuporis I', *SA* 4, (1976) pp.56-62.
Boltunova A.I. 'On the inscription IOSPE, II, 400', *VDI* (1954).
British Museum Catalogue. Roman Coins I. London, 1965.
Burachkov P.O. *General Catalogue of the Coins Pertaining to the Hellenic Colonies which existed in Antiquity on the Northern Coast of the Black Sea*. Odessa, 1884.
Burnett A., Amandry M., Ripollès P. *Roman Provincial Coinage*. Vol. I, London-Paris, 1992.
Callataÿ F. de. 'La Politique monétaire de Mithridate VI, roi du Pont', *Rythmes de la production monetaire de l'antiquite à nos jours*, Louvain-La-Neuve (1987) pp.55-66.
Callataÿ F. de. *L'histoire des guerres Mithridatiques vue par les monnaies*. Louvain-La-Neuve, 1997.
Cohen H. *Description historique des monnaies, médailles imperiales* I. Paris, 1880.
Comstock M., Vermeule C. *Museum of Fine Arts Boston. Greek Coins 1950-1963*. Boston, 1964.
Crawford M.H. *Roman Republican Coin Hoards*. London, 1959.
Dewing A.S. *Collection of Greek Coins*. New York, 1985.
Eckhel J. *Doctrina NumorumVeterum* Vindobone II.
Forrer L. *The Collection of Weber*. Vol. III, part I, 1926.
Friedländer J, von Sallet A. *Das königlishe Münzkabinett*. Berlin, 1877.
Frolova N.A. 'The Copper Coins of Cotys I as a Historical Source', *SA*, 3 (1976) pp.103-11.
Frolova N.A. 'The Coinage of Cotys I, the Son of Aspurgus (45-68 AD)', *Numismaticheski Sbornik GIM*, 5 (1977).
Frolova N.A. 'On the Period of the Reigns of Gepaepyris and of Mithridates III', *VDI* (1977) 3, pp.156-74 = *Essays on the Northern Black Sea Region Numismatics*, Odessa 1995, pp.110-127.
Frolova N.A. 'On the Period of the Reign of Dynamis', *SA*, 2 (1978) pp.49-61 = *Essays on the Northern Black Sea Region Numismatics*, Odessa 1995, pp.41-67.
Frolova N.A. 'Dating the Beginning of Aspurgus's Reign in Bosporus', *VDI* (1979) 1, pp.139-47 = *Essays on the Northern Black Sea Region Numismatics*, Odessa 1995, pp.68-90.
Frolova N.A. 'Coins from the Excavation of Gorgippia 1973-1977', *Symposium "*Gorgippia*"*. Krasnodar, 1980.
Frolova N.A. 'Coins from the Excavation of Phanagoria 1962-1975', *VDI* (1981) 1, pp.100-113.
Frolova N.A. 'The Gold Coins of Mithradates III (338 Be = AD 41) from the Collection of GIM', *VDI* (1986) 4, pp.54-9.
Frolova N.A. 'Bronze Coins of the Bosporus from the End of the 1st Century B.C. to the Beginning of the 1st Century AD', *NE*, 15 (1989) pp.3-18.
Frolova N.A. *Essay on the Northern Black Sea Region's Numismatics*, Odessa, 1995.
Frolova N.A. 'Towards a History of Bosporan Coinage (1st Century BC)', *Ancient Civilizations*, 3, (1996), pp.151-68.
Frolova N.A. 'The History of the Bosporan Coinage of the Ist B.C.', *Numismaticheski Sbornik GIM*, 13 (1998).
Frolova N.A., Karyskovskij P.O., Delfs M., 'Zur Chronologie der Herrschaft Asanders im Bosporos', *Chiron*, 23 (1993) pp.63-81.
Frolova N.A., Maslennikov A.A. 'The Hoard of the 1st Century B.C. Bosporan Coins Found at the Ancient Settlement of "Poljanka" (the Kerch Region)', *Symposium The Exact Sciences Methods in Archaeology*, St Petersburg, 1994.
Frolova N.A., Shelov D.B. 'Coins from excavations at Kepoi 1958-1963', *NSph*, 3 (1965) pp.168-93.

Gajdukevich V.F. *The Kingdom of Bosporus*, Moscow-Leningrad, 1949.
Gajdukevich V.F. *Das Bosporanishe Reich*, Berlin-Amsterdam, 1971.
Giel Chr. *Kleine Beiträge zur antiken Numismatik Südrusslands*. Moscow, 1886.
Giel Chr. *The Bosporan Coins with Monograms BAE, BAM and* , Odessa, 1888, pp.104-13.
Giel Chr. 'A New Acquisition in My Collection', *ZRAO*, 5 (1892) pp.343-60
Giel Ch.Ch. 'Description of Coins Which Have Entered My Collection in 1892 and 1893', *ZRAO*, 7 1895, separate offprint.
Golenko K.V. 'The Date of the Bronze Coins of Panticapaeum. The End of 3rd – 2nd Century B.C.', *KSIIMK*, 58 (1955) pp.131-8.
Golenko K.V. 'On the History of the Currency of the Bosporus in the 1st Cent. B.C.', *NE*, 2 (1960) pp.20-44.
Golenko K.V. 'Bronze Coins of the Time of Pharnaces', *NE*, 2 (1960).
Golenko K.V. 'Bronze Coins of the Cities of Pontos and Paphlagonia in the Time of Mithridates Eupator among Bosporan Finds', *Palestina Symposium 11 (74)*. Moscow-Leningrad, 1964 pp. 58-73.
Golenko K.V. 'The Phantalovski Hoard of Bosporan Didrachms of the 1st Cent. B.C.', *VDI* (1965) 4, pp.141-58.
Golenko K.V. 'Staters from New Acquisitions of GMII', *GMII Reports*, Vol.II. Moscow, 1965.
Golenko K.V. 'Two Coins of Panticapaeum of the 2nd Century. B.C.', *NE*, 5 (1965) pp.56-61.
Golenko K.V. 'The Bronze Coins of Pontus in the Bosporus', *Klio*, 46 (1965) pp.307-22.
Golenko K.V. 'On the Coinage of the Anonymous Bosporan Obols', *NSph*, 3 (1965) pp.41-9.
Golenko K.V. 'Imitations of the Bronze Coins of Pontos and Paphlagonia in the Time of Mithradates Eupator', *VDI* (1966) 3, pp.142-9.
Golenko K.V. 'Some Silver Coins of Panticapaeum During the 2nd Cent. B.C. with Traces of Overstriking', *NE*, 7 (1968) pp.37-42.
Golenko K.V., 'Anonymous Pontic Copper', *VDI* (1969), pp.130-54.
Golenko K.V. 'The Kerch Hoard of Bosporan Coins of the 1st Century. B.C.', *NE*, 9 (1971) pp.38-50.
Golenko K.V. 'The Staters of Asander in the 20 years of his Reign', *NE*, 10 (1972) pp.103-6.
Golenko K.V. 'Coins from the Excavations at Nymphaeum 1939-1970', *NE*, 11 (1974) pp.61-93.
Golenko K.V., Karyszkowski P.O. 'The Gold Coinage of King Pharnaces of the Bosporus', *NC*, 12 (1972) pp.25-38.
Golenko K.V., Shelov D.B. 'Coins from the Excavation of Panticapaeum 1945-1961', *NSph*, 1 (1963) pp.3-65.
Golubzova E.S. *The Northern Black Sea Littoral Between the Centuries BC and AD*. Moscow, 1951.
Heinen H. 'Mithridates von Pergamon und Caesars bosporanische Pläne', *Studien zur Geschichte und Kultur des Altertums*. Band 8. Paderborn-München-Wien-Zürich, 1994, pp.63-79.
Henning R. 'Die Regierungszeit des Asander', *Berliner Münzblätter* 1908.
Imhoof-Blumer F. *Portraitköpfe auf antiken Münzen hellenischer und hellenisierter Völker*. Leipzig, 1885.
Imhoof-Blumer F. 'Die Kupferprägung de mithradatischen Reiches und andere Münzen des Pontos und Paphlagoniens', NZ (1912) pp.169-92.
Ireland S. Frolova N. 'Two Hoards of Bosporan Coins of the 1st Century B.C. from the Ancient Settlement of Poljanka (Kerch)', *Hermathena* 166 (1999) pp.31-43.
Karyszkovski P.O. 'Bosporus and Rome in the First Century AD in the Light of Numismatic Data', *VDI* (1953) 3, pp.179-90
Karyszkovski P.O., Frolova N.A. 'On the History of the Reign of Asander in Bosporus 49/48 – 21/20 B.C.', *The Ancient Black Sea Littora*. Odessa, 1989.
Karyszkovski P.O., Frolova N.A. 'The Reign of Asander in the Bosporus Based on Numismatic Data', (Symposium) *The Black Sea Littoral*, I. Odessa, 1990, pp.89-112.
Karyszkovski P.O., Frolova N.A. 'On the History of the Reign of Asander in Bosporus', *Numismatic Investigations of the History of South-east Europe*, Kishinev, 1990, pp.89-100.
Kazamanova L.N. *Einführung in die antike Numismatik*. Moskow, 1969.
Klawans Z.N. *An Outline of Ancient Greek Coins*. Wisconsin, 1959.
Köhler H.K.E., 'Suite des médailles d'Asander, d'abord de archont, après roi du Bosphore Cimmérien'. *Serapis*, II, 1850.
Köhne B.V., *Description of the Museum of Prince V.V. Kochubei and Investigation into the History and Numismatics of the Greek Colonies in Russia and Likewise of the Kingdoms of Pontos and of the Cimmerian Bosporus*, Vol. I. St Petersburg, 1857.

Krushkol Yu.S. 'Coins with Monograms from the Patraeus Hoard of 1950 (Taman)', *VDI* (1952) 3, pp. 139-46.
Krushkol Yu.S. 'The Patraeus Hoard of 1950', *KSIIMK*, 66 (1956) pp.116-17.
Kunisz A.A. *Recherches sur le monnayage et la circulation monétaire sous le règne d'August*, Waszawa, 1976.
Latyshev V.V. *ΠΟΝΤΙΚΑ*, St Petersburg., 1909.
Leschhorn W. *Antike Ären.Zeitrechnung, Politik und Geschichte im Schwarzmeerraum und in Kleinasien, nördlich des Tauros*. Stuttgart, 1993.
Mashkin N.A. *The Principate of Augustus*. Moscow-Leningrad, 1949.
Meynerts. *Revue Belge de Numismatique*, 3, 1847.
McGing B.C. *The Foreign Policy of Mithridates VI Eupator King of Pontus*. Leiden, 1986.
Mionnet T.E. *Description des médailles antiques grecques et romaines. Suppl. II*, Paris, 1822.
Mionnet T.E. *Description des médailles antiques grecques et romaines. Suppl. IV*, Paris, 1829.
Minns H.E. *Scythians and Greeks*. Cambridge, 1913.
Molev E.A. 'The Power of Mithridates in the Bosporus', Symposium, *The Ancient World and Archaeology*, II. Saratov, 1974.
Molev E.A. *Mithridates Eupator*, Saratov, 1976.
Molev E.A. *Bosporus in the Hellenistic Period*, Nizhnij Novgorod, 1994.
Molev E.A. *The Ruler of Pontos*, Nizhnij Novgorod, 1995.
Nanteuil H. de. *Collection des monnaies grecques*. Paris, 1925.
Nawotka K. 'The Attitude Towards Rome in the Political Propaganda of the Bosporan Monarchs', *Latomus*, 48 (1989) pp.326-38.
Nawotka K. 'Asander of the Bosporus: His Coinage and Chronology', *AJN*, 3-4 (1991-2) pp.21-48.
Novichenkova N.G. 'A New Find of the Yalta Archaeology Expedition in 1983', *Symposium of the Institute of Archaeology of Russia*, March, 1984.
Oreshnikov A.V. *Zur Münzkunde des Cimmerischen Bosporus*. Moscow, 1883.
Oreshnikov A.V. *The Cimmerian Bosporus in the Period of the Spartocids from Inscriptions and Royal Coins*, Moscow, 1884.
Oreshnikov A.V. *Catalogue of the Collection of Antiquities of Count A.S. Uvarov*. VII. Moscow, 1887.
Oreshnikov A.V. 'Pythodoris and her Origin in the Pontic Kingdom', *IAK*, 34 (1902).
Oreshnikov A.V. *Excusus on the Ancient Numismatics of the Black Sea Coast*, Moscow, 1914.
Perl G. 'The Eras of the Bithynian, Pontic and Bosporan Kingdoms', *VDI* (1969) 3, pp.39-69.
Pink K. 'Die Triumviri Monetales unter Augustus', *NZ*, 71 (1946).
Podshivalov A. *Beschreiburg der unedirten und wenig bekannnten Münzen von Sarmatia Europaea, Chersonesus Taurica und Bosphorus Cimmerius aus der Sammlung A.M. Podshiwalov*, Moscow, 1882.
Podshiwalov A.M. *The Moscow Public and Rumijanzev Museum. Numismatic Department*, Vol.I, Moscow, 1884.
Podshiwalov A.M. 'The Coins of the Cimmerian Bosporos Kings of the Spartocid and Achaemenid Dynasties', *ZOOID*, 15 (1889) pp.112-40.
Price M.J. 'Mithridates VI Eupator, Dionysus and the Coinages of the Black Sea', *NC*, 1968, pp.1-12.
Price M.J. *Sylloge Nummorum Graecorum IX, British Museum. The Black Sea*. London, 1993.
Reinach Th. *Trois Royaumes de l'Asie Mineure*. Paris, 1888.
Robinson-Walker-Jenkins, Carson. *The British Museum Quarterly*. XV, 1952.
Rostovtzeff M.I. 'A Bronze Bust of the Bosporan Queen Dynamis and the History of the Bosporus at the Time of Augustus', *Drevnosti*, 25 (1916), pp.1-31.
Rostovtzeff M.I. 'The Bronze Coins of Dynamis and Aspurgos', *ITUAK*, 54 (1918).
Rostovtzeff M.I. 'Queen Dynamis of Bosporus', *JHS*, 39 (1919) pp.82-109.
Rostovtzeff M.I. *Iranians and Greeks in the South of Russia*. Oxford, 1922.
Rostovtzeff M. *Scythien und der Bosporus*. Band II. Wiederentdeckte Kapzel und verwandtes. Stuttgart, 1993.
Sallet A. von. *Beiträge zur Geschihchte und Numismatik der Könige des Cimmerischen Bosporus und des Pontus*, Berlin, 1886.
Sestini D. *Lettere e dissertazione numismatiche VI*. Berlin, 1804.
Sestini D. *Descrizione delle medaglie antiche del Museo Hedervariano del Bosfore Cimmerio fino all'Armenia Romana*. P. II. Firenze, 1838.
Shelov D.B. *The Ancient World in the Northern Black Sea Littoral*, Moscow, 1956.

Shelov D.B. 'Materials toward the History of Monetary Circulation in the Cities of the Bosporus in the VIth – Ist Cent B.C.' *NE*, 5 (1965) pp.31-50.
Shelov D.B. *Tanais and the Lower Don in the IIIrd – Ist cent. B.C.*, Moscow, 1970.
Shelov D.B. 'Machares as King of Bosporus', *VDI* (1978), 1, pp. 55-72.
Shelov D.B. *Coinage of the Bosporus VI-II Centuries BC*, Oxford, 1978.
Shelov D.B. 'On the History of the Currency of the Bronze Coins of Panticapaeum', Symposium, *Numismatics of the North Black Sea Coast*. Kiev, 1982, pp.45-50.
Shelov D.B. 'The Cities of the Black Sea Coast and Mithridates Eupator', *VDI* (1983) 2, pp.40-58.
Sherwin-White A.N. *Roman Foreign Policy in the East 168 B.C. to AD I*. London, 1984.
Sibirskij – Prince A. Sibirskij. *Catalogue des médailles du Bosphore Cimmérien précédé d'études sur l'histoire et les anantiquités de ce pays*. St Petersburg, 1859.
Spasski G. *Archaeological Numismatic Symposium*, Moscow, 1846.
Spasski G. *The Cimmerian Bosporus*, Moscow, 1848.
Trésor de Numismatique et de Glyptique ou Recueil Général de Medailles, Monnaies, Pierrres Gravées, Bas Reliefs etc. Paris, 1849
Terlecki W. *Die Münzen des Kimmerischen Bosporus unter Rheskouporis // Zapiski Numizmaticzne*. Lwów, 1928.
Vinogradov Y.G. 'Epigraphy in the USSR' *Archeologysk Vestnik // Acta Archaeologica*, XXXI, 1980.
Von Aulock H. *Sylloge Nummorum Graecorum, Deutschland. Sammlung v. Aulock*, Berlin 1957-68.
Wroth W. Pontos, *Bithynia, Paphlagonia and the Kingdom of Bosporus* // BMC, L, 1889.
Waddington W.H. 'Sur la chronologie des rois du Pont et du Bosphore et des princes d'Olba', *RevNum* 1886.
Waddington W.H., Babelon E., Reinach Th., *Recueil général des monnaies grecques d'Asie Mineure*. T.1, fasc.1. Paris, 1925.
Yazenko I.V. 'The Queen Gepaepyris Dish from Scythian Neapolis', *Istoriko-Archaeologicheski Sbornik*. Moscow, 1962.
Zaginailo A.G. 'The Gold Bosporan Coin of Mithridates Eupator', *KSJGAM*, 1963.
Zhebelev S.A. 'The Last Pairisades and the Scythian Uprising in the Bosporus', *The Northern Black Sea Littoral*. Moscow-Leningrad, 1953.
Zograph A.N. *Ancient Coins*, *MIA*, 1951.
Zograph A.N. *Ancient Coinage*. Part II, BAR. Supplementary Series 33. Oxford, 1977.

Monograms

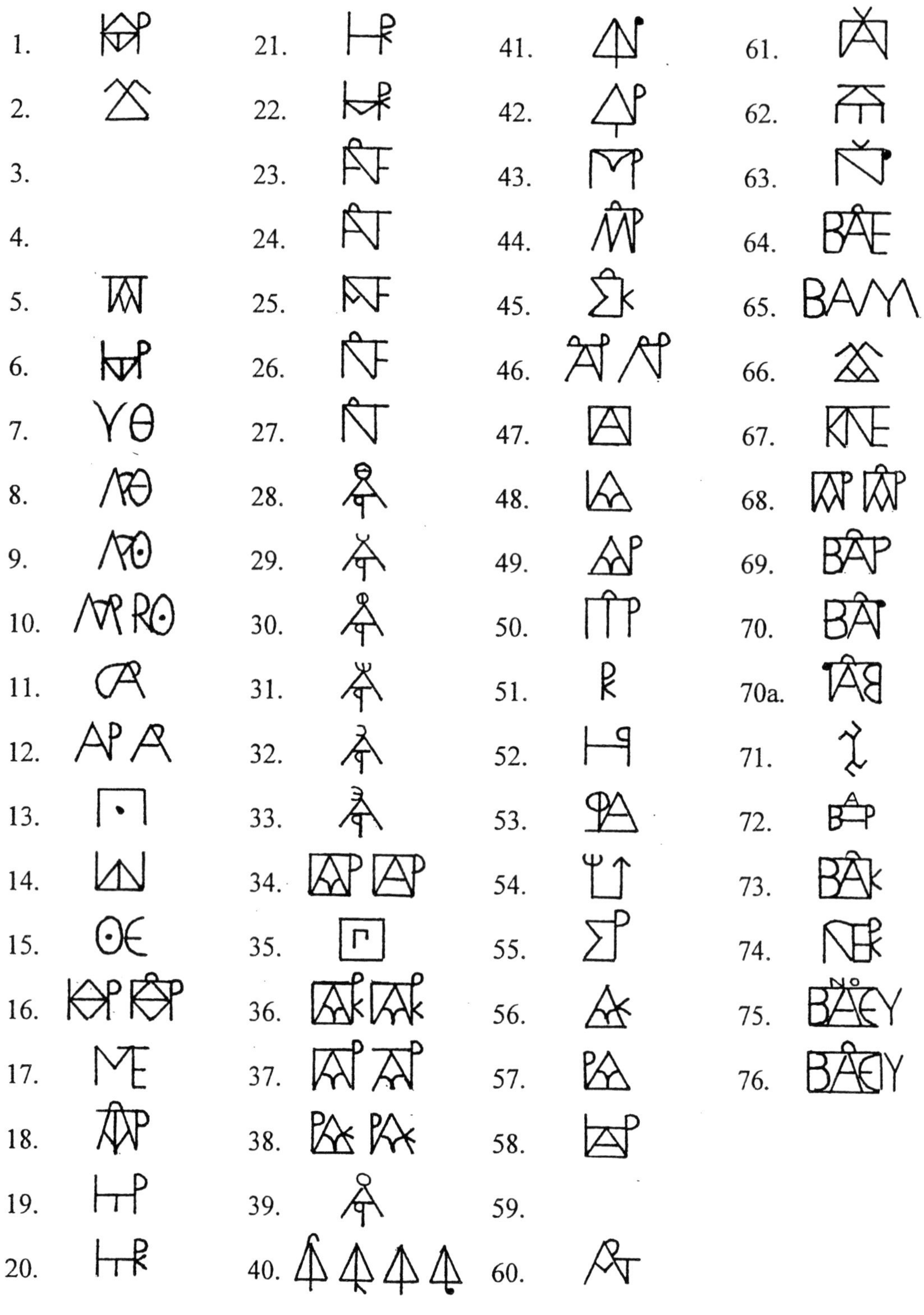

Monograms 3, 4, and 59 have been omitted since they duplicate others or were found not to exist.

Plate I

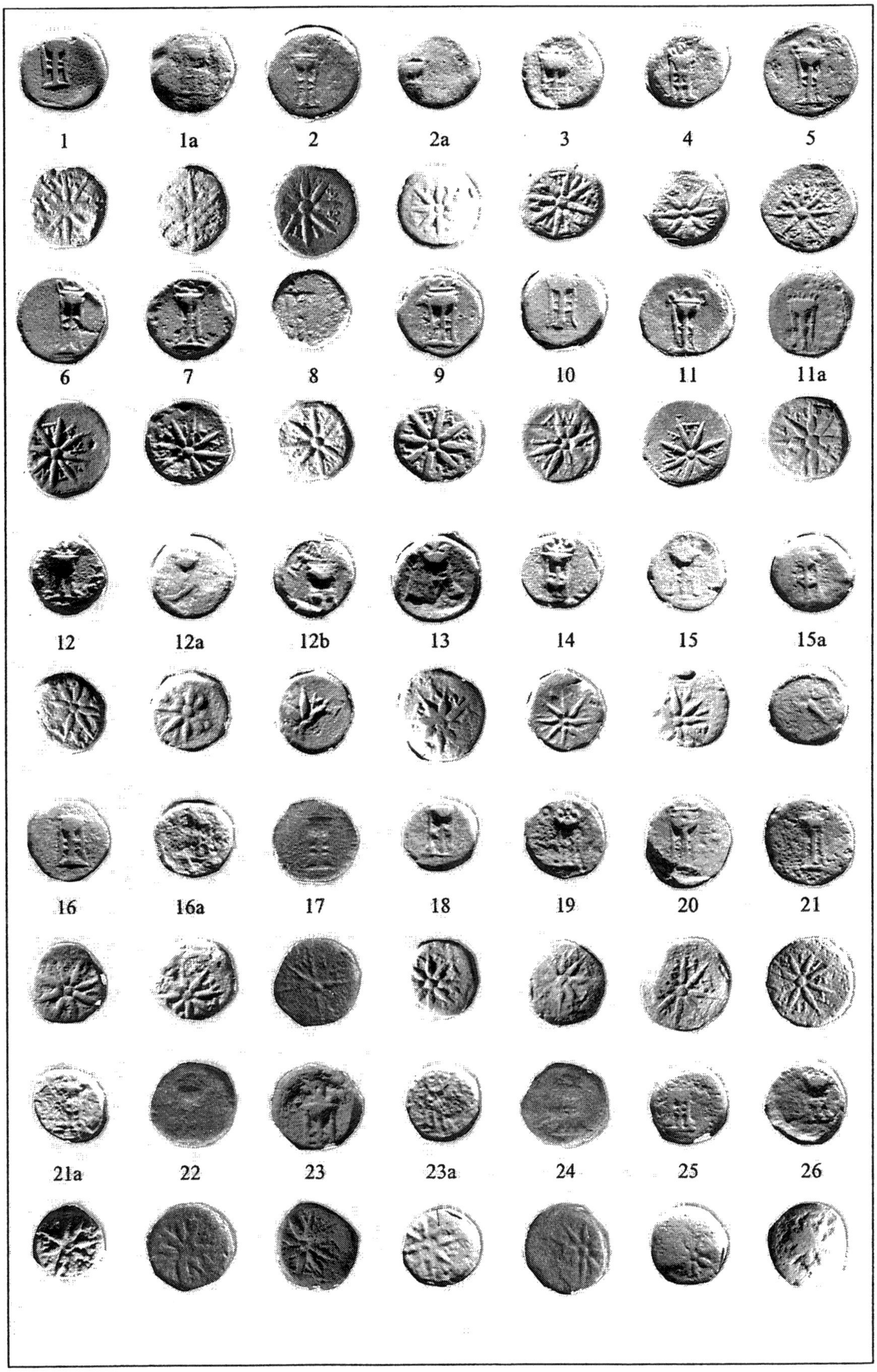
1 1a 2 2a 3 4 5
6 7 8 9 10 11 11a
12 12a 12b 13 14 15 15a
16 16a 17 18 19 20 21
21a 22 23 23a 24 25 26

Plate II

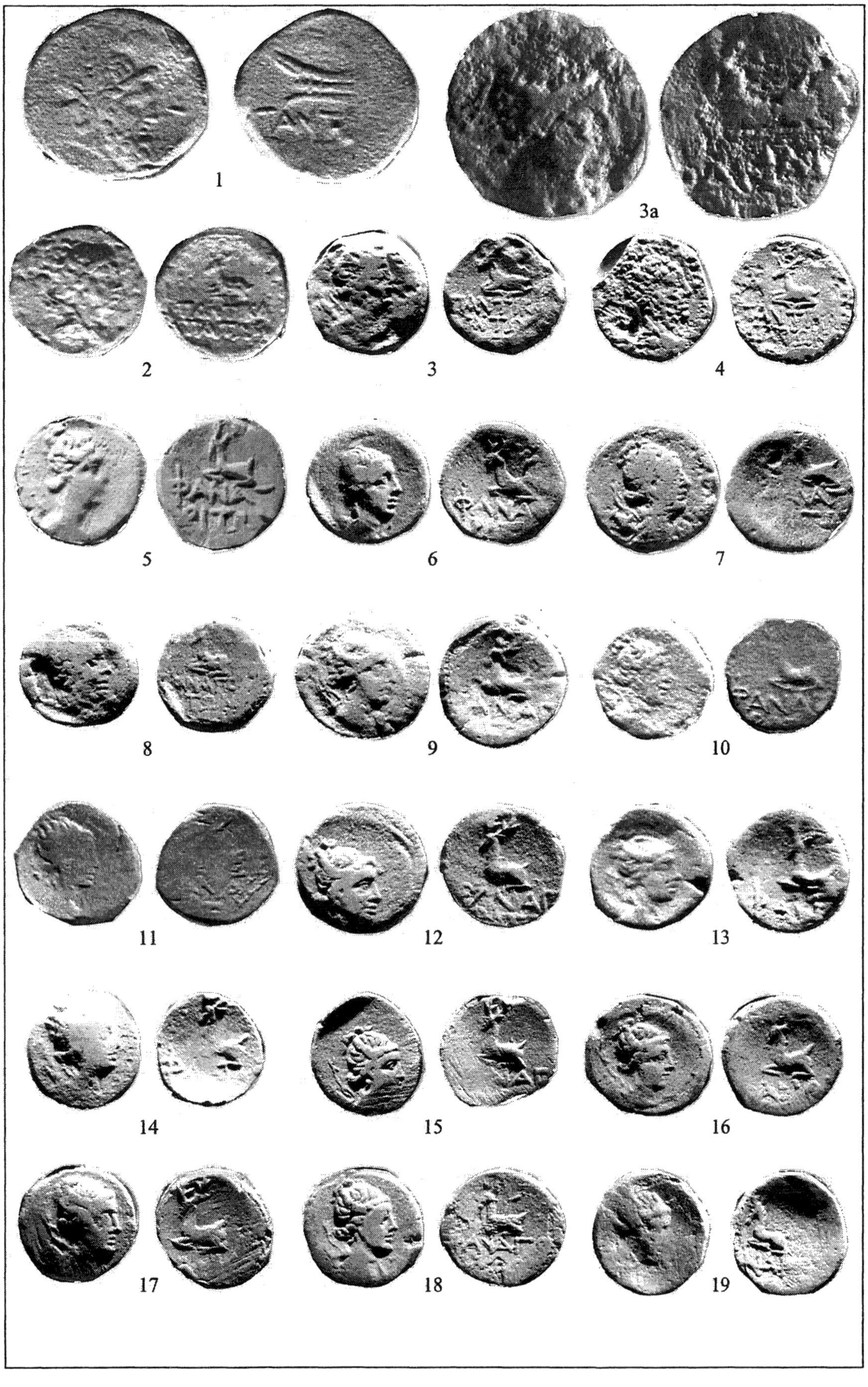

1

2

3

4

5

6

7

8

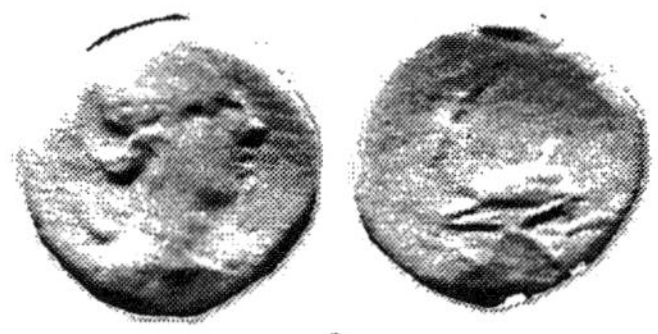
9

10

11

12

13

14

15

16

17

18

19

20

21

Plate IV

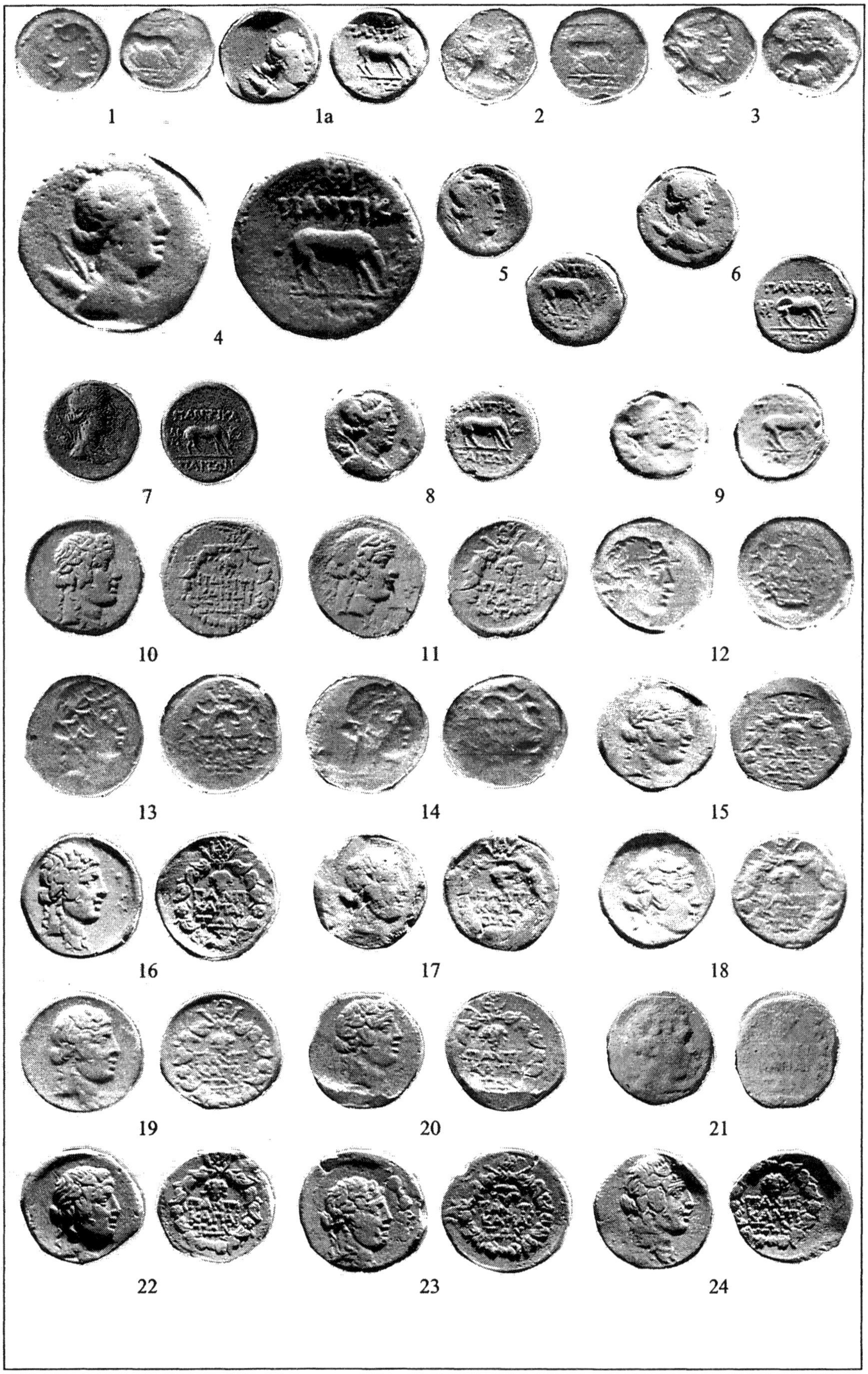

Plate V

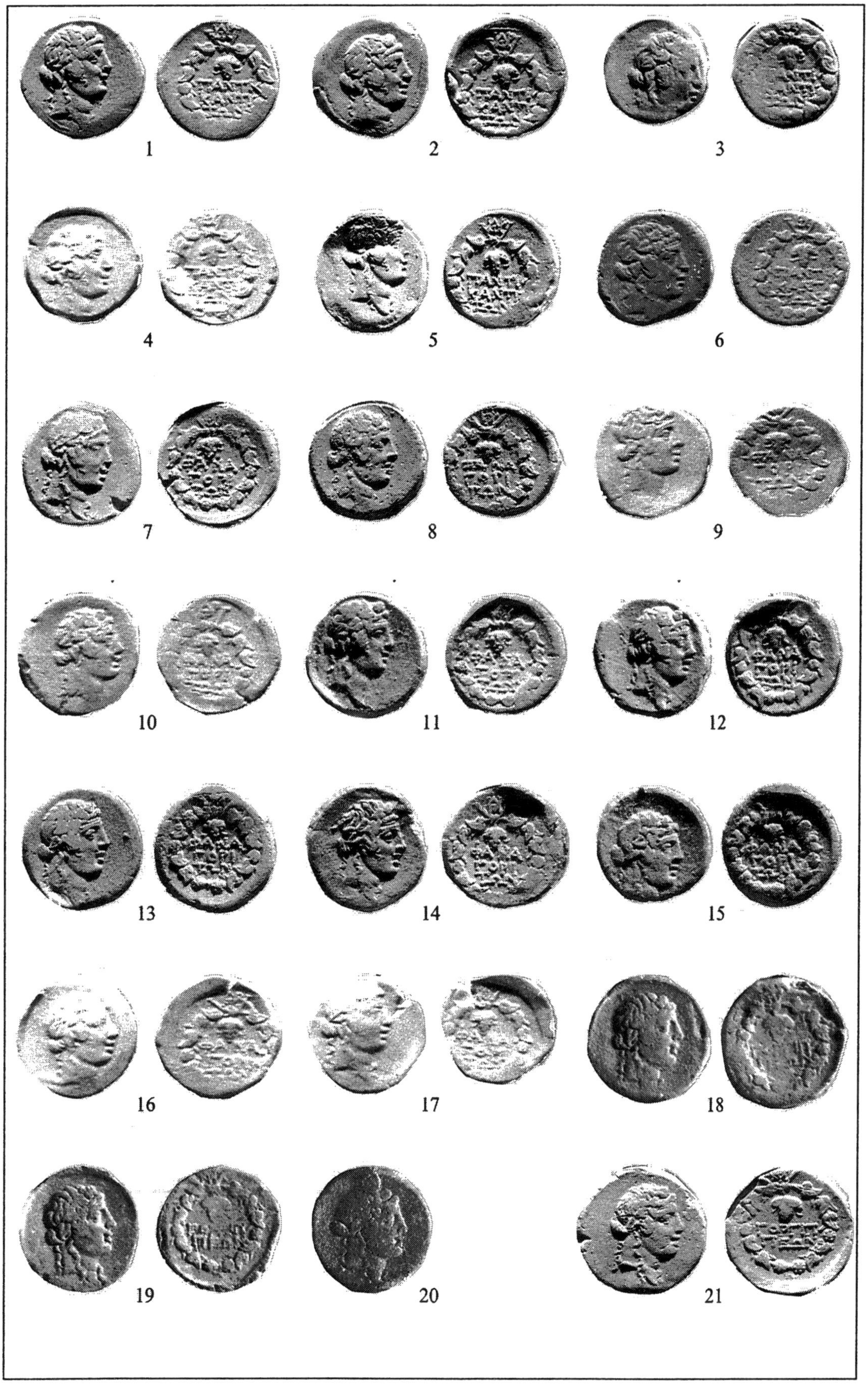

1 2 3 4 5 6 7 8 9 10 11 12 13 14 15 16 17 18 19 20 21

Plate VI

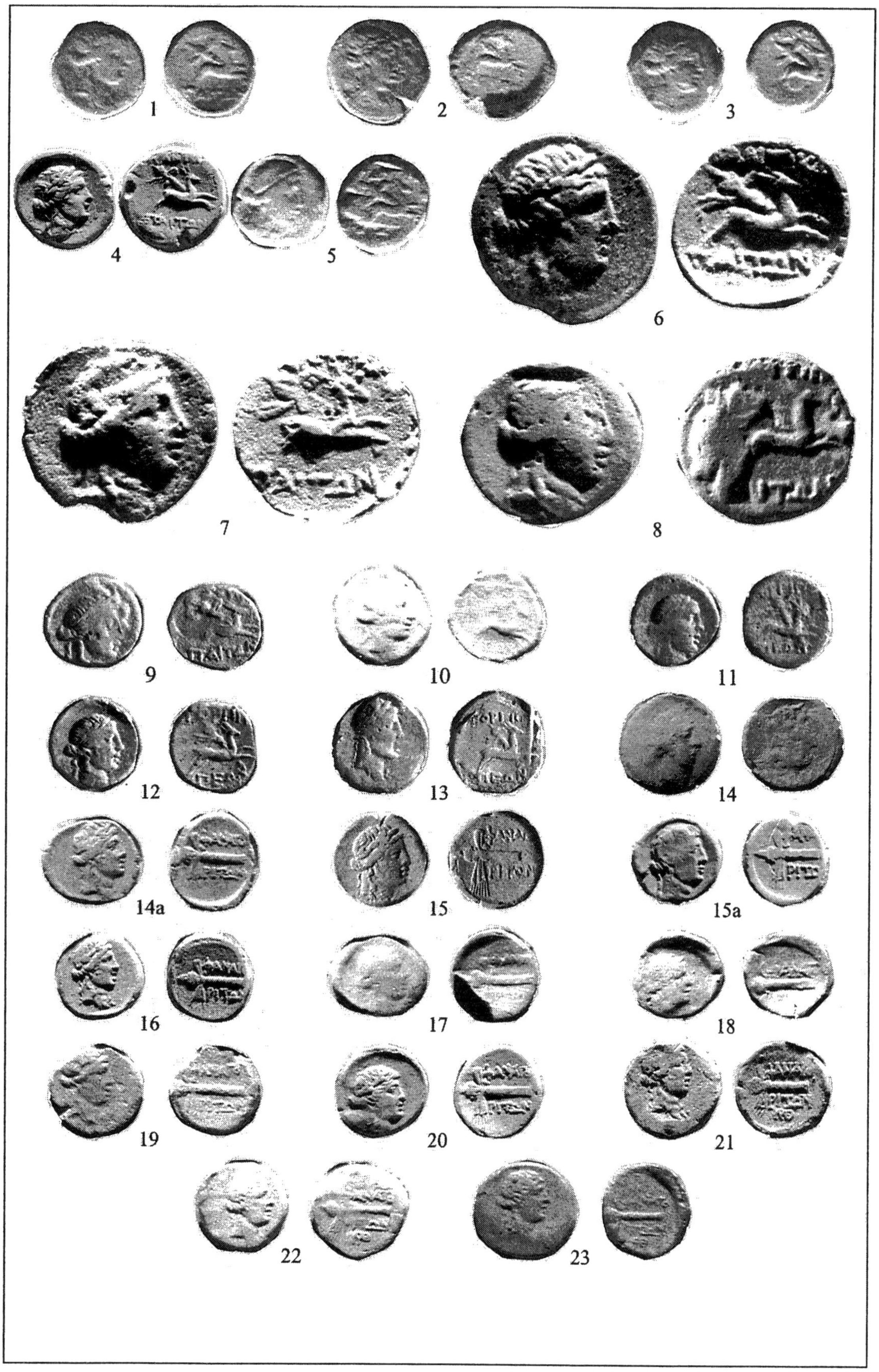

Plate VII

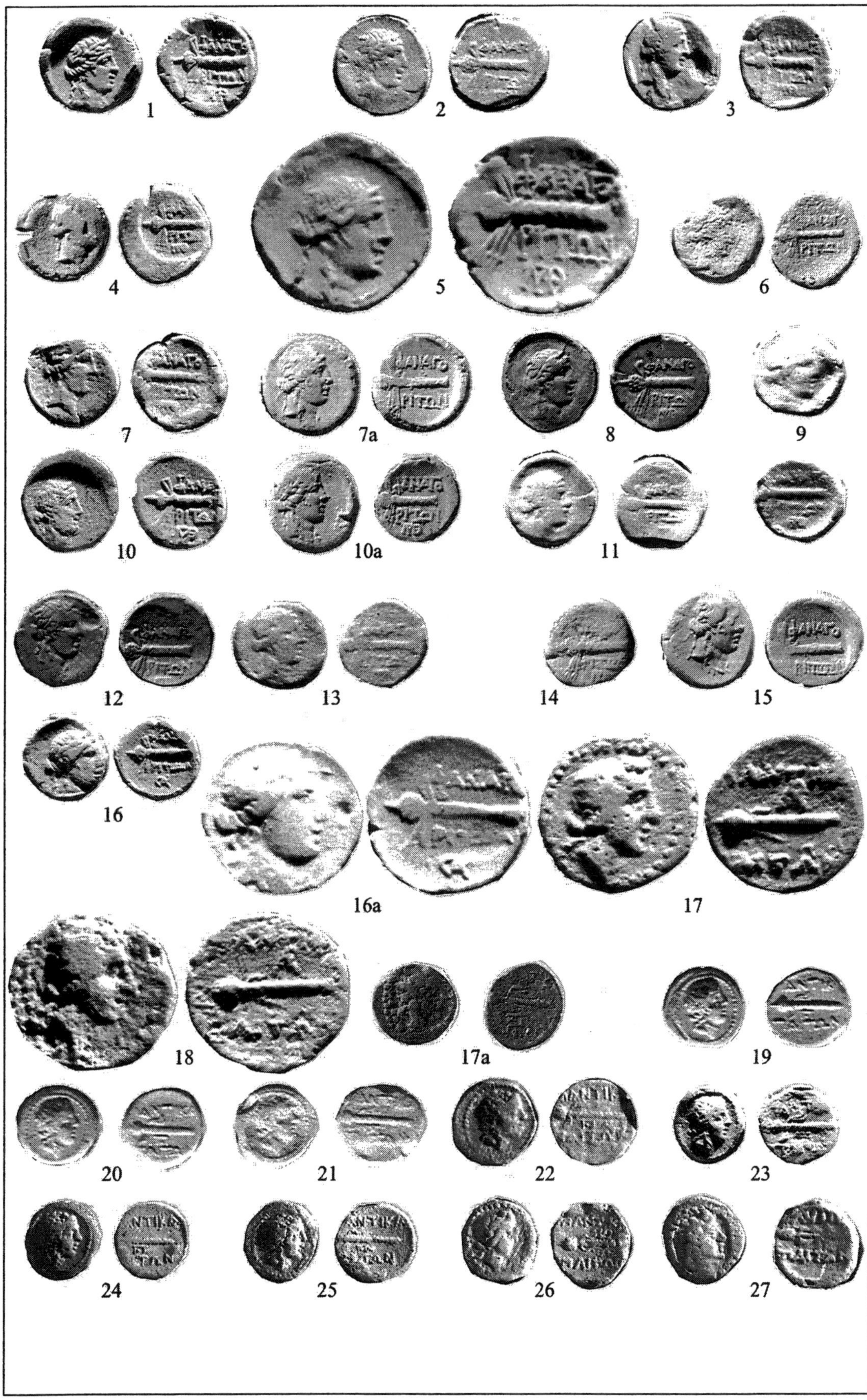
1
2
3
4
5
6
7
7a
8
9
10
10a
11
12
13
14
15
16
16a
17
18
17a
19
20
21
22
23
24
25
26
27

Plate VIII

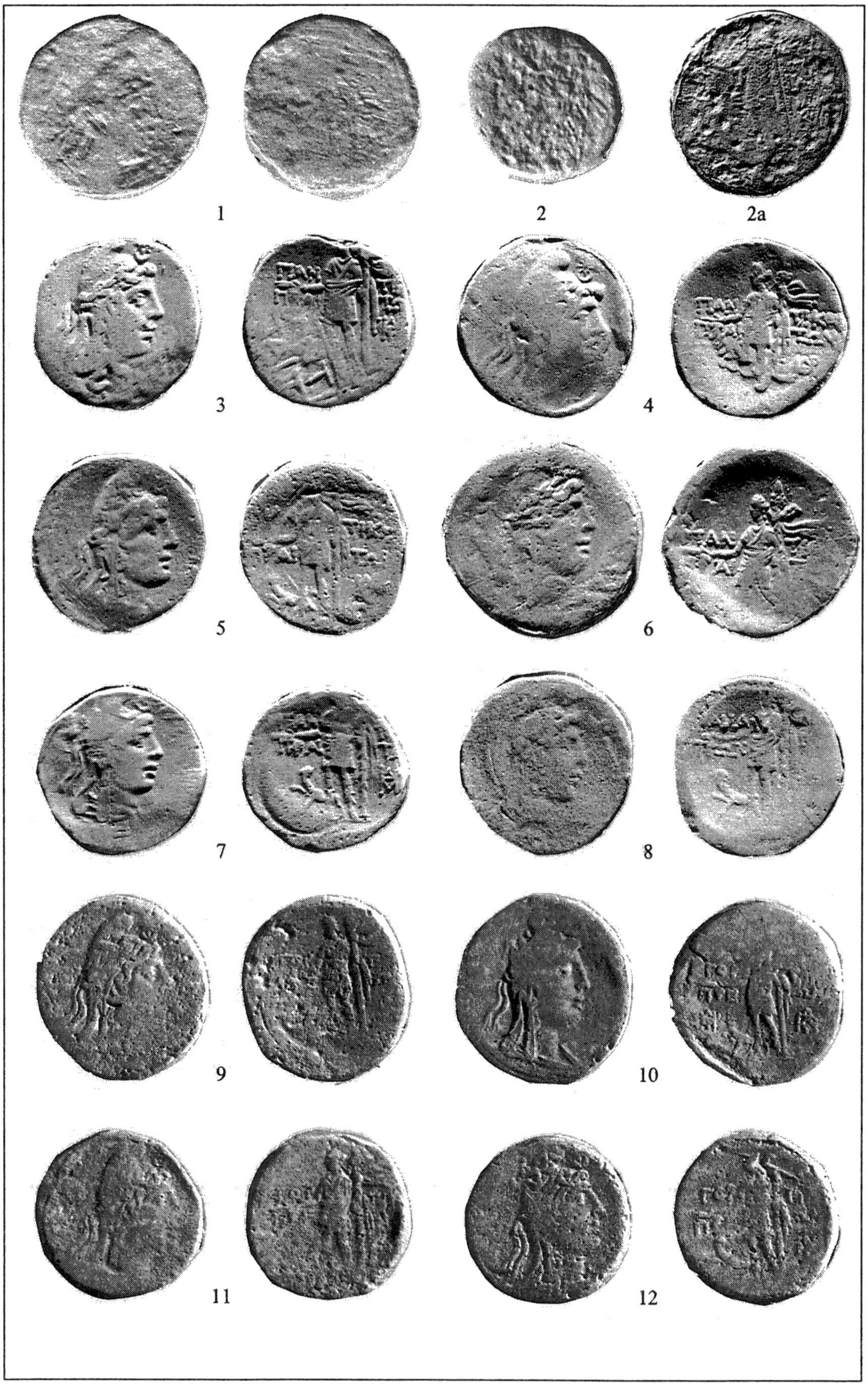

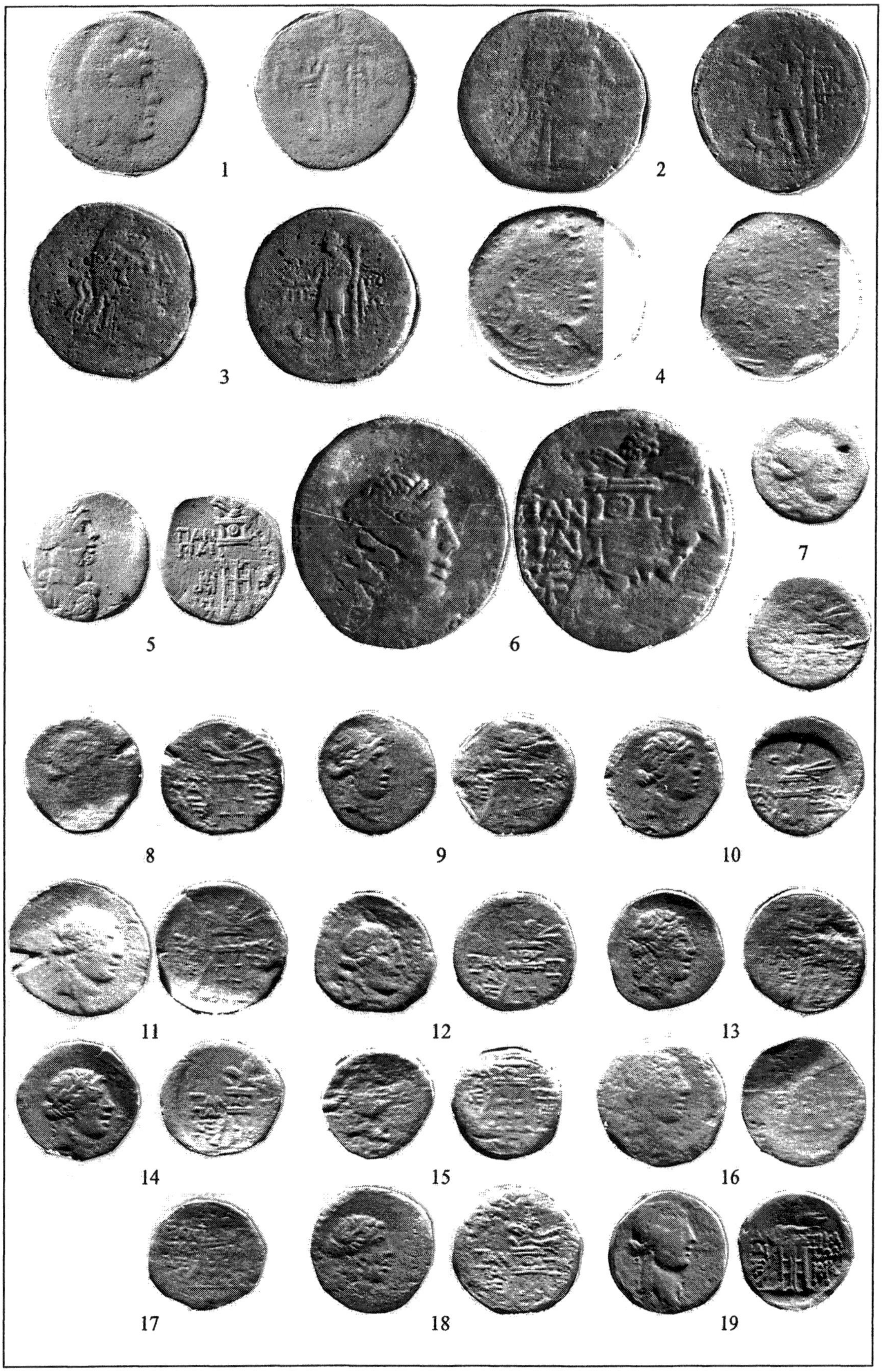
1
2
3
4
5
6
7
8
9
10
11
12
13
14
15
16
17
18
19

Plate X

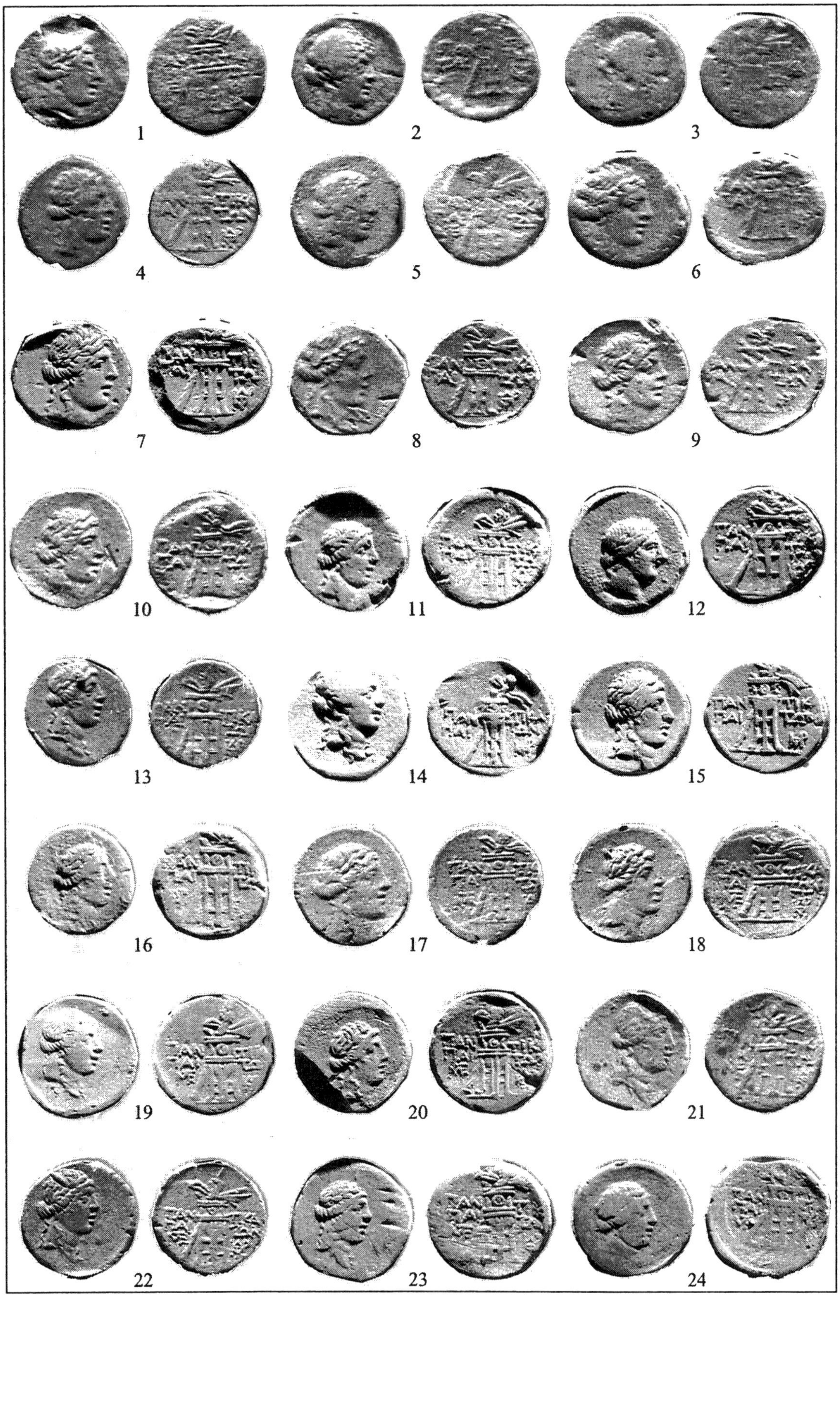

Plate XI

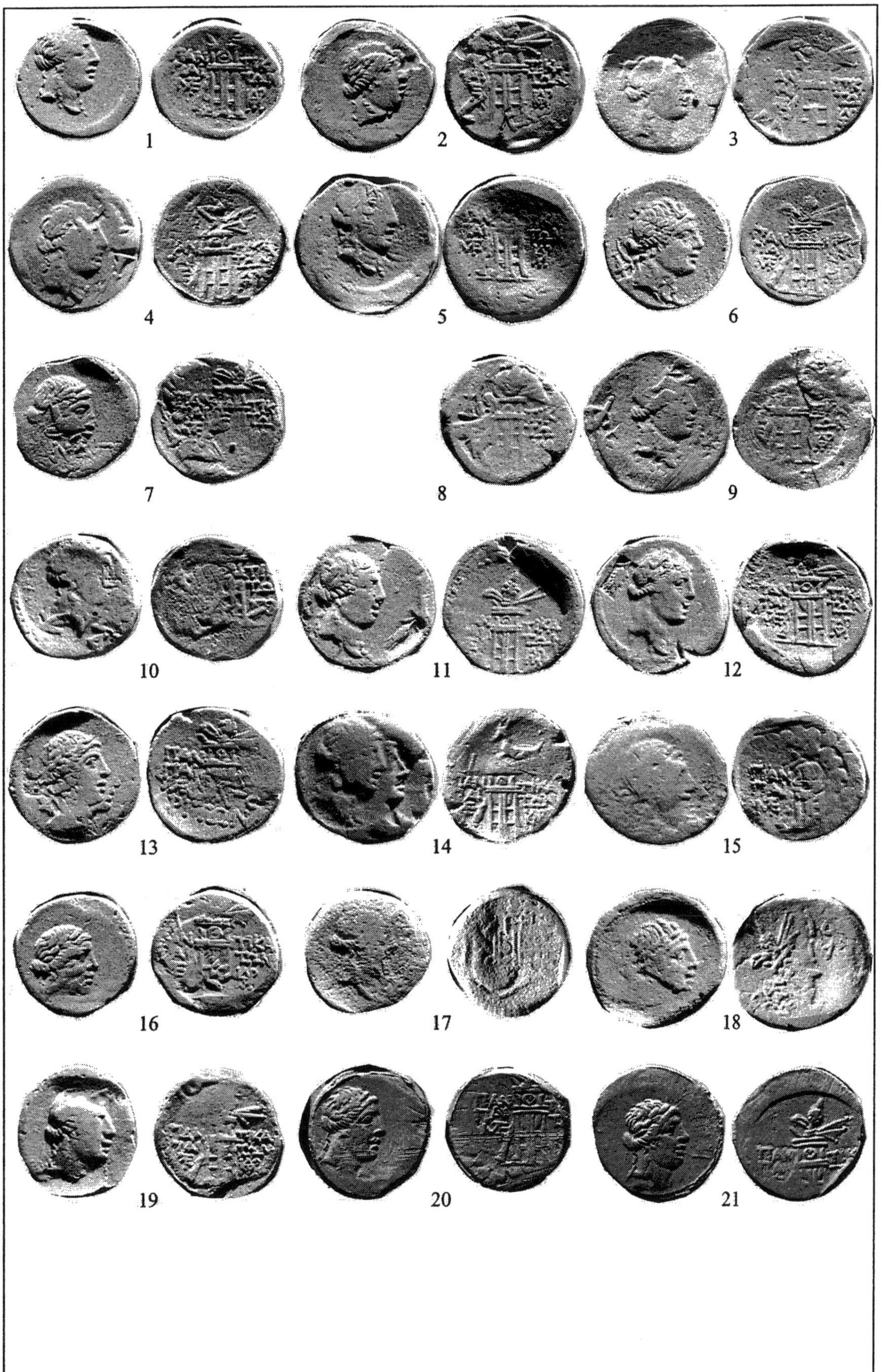

Plate XII

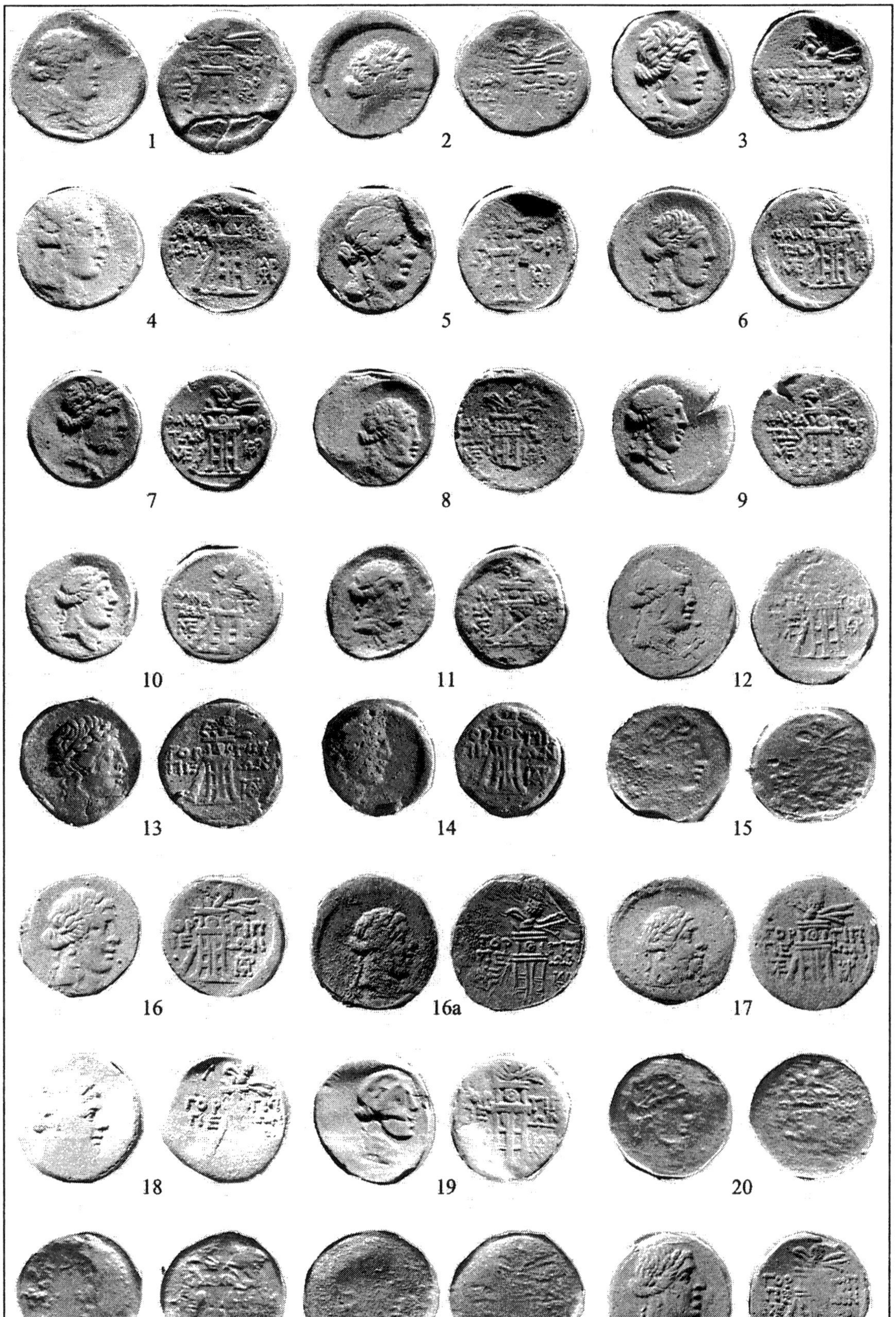

1
2
3
4
5
5a
6
7
8
9
10
11
12
13
14
15
15a
16
17
12a

Plate XIV

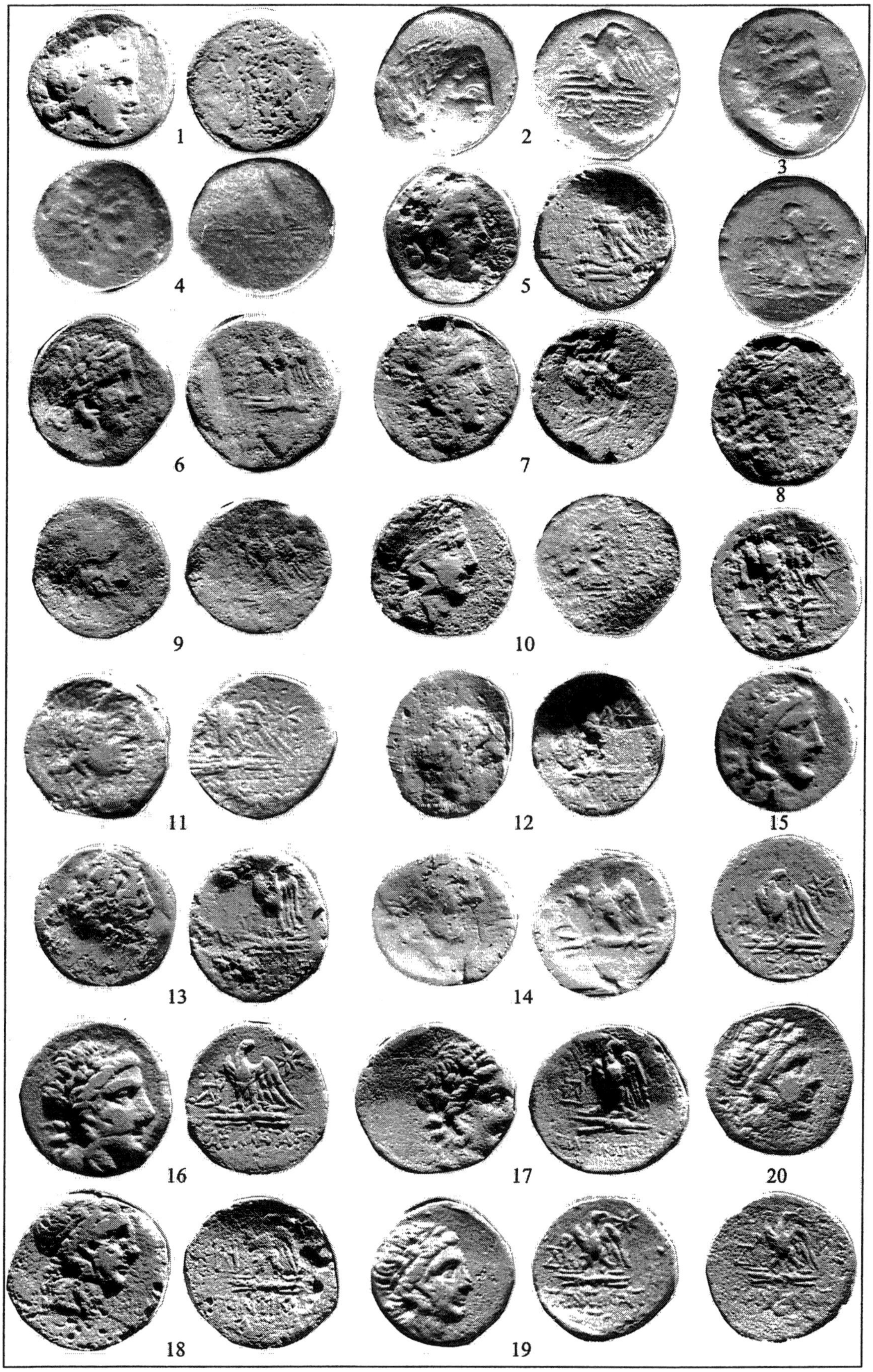

Plate XVI

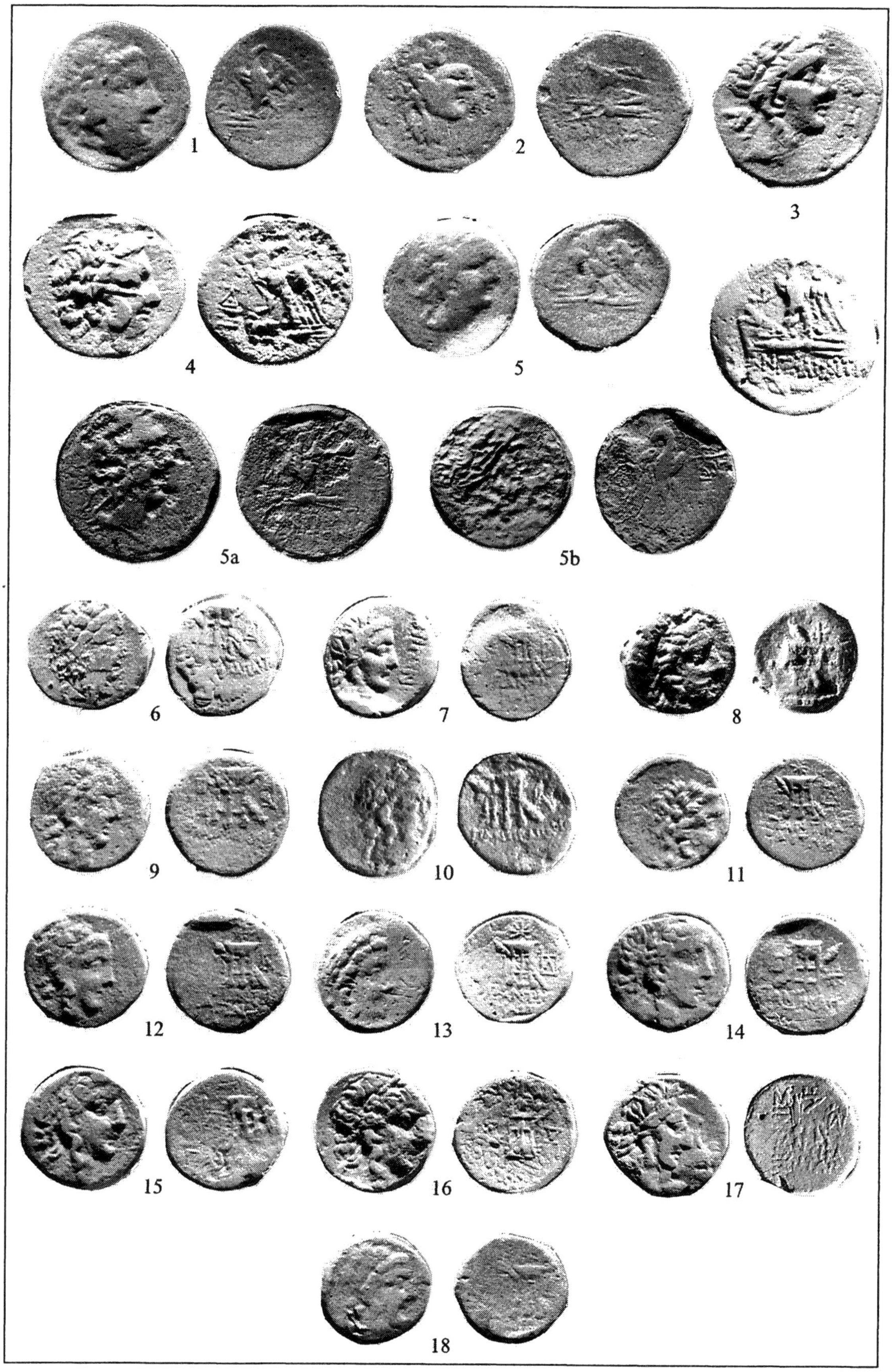

Plate XVII

1

2

3

4

5

6

7

8

9

10

11

12

13

14

15

16

Plate XVIII

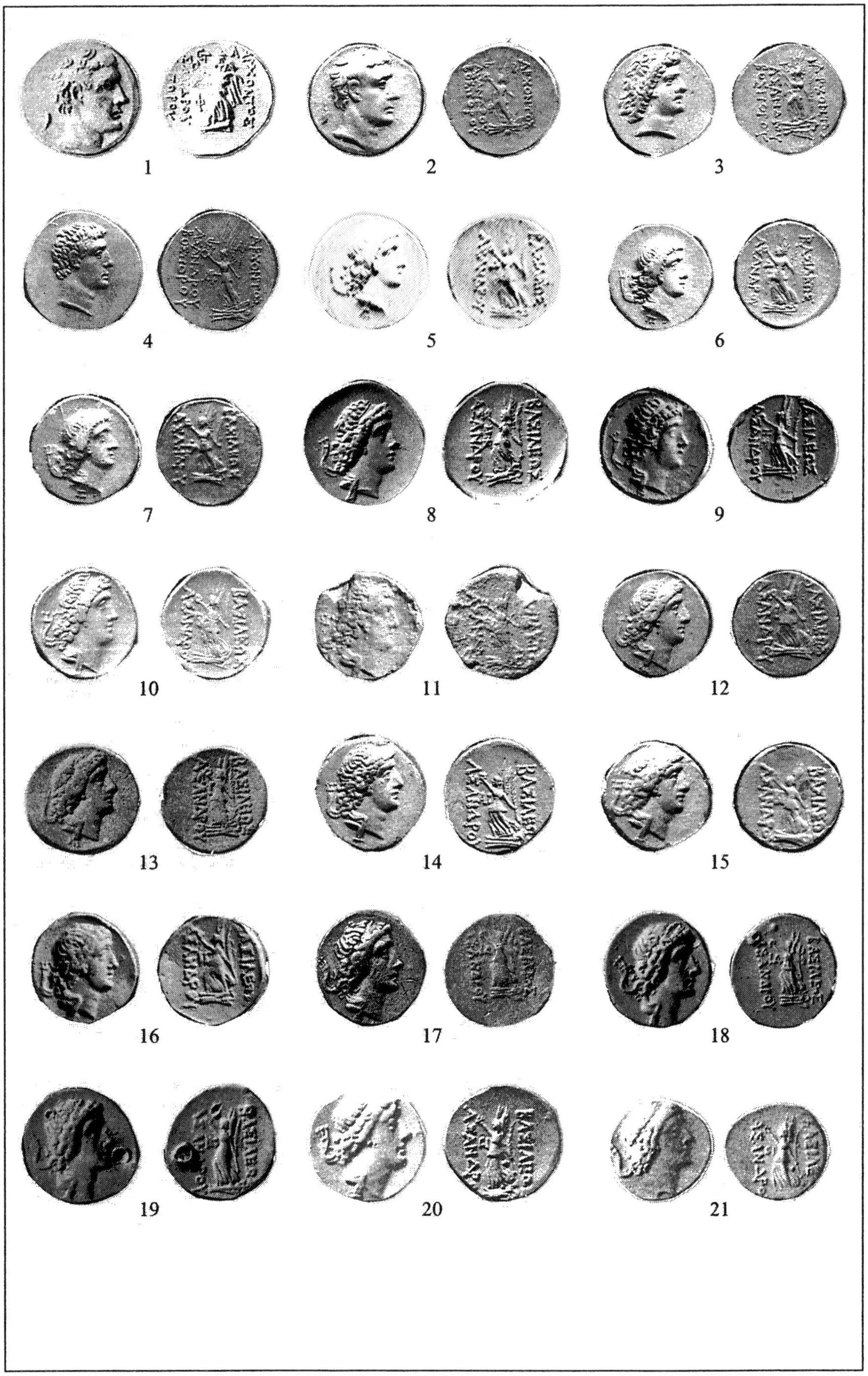

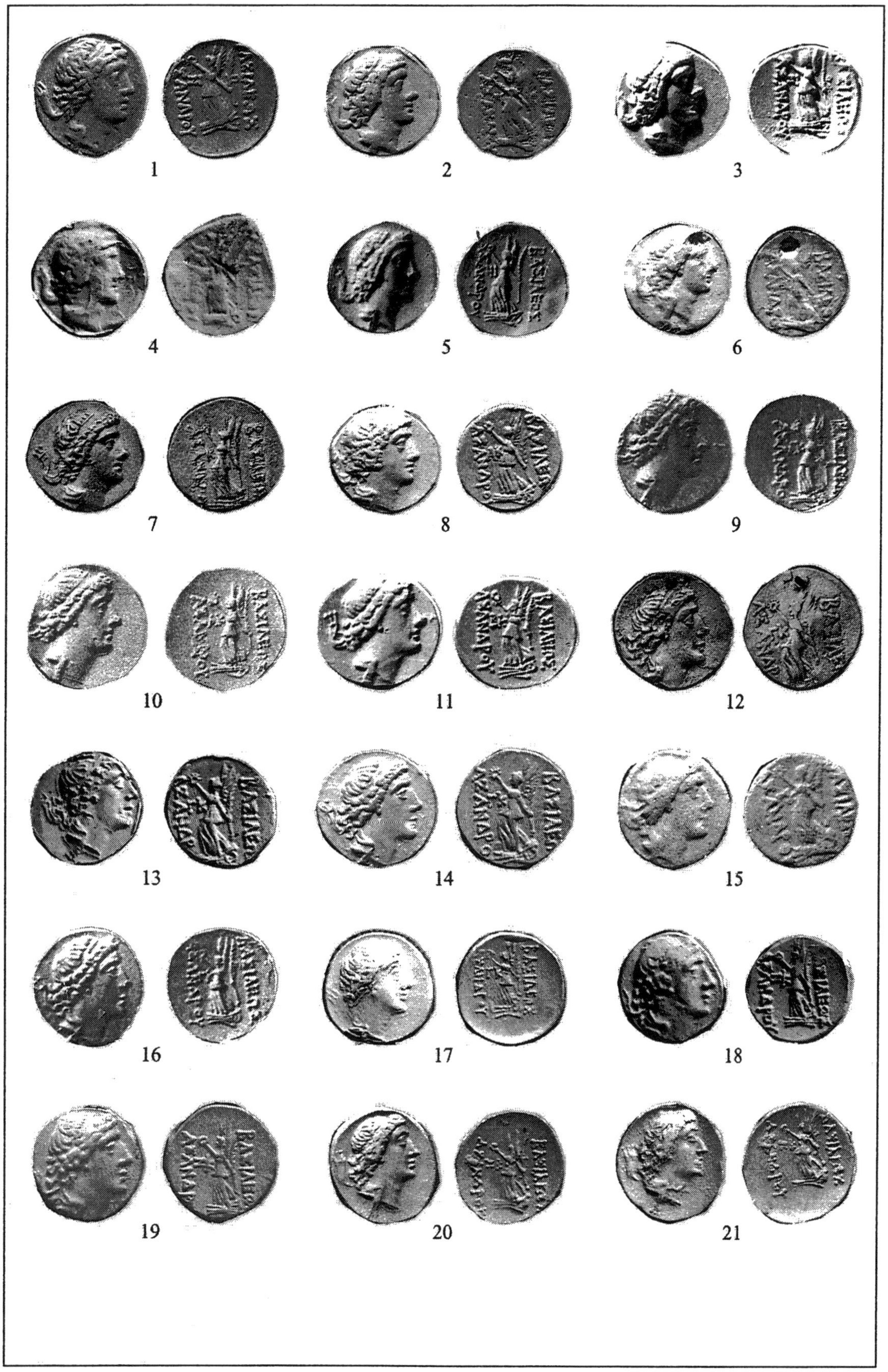
1
2
3
4
5
6
7
8
9
10
11
12
13
14
15
16
17
18
19
20
21

Plate XX

1

2

3

4

4a

5

6

7

8

9

10

11

12

13

14

15

16

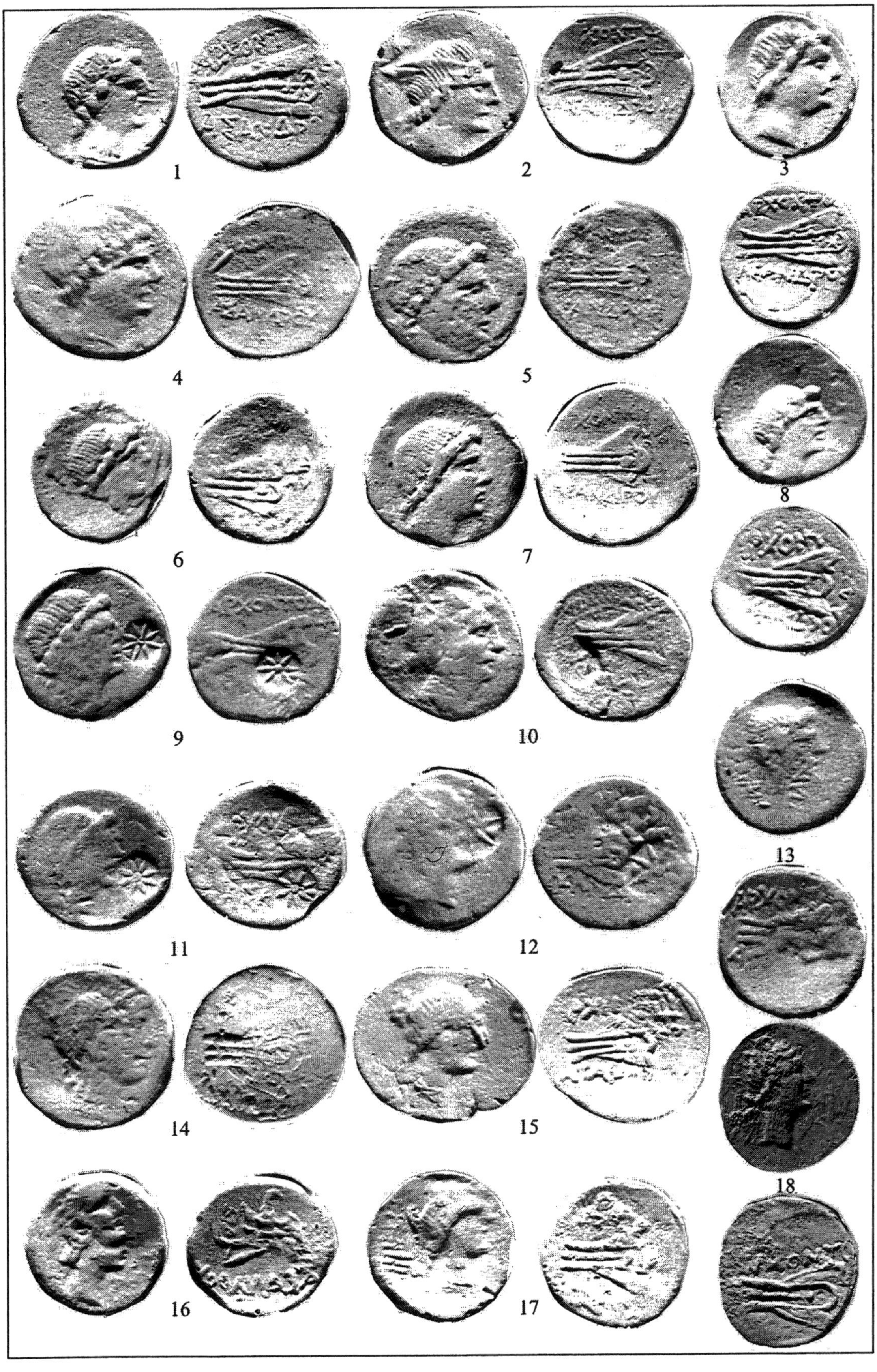

Plate XXII

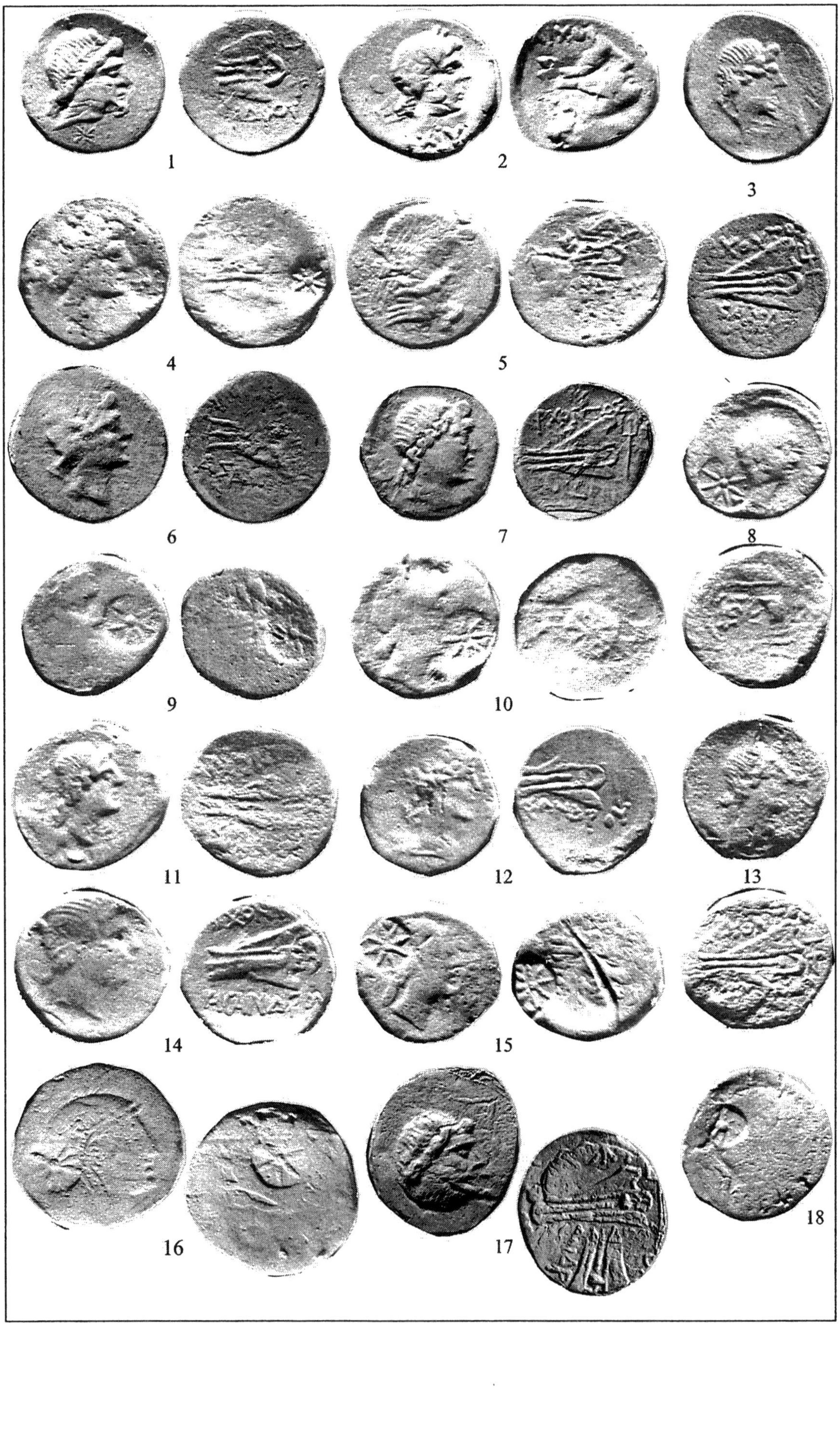

Plate XXIII

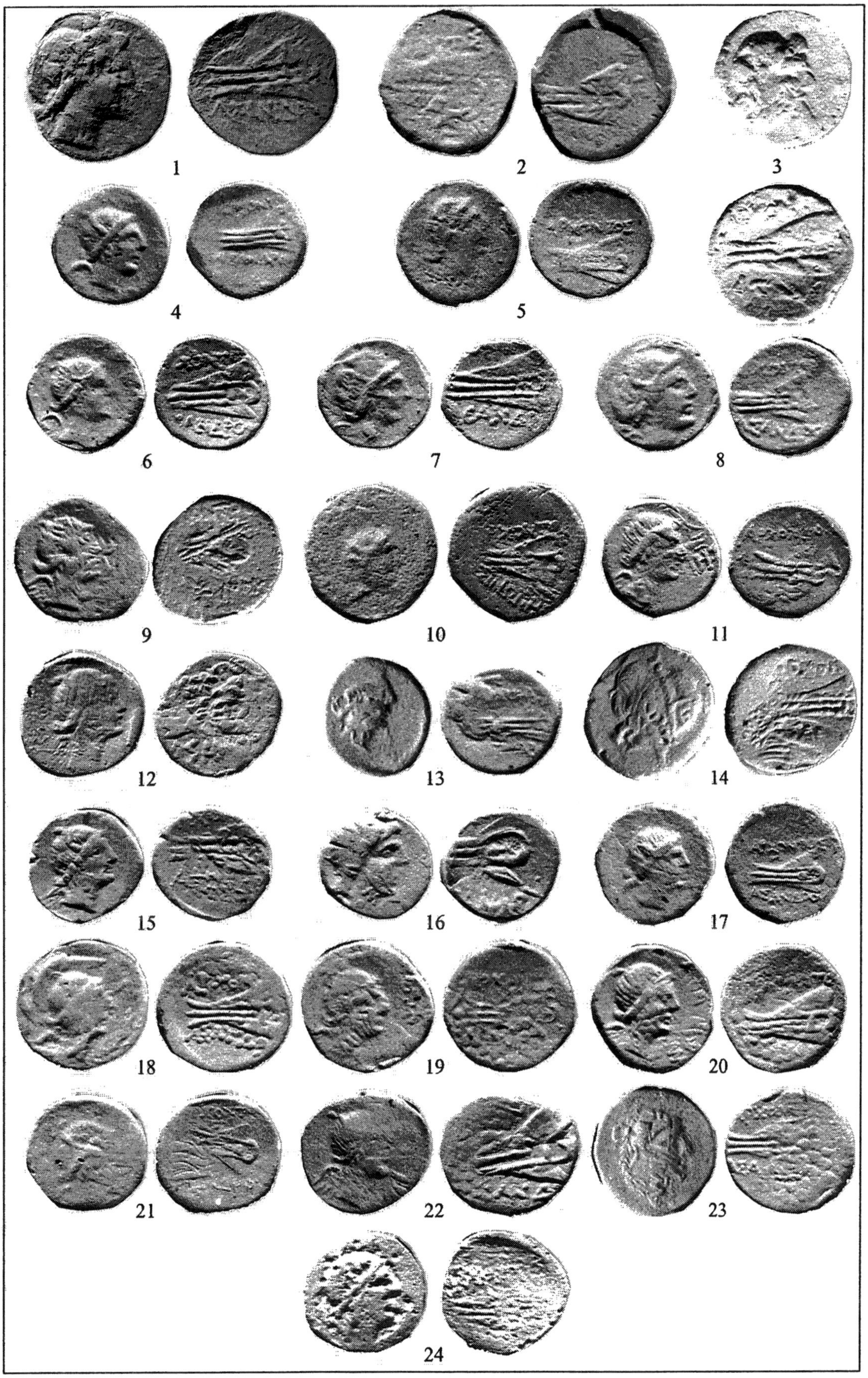

Plate XXIV

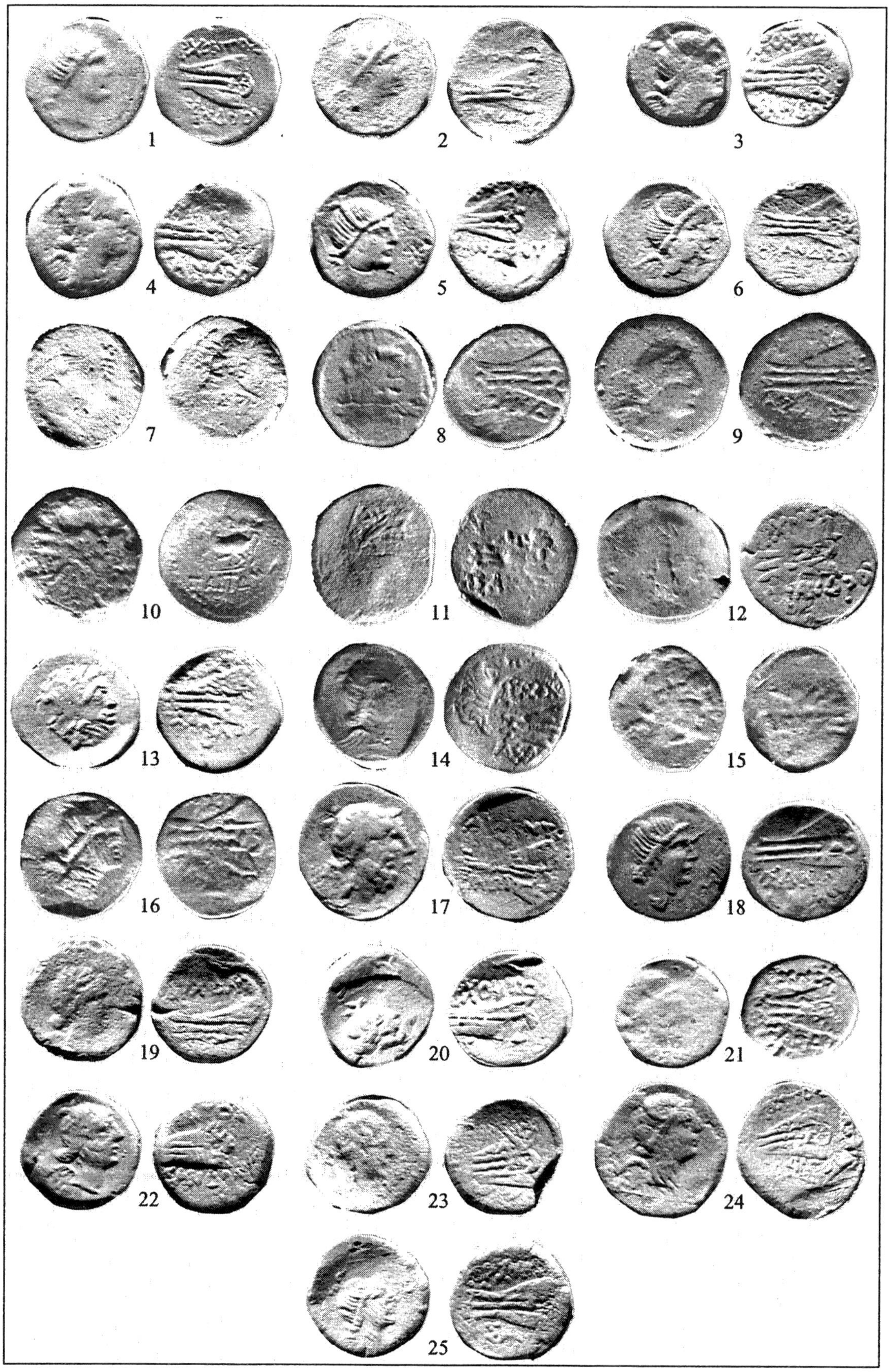

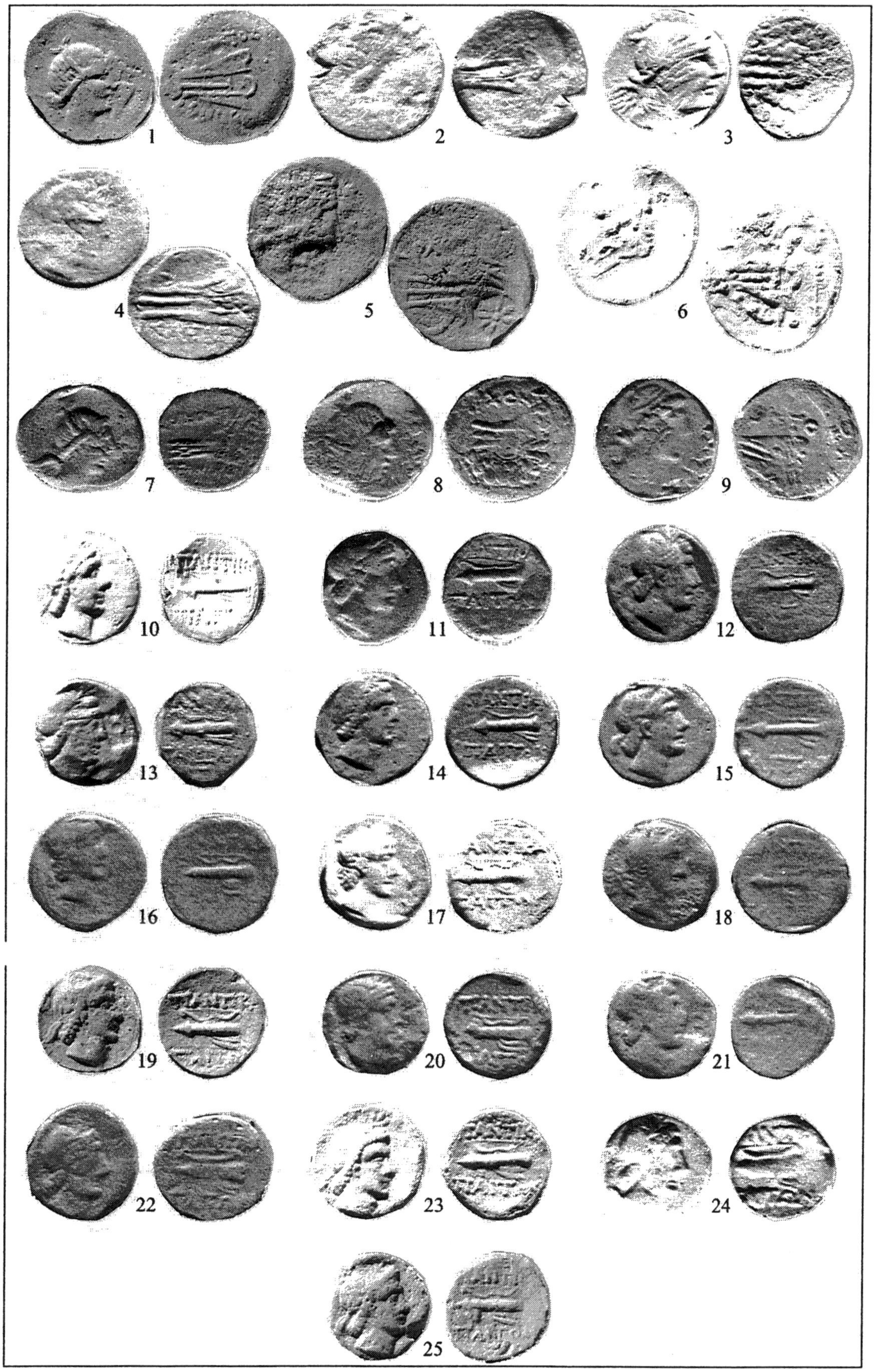

Plate XXVI

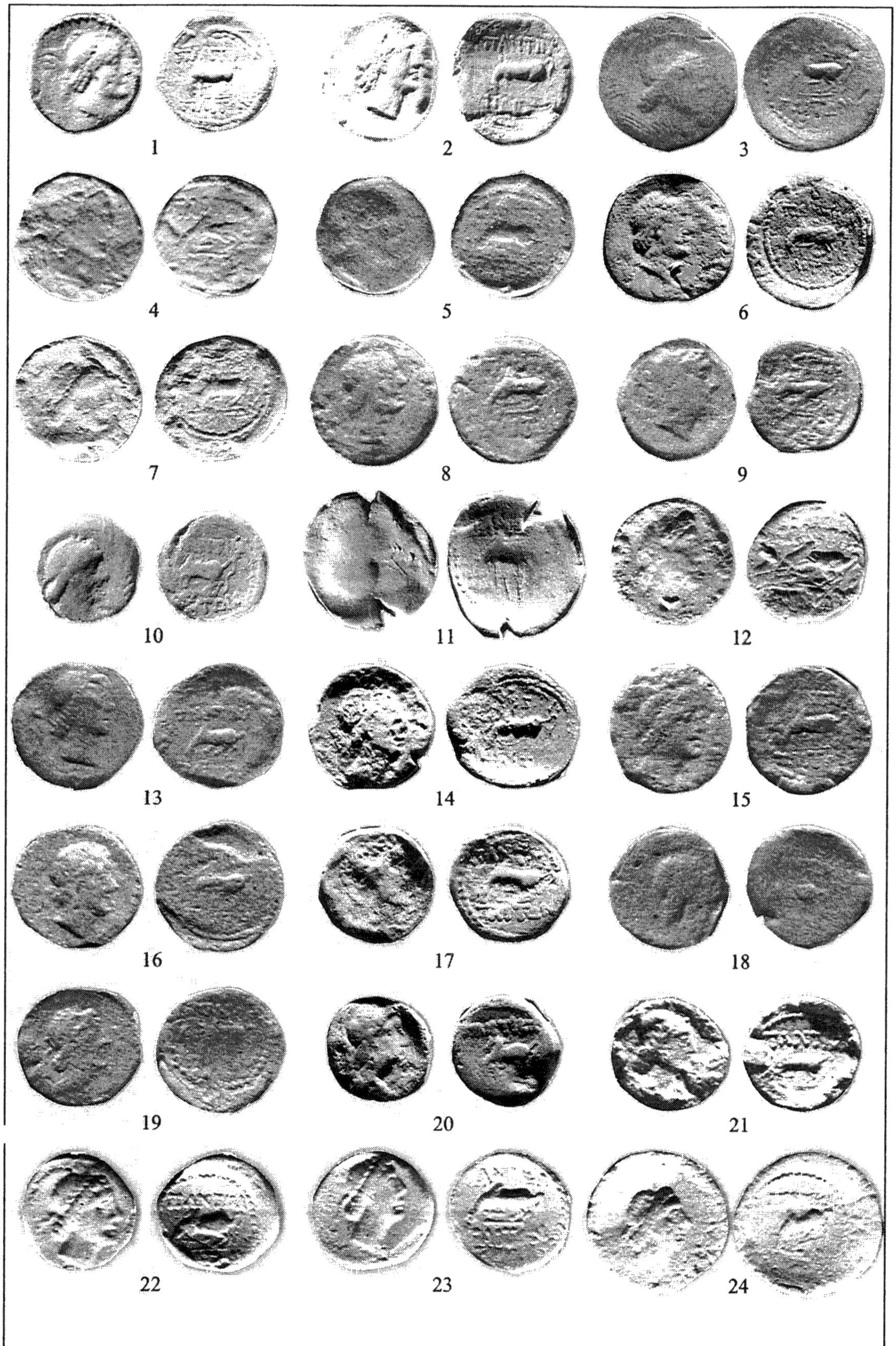

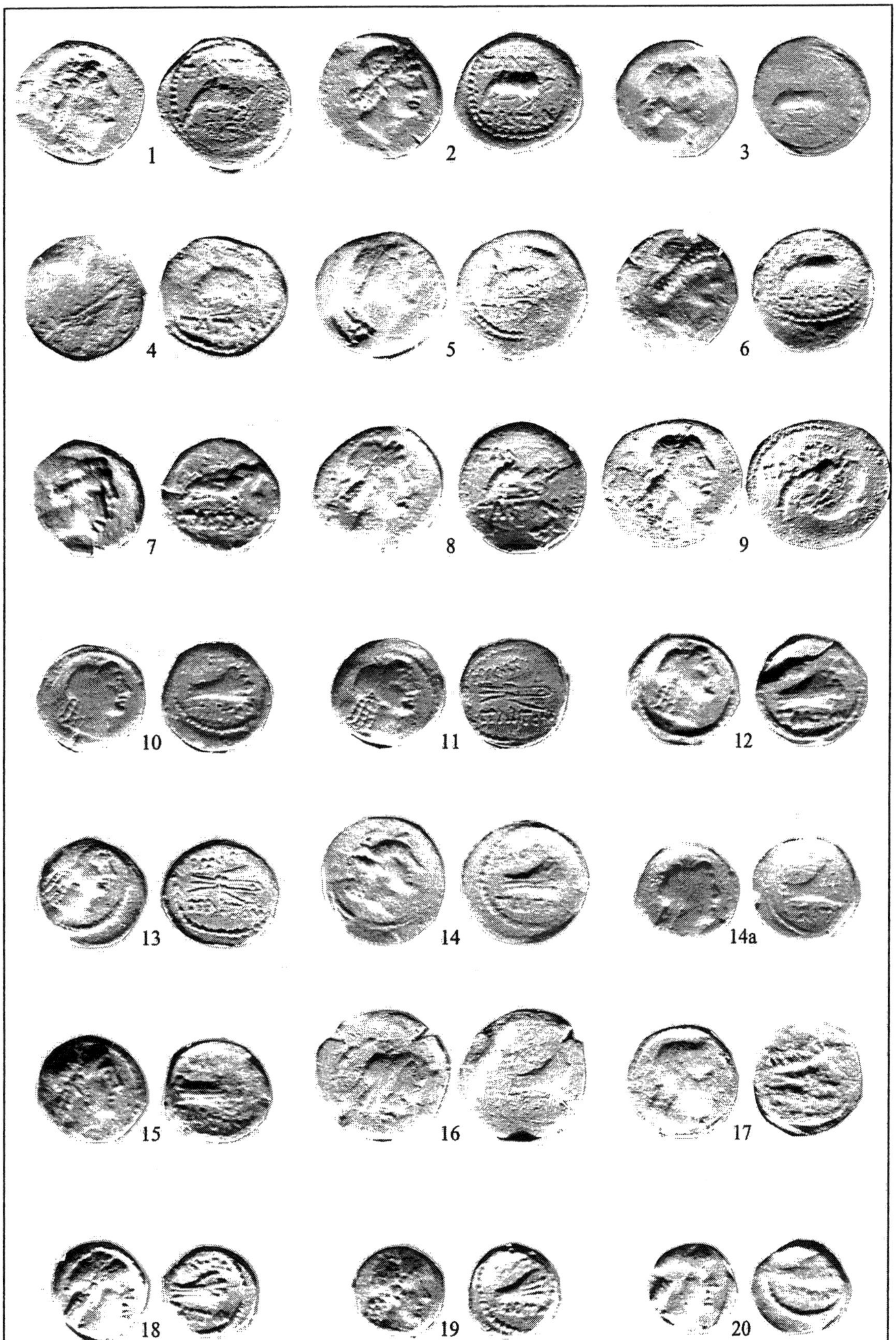
1
2
3
4
5
6
7
8
9
10
11
12
13
14
14a
15
16
17
18
19
20

Plate XXVIII

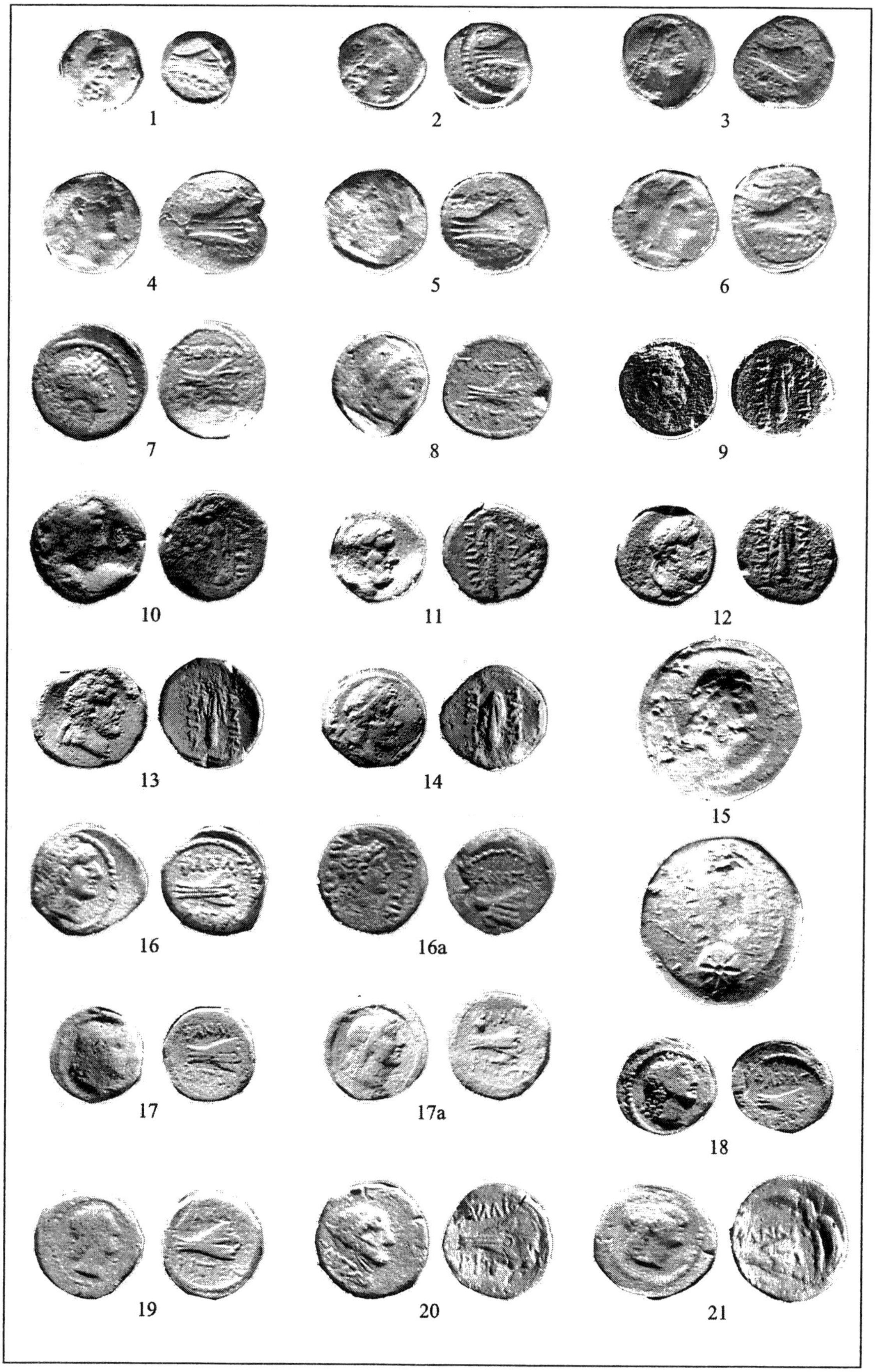

1 2 3 4 5 6 7 8 9 10 11 12 13 14 15 16 16a 17 17a 18 19 20 21

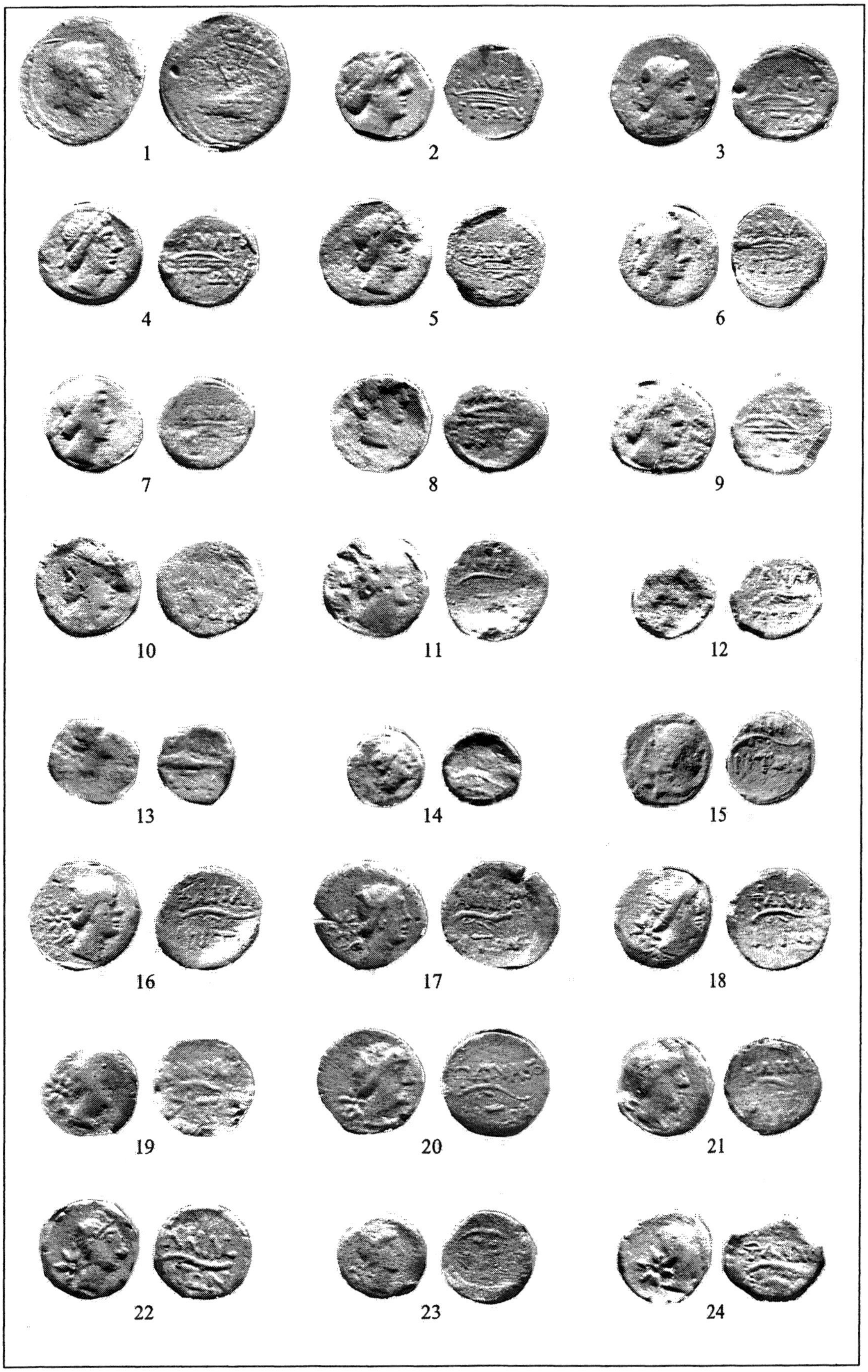
1
2
3
4
5
6
7
8
9
10
11
12
13
14
15
16
17
18
19
20
21
22
23
24

Plate XXX

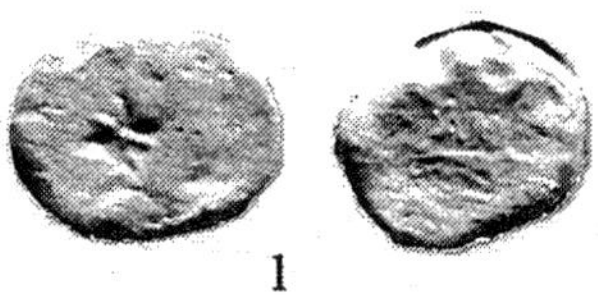

1

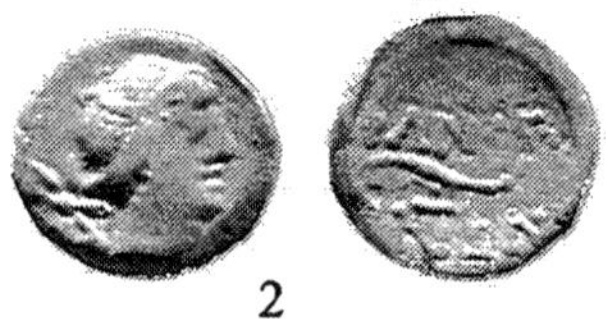

2

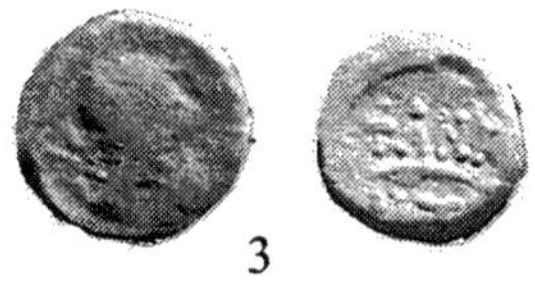

3

4

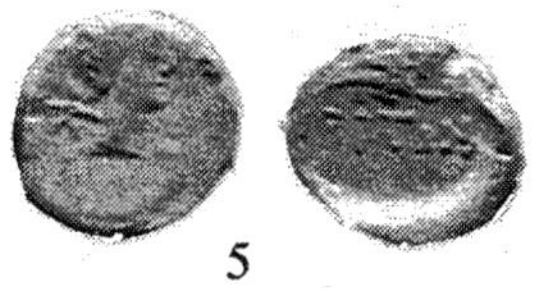

5

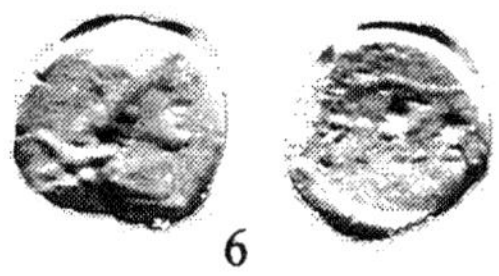

6

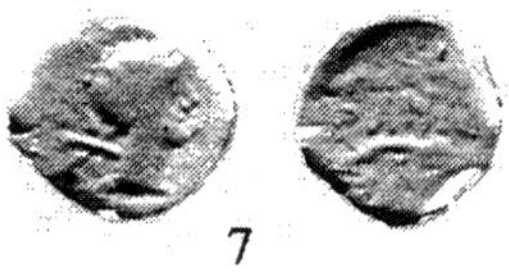

7

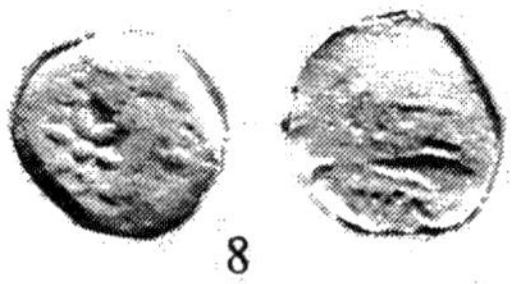

8

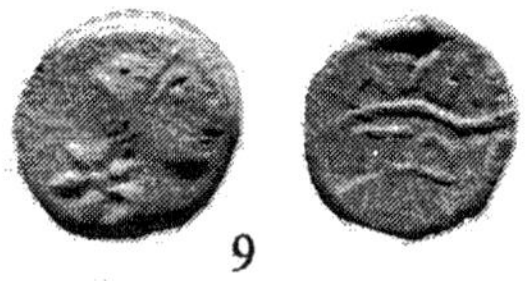

9

10

11

12

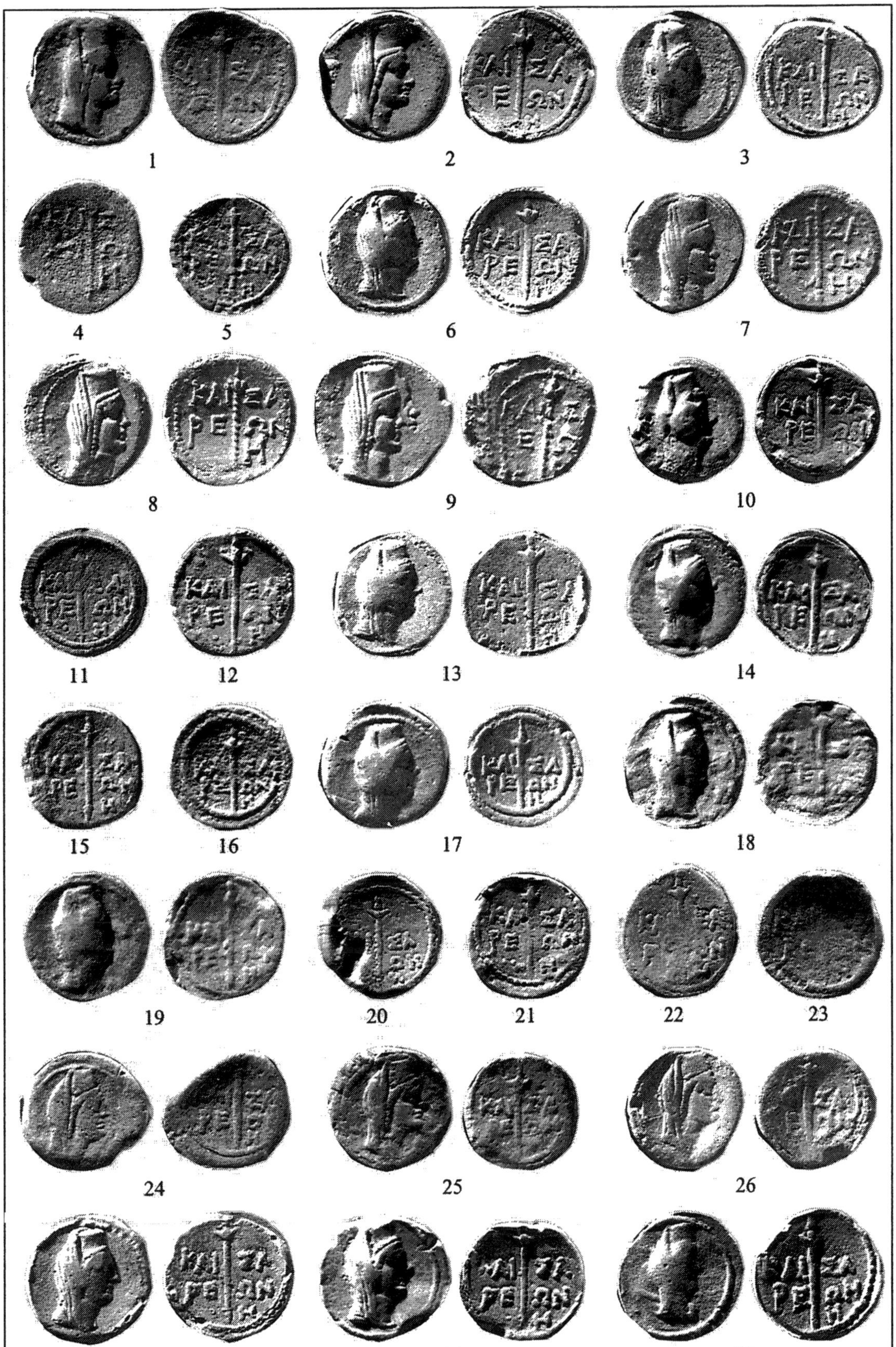
1
2
3
4
5
6
7
8
9
10
11
12
13
14
15
16
17
18
19
20
21
22
23
24
25
26
27
28
29

Plate XXXII

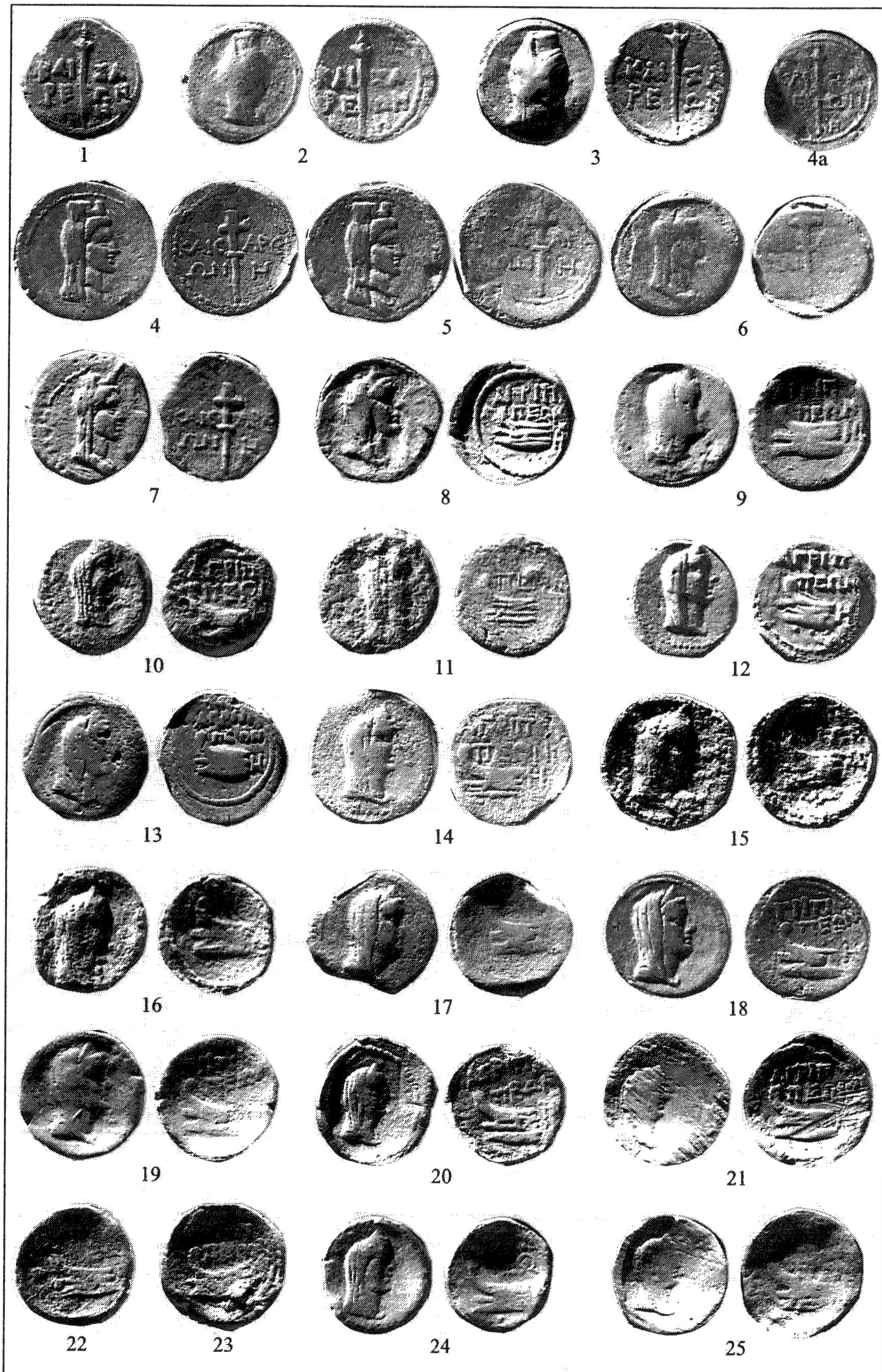

Plate XXXIII

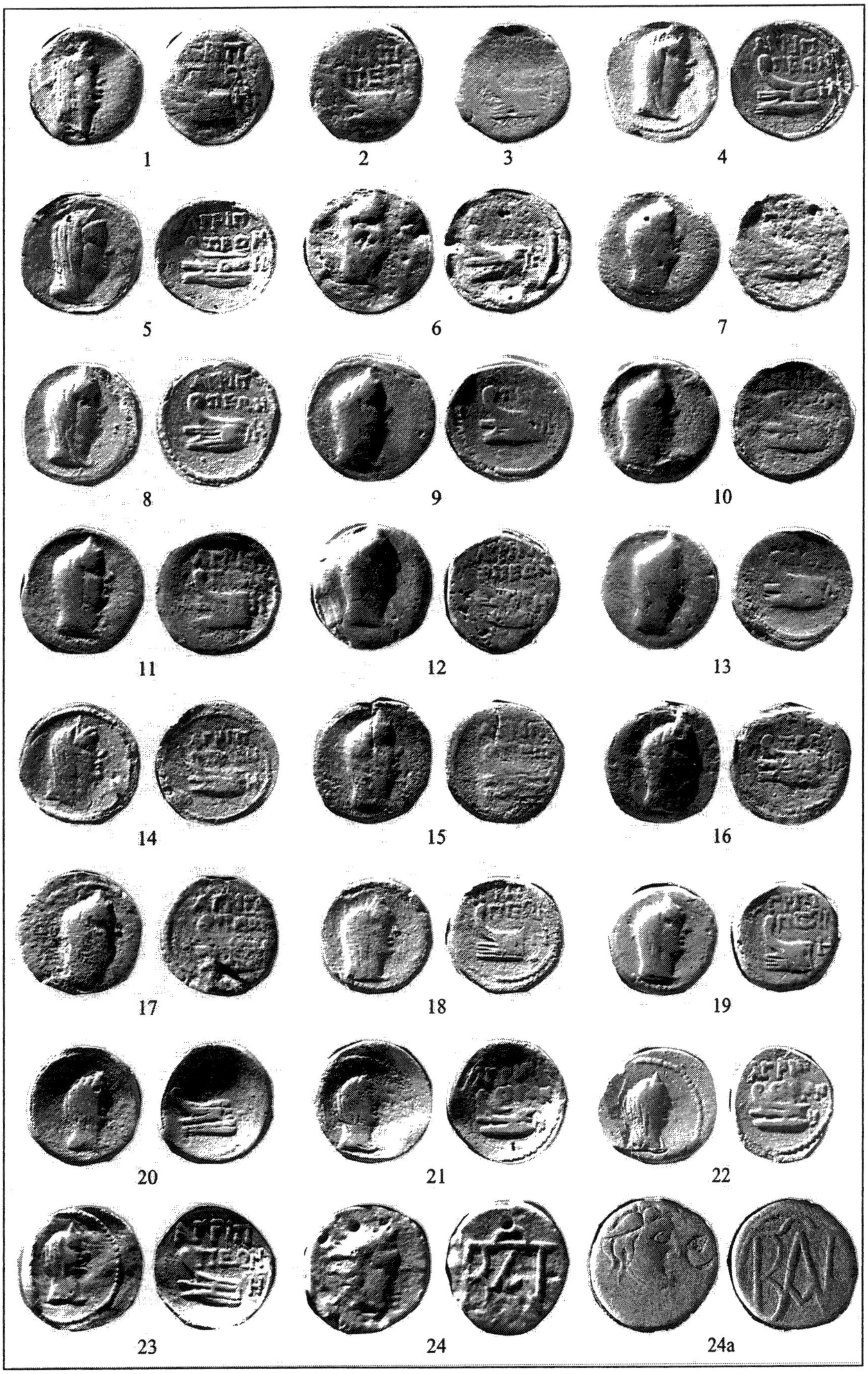

Plate XXXIV

1 2 3 4 5 5a 6 7 8 9 10 11 12 13 14 15 16 16a 16b 18 17 19 20 21

1
2
3
4
5
6
7
8
8a
9
10
11
12
13
14
15
16
17
18
19
20
21
22
23
24
25
26

Plate XXXVI

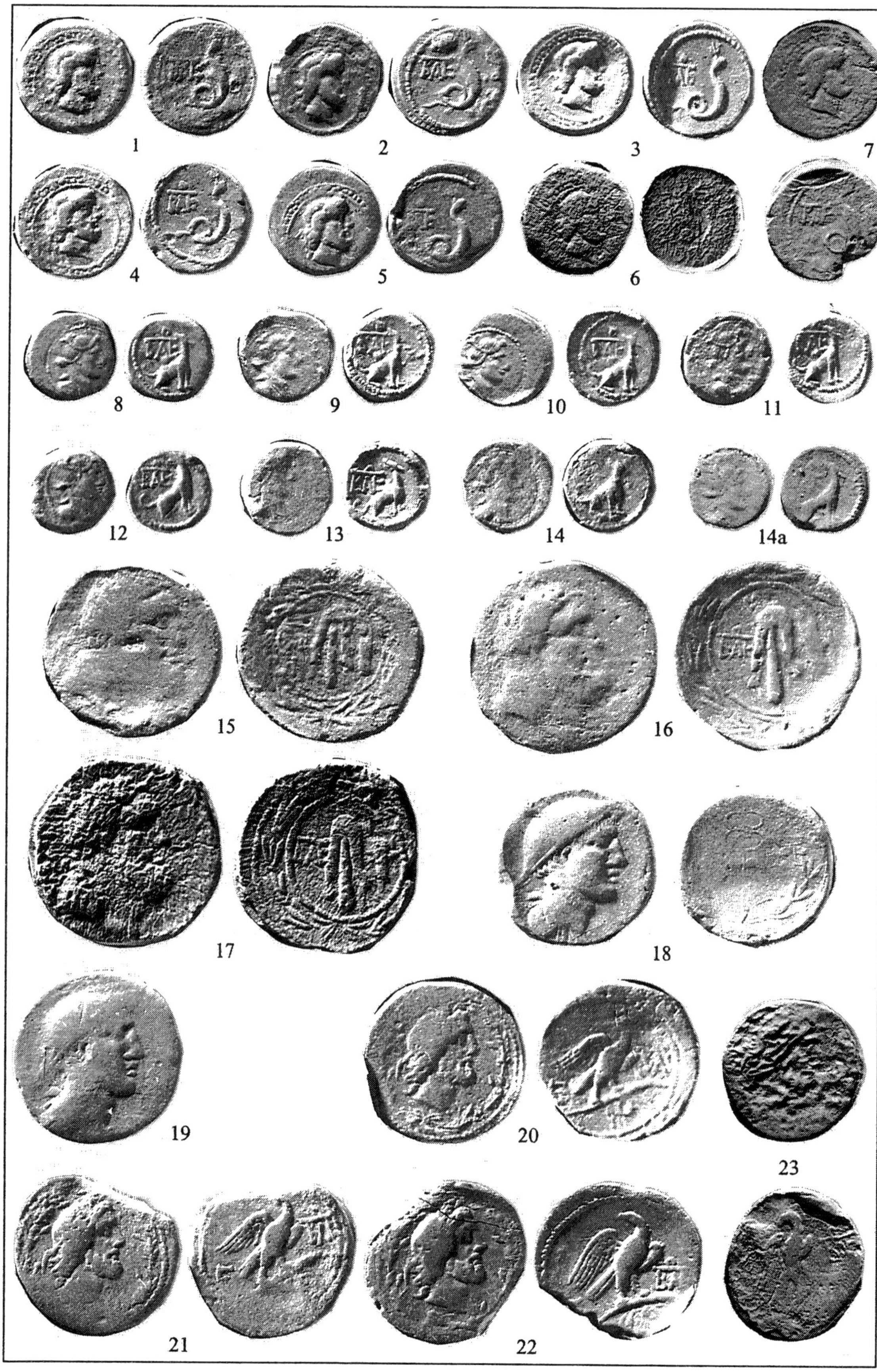

Plate XXXVII

Plate XXXVIII

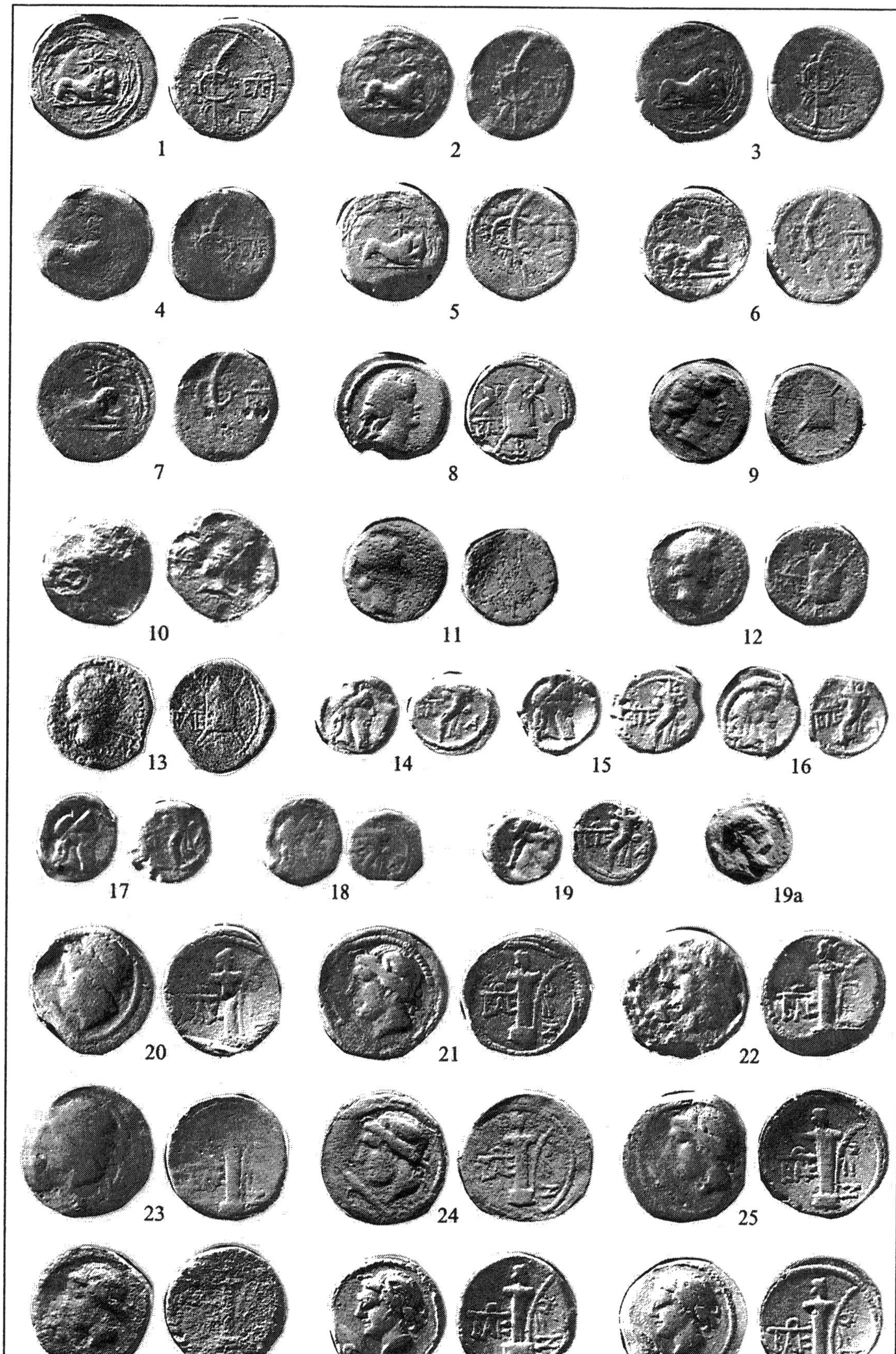

Plate XXXIX

1
2
3
4
5
6
7
8
9
13
10
11
12
14
15
16
17
18
19
20
21
22
23
24
25
26
30
27
28
29

Plate XL

1

2

3

4

5

6

7

8

9

10

11

12

13

14

15

16

17

18

19

20

21

22

23

24

Plate XLII

Plate XLIII

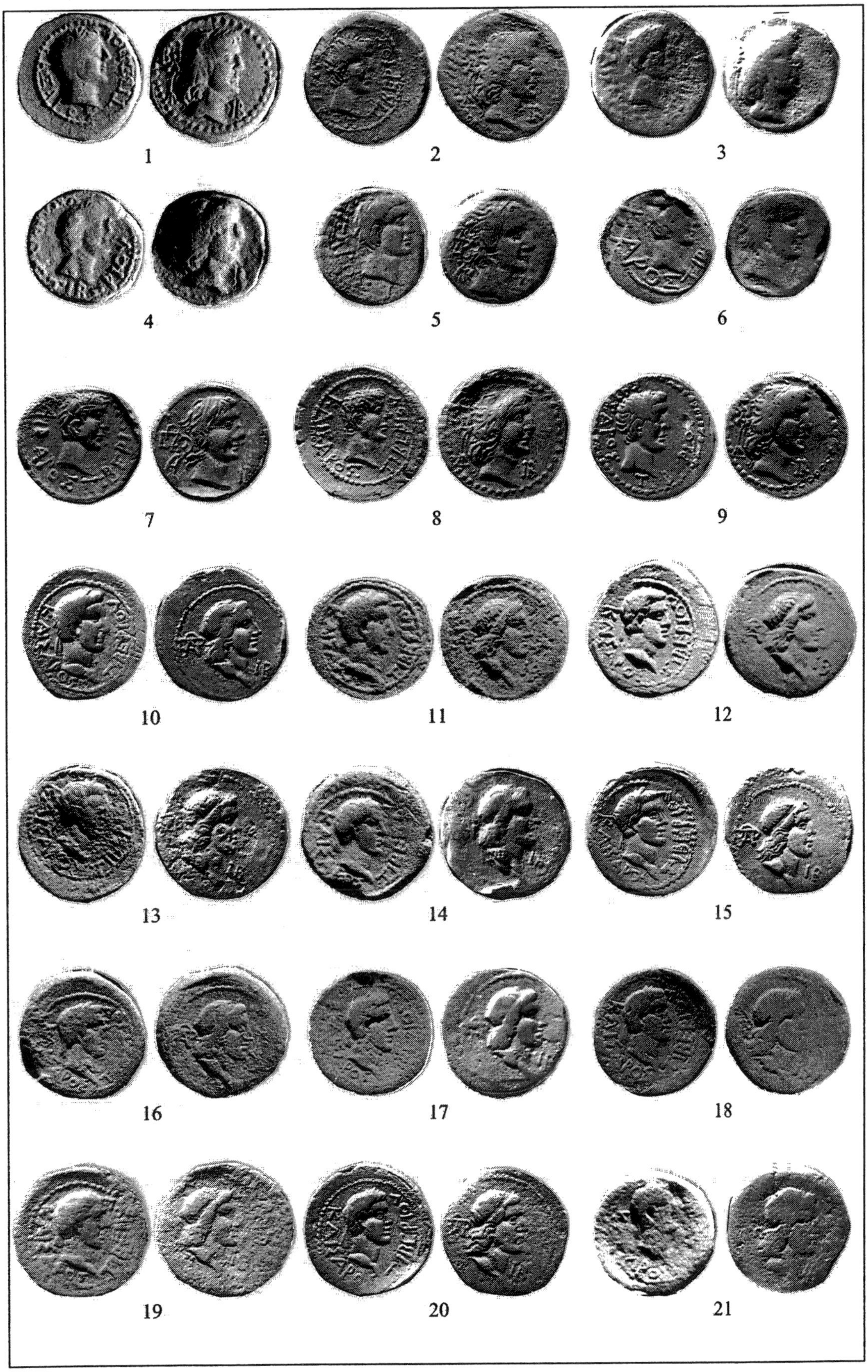

Plate XLIV

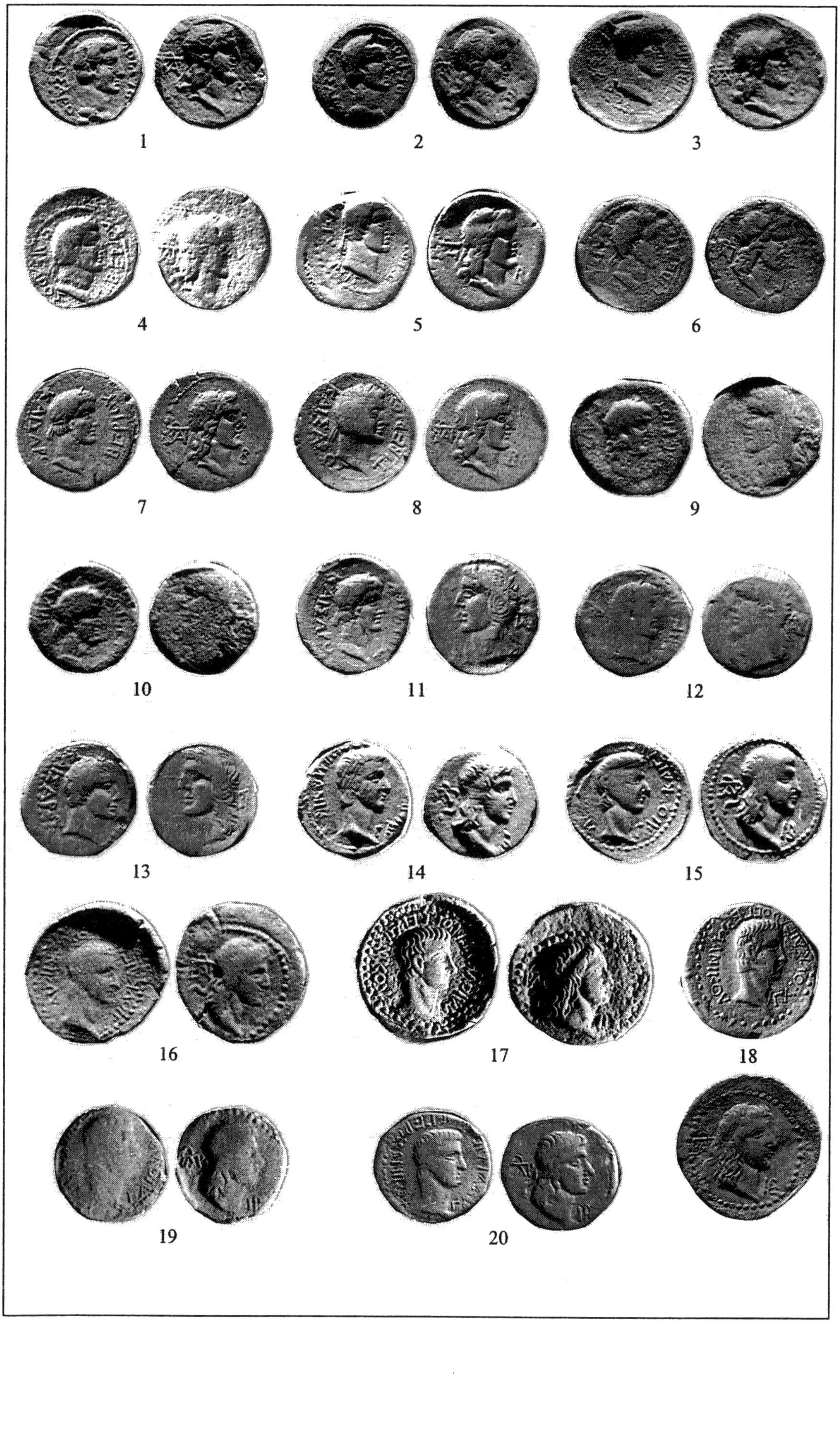

1 2 3 4 5 6 7 8 9 10 11 12 13 14 15 16 17 18 19 20

Plate XLV

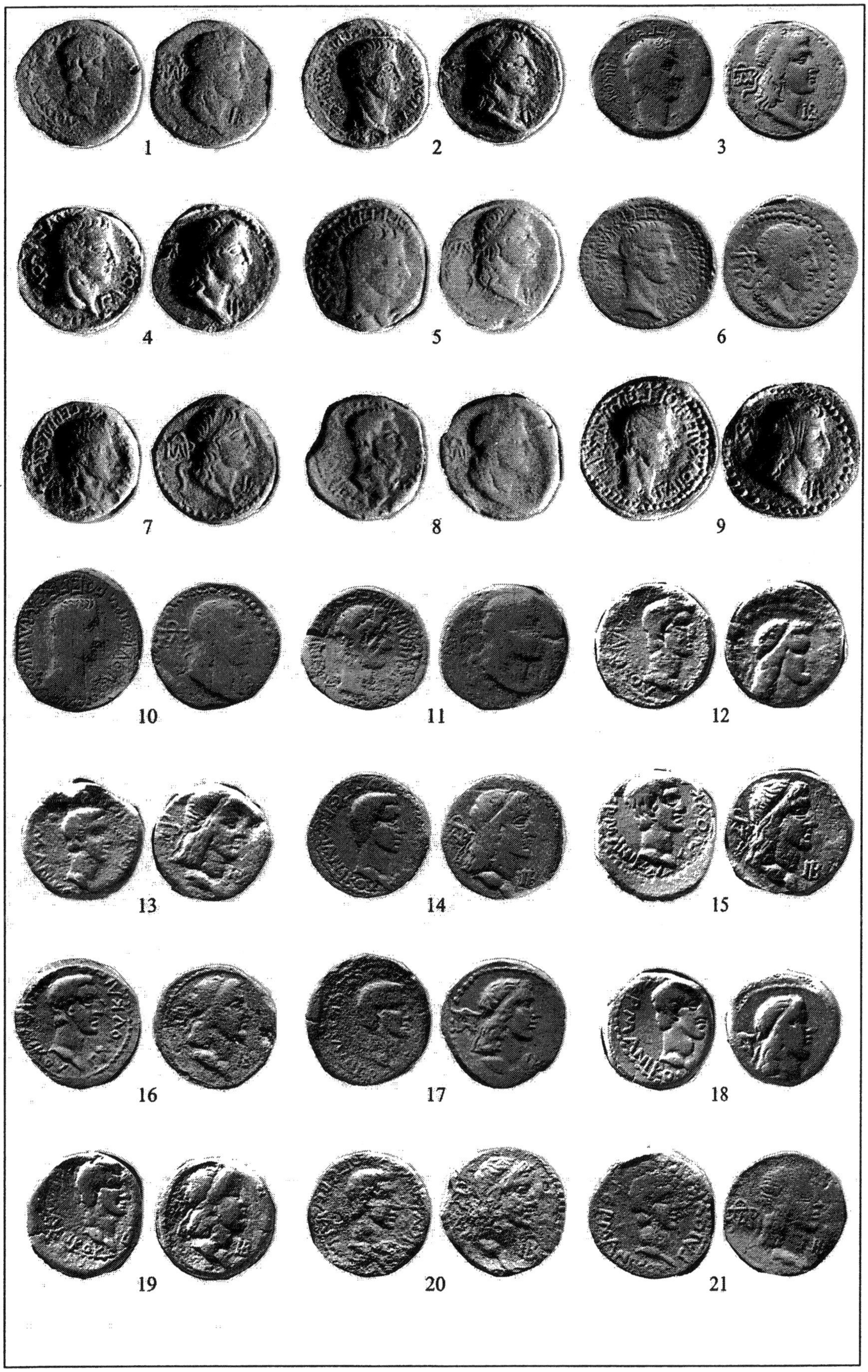

Plate XLVI

Plate XLVIII

Plate XLIX

Plate L

1
2
3
4
5
6
7
8
9
10
11
12
13
14
15
16
17
18
19
20
21
22
23
24

Plate LII

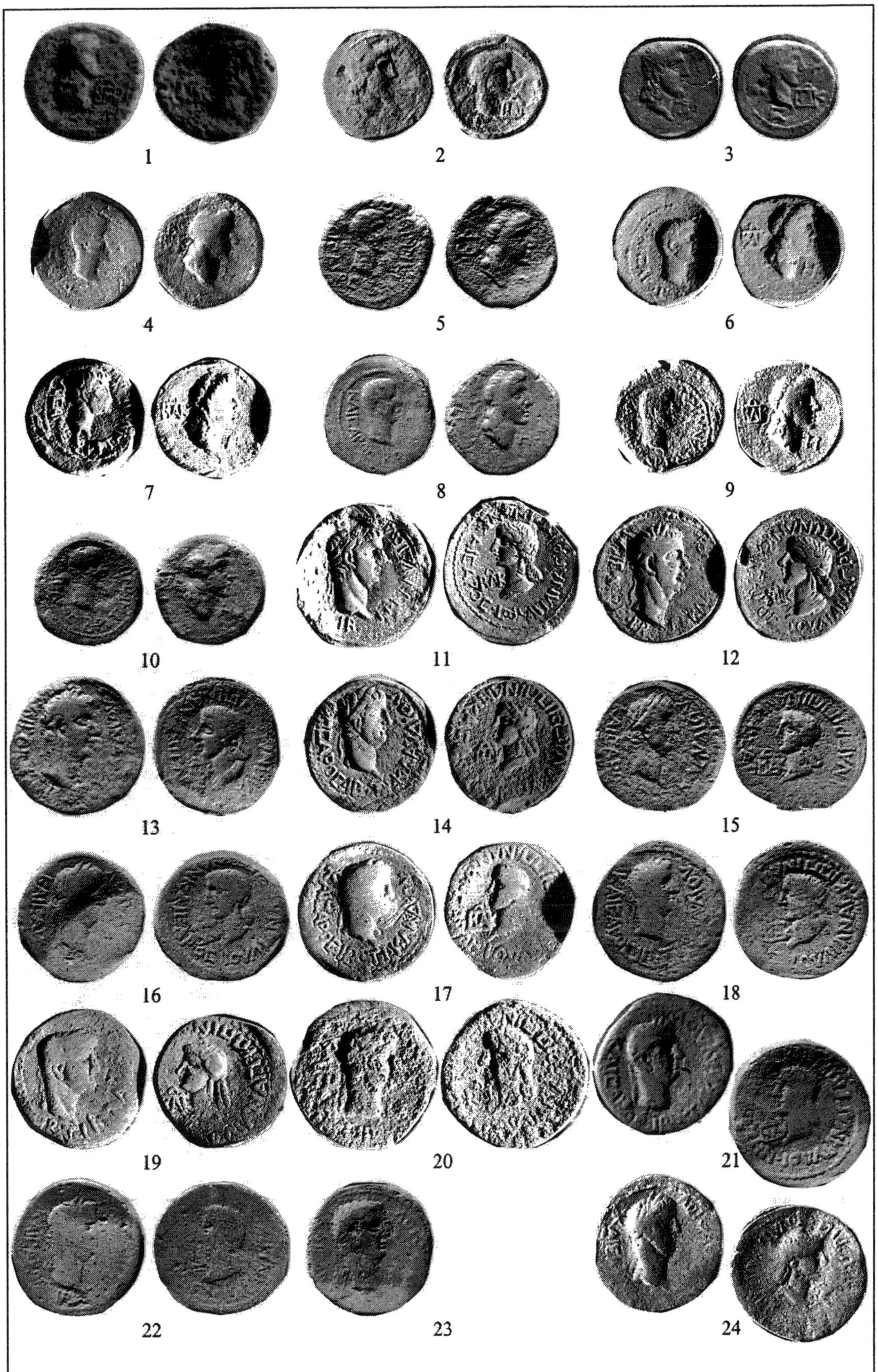
1
2
3
4
5
6
7
8
9
10
11
12
13
14
15
16
17
18
19
20
21
22
23
24

Plate LIV

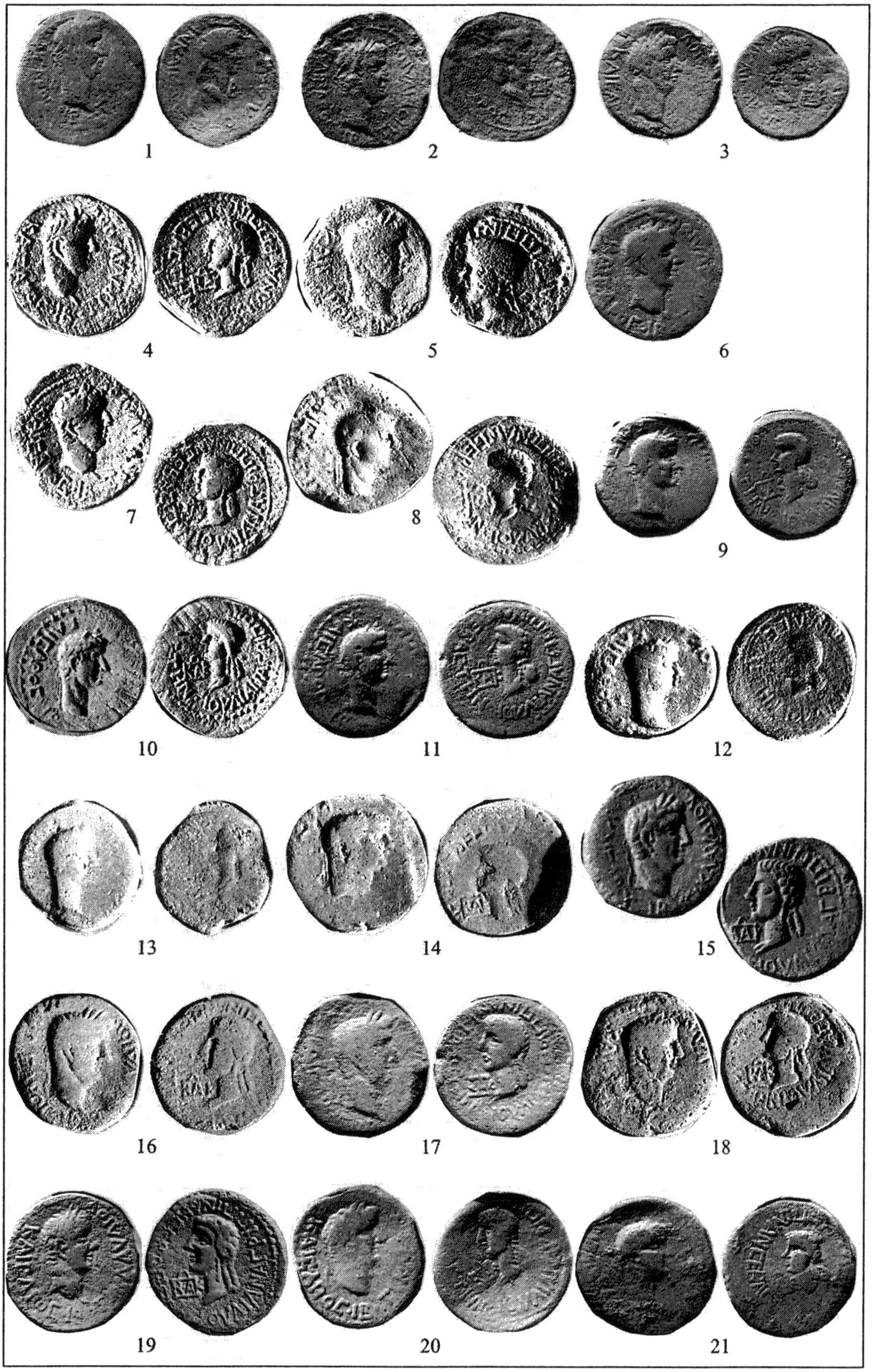

Plate LV

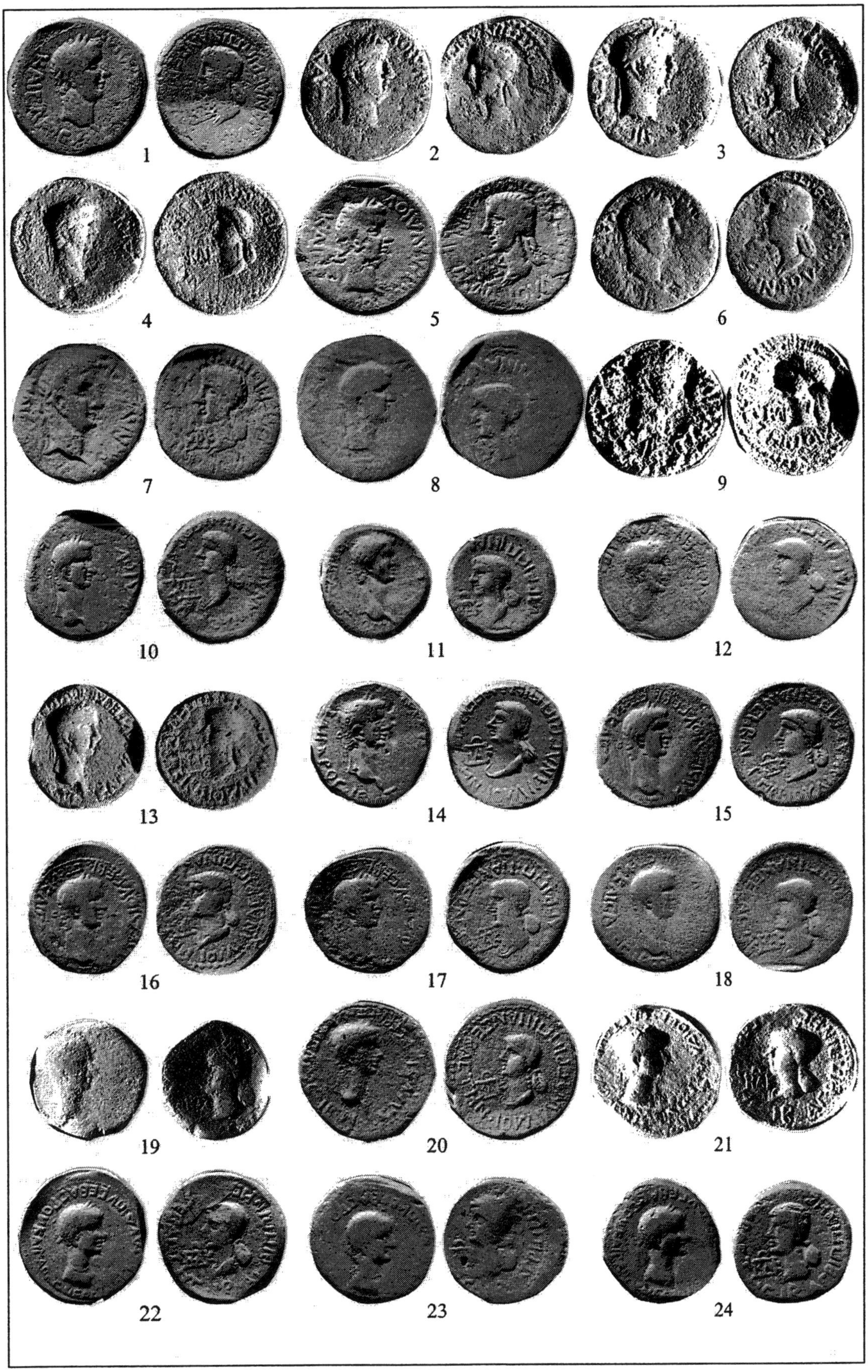

Plate LVI

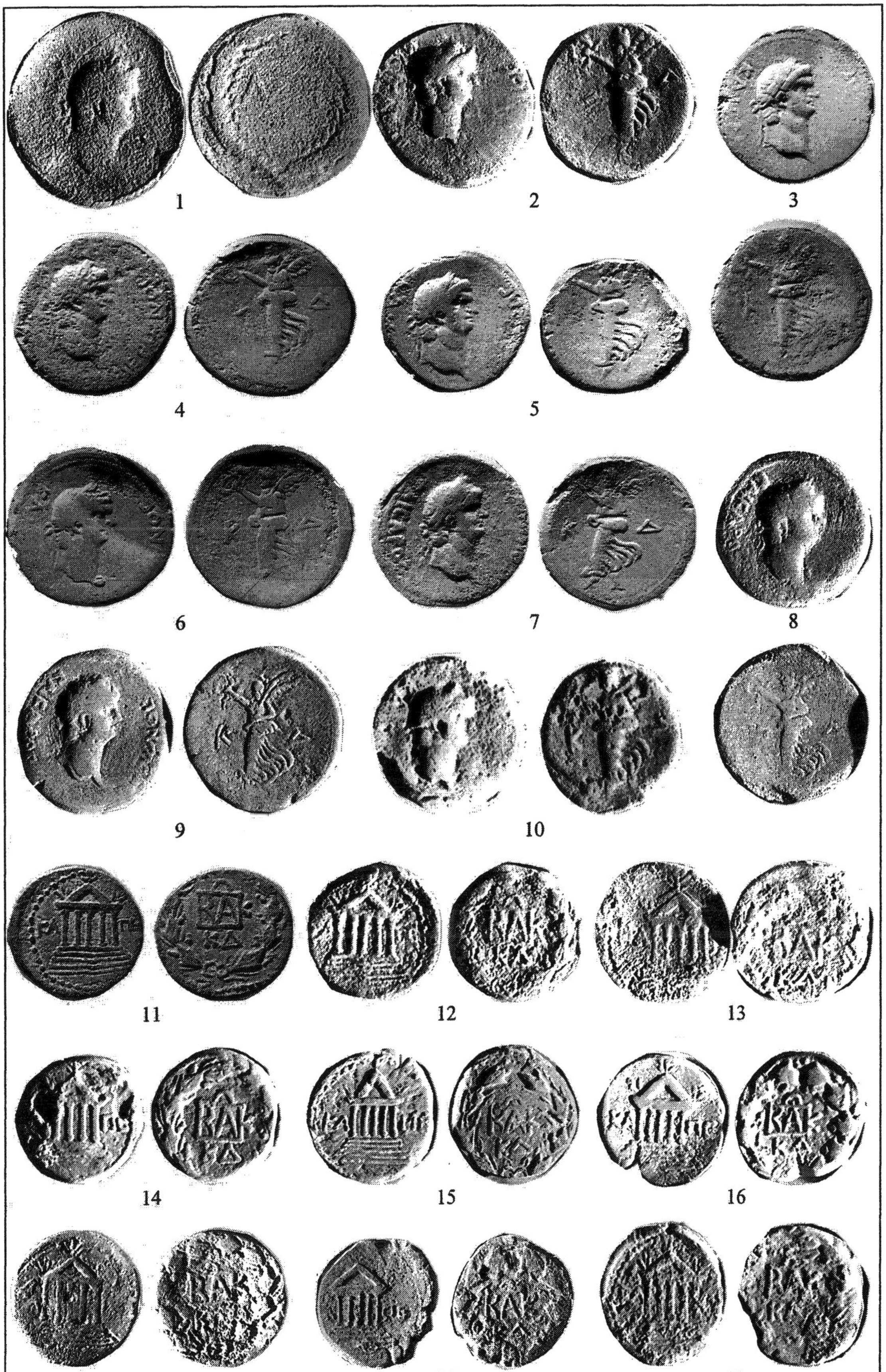
1
2
3
4
5
6
7
8
9
10
11
12
13
14
15
16
17
18
19

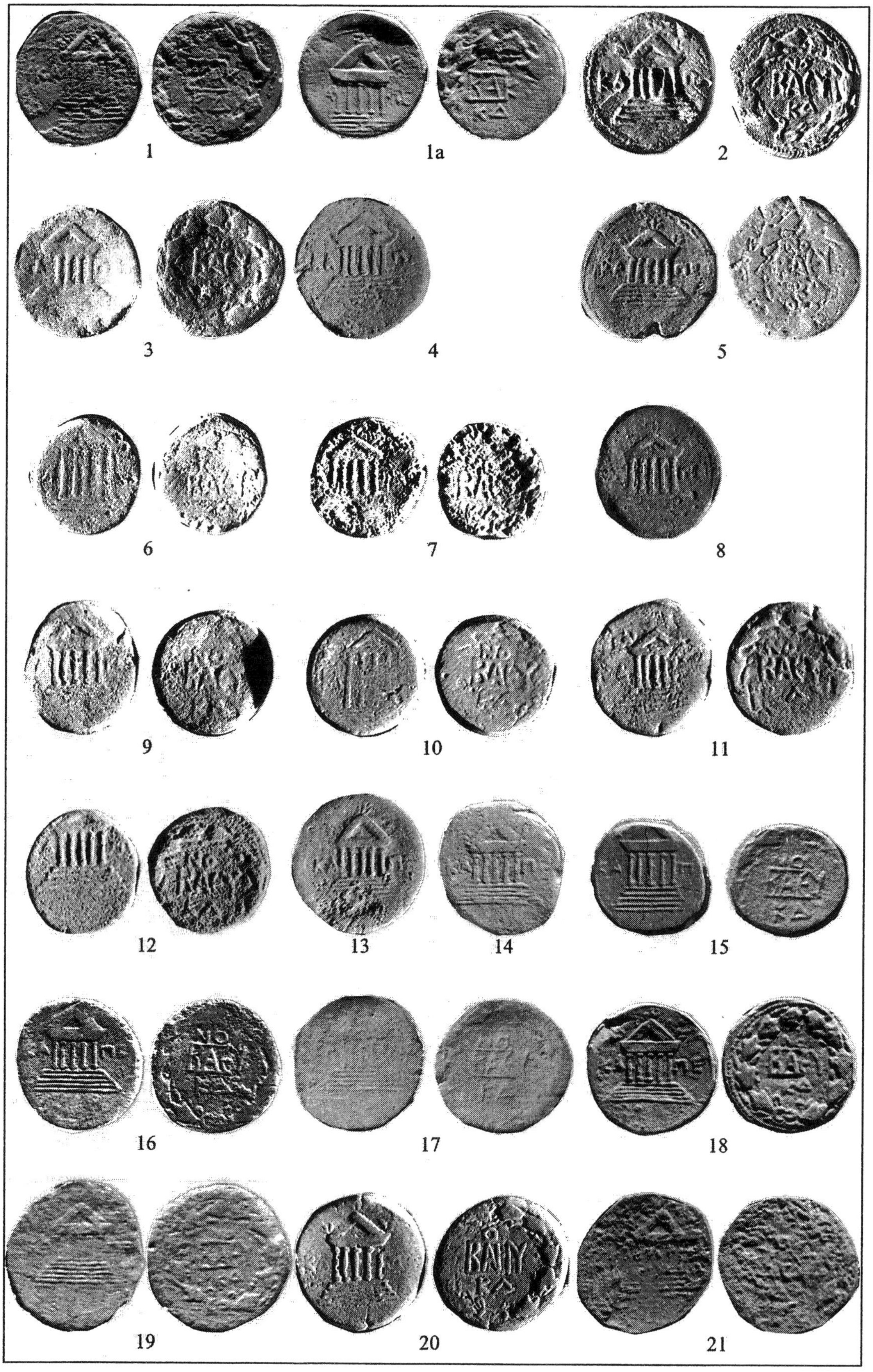
1
1a
2
3
4
5
6
7
8
9
10
11
12
13
14
15
16
17
18
19
20
21

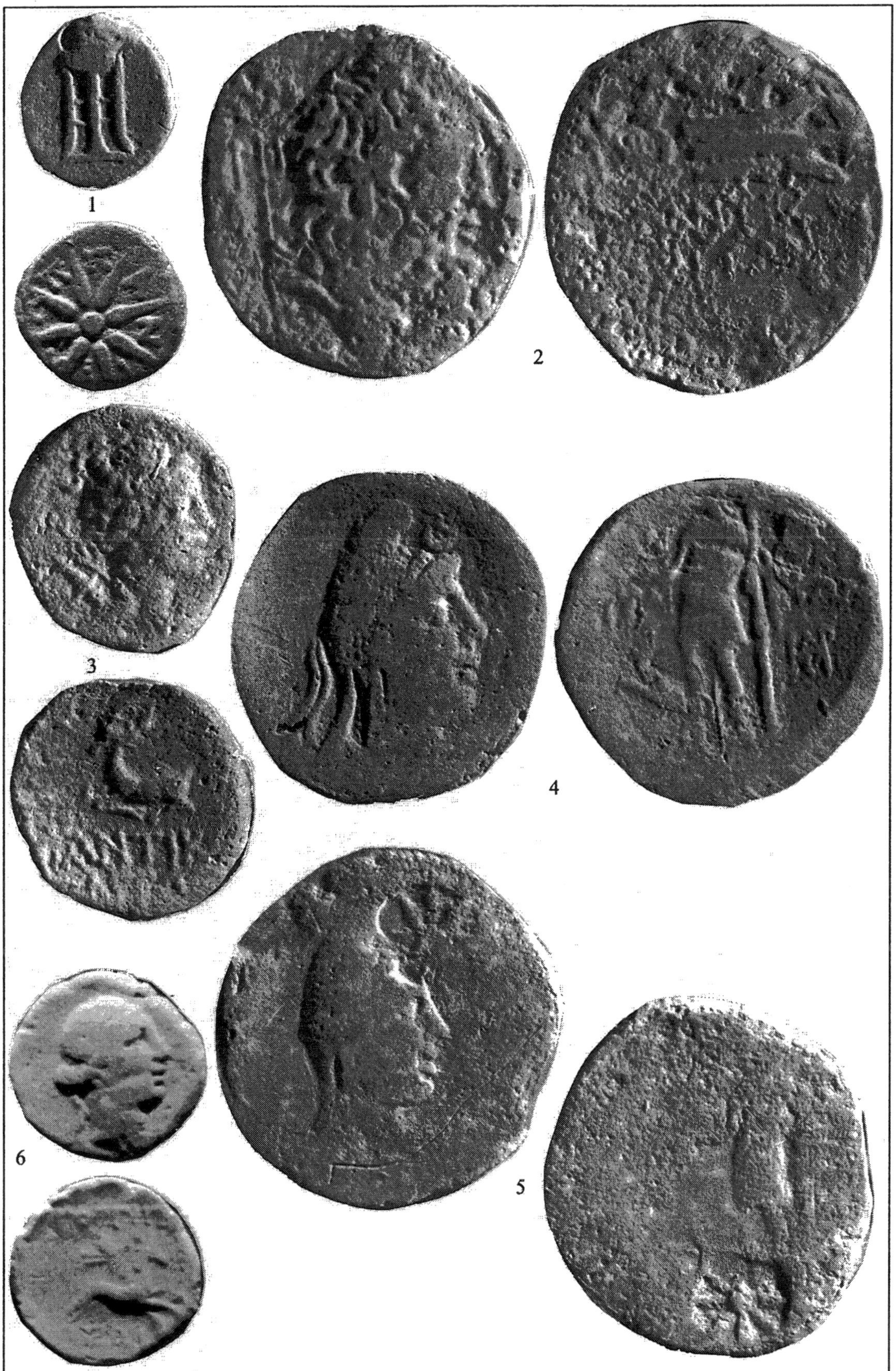

Plate LX

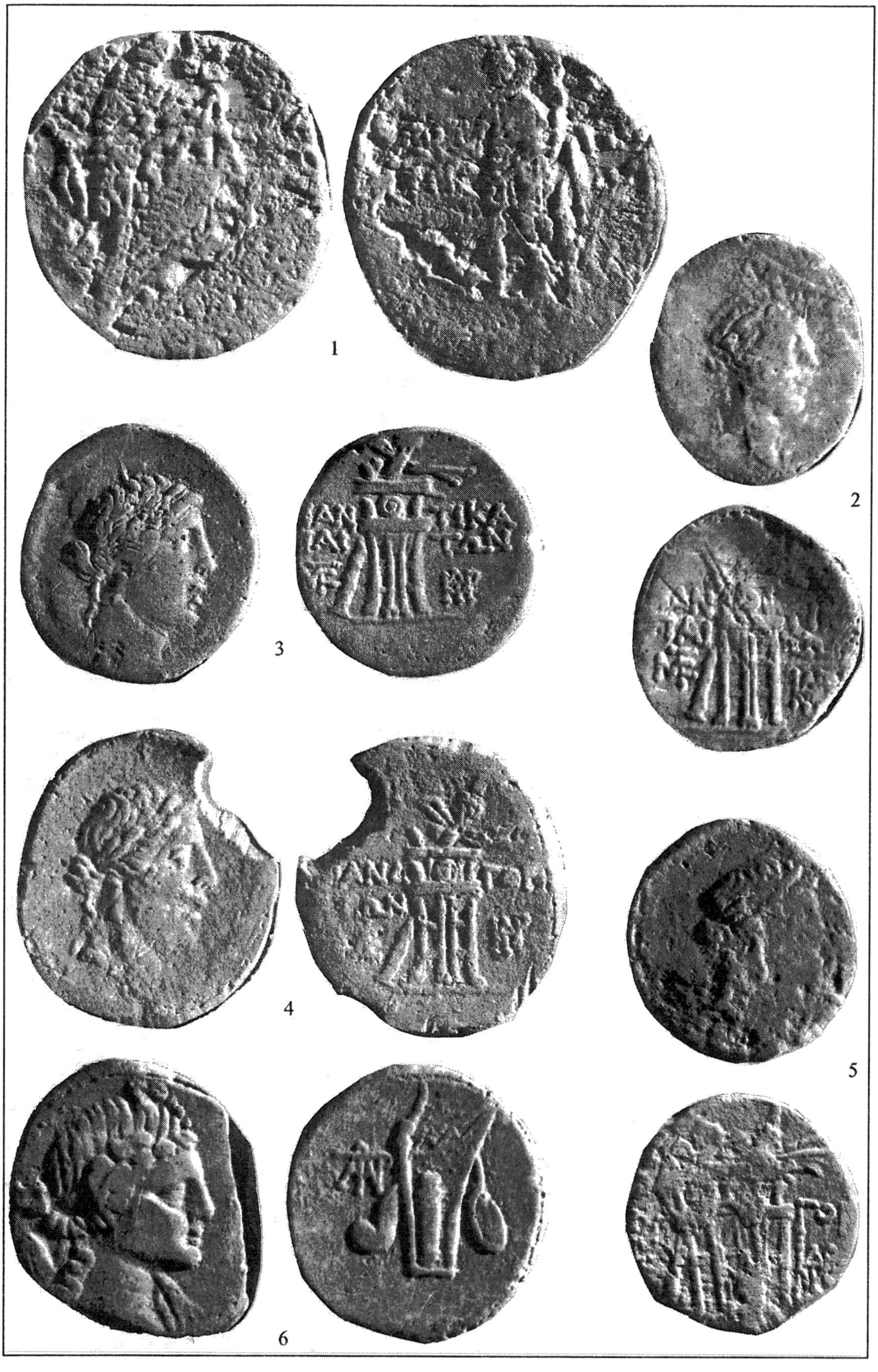

Plate LXII